3-1-71

THE SUCCESS
of
MODERN PRIVATE ENTERPRISE

THE SUCCESS
of
MODERN PRIVATE ENTERPRISE

Compiled by

Roland W. Bartlett

Professor, Agricultural Economics, Emeritus
University of Illinois
Urbana

The Interstate Printers & Publishers, Inc.
Danville, Illinois

LIBRARY OF CONGRESS CATALOG CARD NO. 70-106133

PRINTED IN U.S.A.

Preface

During the past two decades the greatest economic progress has been made in those countries where private enterprise is dominant rather than in those countries where centralized planning is dominant. Monopolies which flourished under a system of exploitative capitalism have generally been replaced by competition in the principal industrial countries of the free world. The colonial economics, the robber baron, and the other types of exploitative capitalism which, historically, were characteristic of private enterprise, have largely been replaced by a system of private enterprise centered upon efficient production and distribution in supplying goods and services wanted by consumers.

Despite substantial economic gains, particularly in the heavy-goods industries, the last 50 years of state control in Soviet Russia have resulted in living standards that are now substantially lower than in most countries in free Europe—and much lower than in the United States—where the principal incentive for innovation and improvement has been private enterprise. The greatest failure of central planning is in the production of agricultural products and other consumer goods. Developing countries may well wonder why 33 out of every 100 workers are required to feed Russia's population and why, in a bad crop year, Russia must still import food from other countries, when other European countries need less than half this number (on the average) to feed their people. Russian collective and state farms with all their engineers, craftsmen, and scientists under centralized control have failed to attain the productivity of countries such as France, where, under private enterprise, less than 18 percent of the workers produce more than enough food to meet the needs of its own population. Many Russian farm workers must be released for other jobs before their country's living standards can be increased to equal those in the free European countries or even approach those in the United States.

Labor efficiency under modern private enterprise is directly related to efficiency by consent. This relationship is in sharp contrast to the situation in countries with highly centralized planning, where most workers have little chance to play any part in attaining greater productivity. Labor unions have played an important part in attaining efficiency and have made possible high real wages by helping to attain high productivity. More than one out of every three workers in the United States is a union member.

As stated, in no place is the contrast between private enterprise and state control sharper than in the field of agriculture. Under private enterprise in the United States only 6 percent of its people are needed to feed its population or less than a fifth of the 33 percent required in Soviet Russia. This remarkable agricultural production record of the United States has resulted not only from the application of modern technology by individual farm operators but also from the growth of farmer cooperatives which have been the pacesetters in the efficient purchase of farm supplies and in the marketing of farm products.

Every economic or political system ever in existence has at one time or another been subjected to attack by some of those living under it. Under a system of private enterprise, a discontented individual may, on his own initiative, go about increasing his income. His discontent about his income can be directed against himself and not against the system. In this way he is likely to become a more productive member of society, obtain a higher income, and resolve his discontent.

Under a system of state control, however, it may be just possible for a younger person to attain a higher echelon in the state bureaucracy, but for the ordinary man there is only a remote chance of his being permitted to change his status so as to get a higher income. A few may attain the heights of income and power; the masses of people never do. Since the survival of any economic or political system depends on its ability to resolve the forces of discontent within it, private enterprise has a far greater chance of survival than does centralized control as it has historically operated.

While the articles in this book show a wide divergence, both in the ideas expressed and in the method of expression, they have one thing in common. Each of the writers of these articles was a firm believer in the system of private enterprise as it operates in free Europe and in the United States. This collection of their efforts should help clear up some of the confusion about the relative merits of state-controlled and private-enterprise economies. Finally, I express my sincere appreciation to the publishers who gave me permission to reproduce the articles included in this book.

ROLAND W. BARTLETT

Contents

Part I

INTRODUCTION

INTRODUCTION

Roland W. Bartlett

The world has been, is, and always will be beset with troubles. Probably the greatest problem today is hunger, with about half of the three and one-half billion people in the world going to sleep every night with hunger pains. The problem of hunger looms still greater with the population explosion, for it is estimated that by the year 2000 there will be about seven billion people and that the greatest increases will have taken place in the areas of the world least able to feed them.

Poverty is the underlying cause of hunger, as well as disease, lack of education, and of a thousand and one other deprivations of the things that give an individual hope for the future. Aside from poverty, hunger, and disease, even the industrial nations of the world have problems such as unemployment, air and water pollution, racial inequality, slums, and so forth. The crucial question is: How can poverty be alleviated both in the developing nations of the world and in the lower-income groups of the industrial nations? This book of readings tries to answer this question by asking and answering others: Why have some countries been able to cope with basic problems such as poverty and hunger so much better than other countries? Why is the gross national product (GNP) per person for the 13 countries in the European Common Market and the European Free Trade Area 52 percent higher, and for the United States nearly 200 percent higher, than that in Russia? Why do food expenditures in free Europe and the United States take so much smaller a part of total consumer income than in Russia? Why is the proportion of the labor force in agriculture so much lower in the other major industrialized countries than it is in Russia? What economic systems, groups, and approaches can increase productivity and increase low incomes?

There are no simple answers to these questions. Factors such as history, natural resources, and the social characteristics of people differ from country to country. Despite these differences, however, the fact is that since World War II the greatest progress in improving standards of living has been made in the countries whose economies were based primarily upon private enterprise in contrast to centralized planning by government. The premise underlying this book of readings is that modern private enterprise is at least a large part of the answer to most of the questions we have posed.

Private Enterprise Versus Centralized Control

Unfortunately, many people not familiar with modern American private enterprise still speak in terms of the era of the "robber baron." This era, however, is long past, as Professor Sumner Slichter points out in his paper "The Growth of Competition" (Chapter 2). His article is a classic which should be read by everyone interested in the economic progress which has taken place in the United States since World War II. It is also an extension of Dr. Raymond W. Miller's valuable discussion of the difference between modern private enterprise and monopolistic private enterprise, "Can Capitalism Compete?" (Chapter 1).

Unfortunately, too, many people still speak of modern private enterprise in terms of colonialism and other exploitative types of capitalism which prevailed during the late nineteenth century and the early twentieth century. Skeptics point to the fact that, in the past, monopoly rather than competition has been the rule rather than the exception for many countries where private enterprise was in effect. It is true that before World War I, there were 13 empires (see Table 1) with their monopolistic types of capitalism covering the trade areas of the world, but sharp changes have taken place since then, most dramatically in the empires which formerly were integral parts of the European countries. In 1912-13, Austro-Hungary, Belgium, Great Britain, France, Germany, Italy, and the Netherlands had empires that covered 21,285 square miles and had a total population of about 750 million people. By 1965, the area of these empires had been reduced to 1,127 square miles (5 percent of what it had been), and their population was down to about 288 million (38 percent of what it had been, and this considering the great growth of the world population in those years). These statistics reflect the loss of colonies, which forced a sharp change in the trading patterns of the seven countries, once empires, but now without a market outlet for manufactured goods at monopoly prices. Five of the countries, namely Belgium, France, West Germany, Italy, and the Netherlands, have now joined together into the European Economic Community[1] to effectuate greater efficiency in the production and sale of goods and services. Within the EEC, competition under private enterprise has to a considerable degree replaced monopoly, with substantial increases in productivity. The rise of West Germany under private enterprise, following the ruins of World War II, has been one of the marvels of the twentieth century. Ludwig Erhard's role in this rise is well known, and his 1946 and 1947

[1] The EEC also includes Luxembourg.

Table 1. Empires of the World, 1912-13 and About 1966[1]

	1912-13		*About 1966*		*Percent of 1912-13*	
	Area square miles (thousands)	*Population (millions)*	*Area square miles (thousands)*	*Population (millions)*	*Area*	*Population*
Austro-Hungarian	261	51.3	68	17.6	26.0	34.3
Belgian	911	21.4	12	9.5	13.2	44.4
British[2]	12.960	436.2	447	67.5[1963-67]	3.4	15.5
Chinese[3]	4.277	400.0	3.760	773.1[-]	87.9	193.2
French	4.411	82.8	275	51.2[1963-67]	6.2	61.8
German	1.236	77.6	(West) 137	76.7[1964]	1.1	98.8
Italian	711	33.8	116	52.7	16.3	155.9
Japanese	256	63.9	143	98.9	55.8	154.8
Netherlands	795	45.2	72	13.0[1964-66]	9.1	28.8
Ottoman (Turkish)	759	23.8	296	32.9	39.0	138.2
Portuguese	839	14.2	838	23.0[1960-66]	100.0	161.9
Russian[4]	8.660	166.2	8.647	235.0[1967]	99.8	141.3
Spanish	312	19.9	313	32.2[1960-66]	100.0	161.8

[1] Sources: *Encyclopedia Britannica*, 1912 and 1957 eds.
The World Almanac and Encyclopedia for 1913, also 1914.
The World Almanac and Book of Facts, 1968
See pertinent headings in each.

[2] Aden and South Arabia were to gain independence in January, 1968. Total area, 111,075 square miles, and total population, 1,250,000.

[3] The Chinese Republic was established in 1948.

[4] The Union of Soviet Socialist Republics was established (after the Bolsheviks overthrew the Russian government in 1917).

articles (Chapter 3) for private enterprise in West Germany, when this statesman was faced on all sides by those favoring centralized planning for the country, are historical landmarks as well as cogent expositions of the alternatives.

Meanwhile, the area of both Portugal and Spain has remained very close to that before World War I, and both countries have had substantial increases in population. Living standards in these countries are substantially below those in other countries in free Europe. This is even more true of the Ottoman Empire, now Turkey, whose area was sharply reduced after World War I, but whose population increased substantially. The historical event most pertinent to our questions, however, occurred in 1917, when the Bolsheviks overthrew the czarist regime which controlled the Russian Empire. Then, in 1948, the Communists became rulers of China after having forced the Nationalist government out of the country. For Russia and China, the present areas are close to those of before World War I, but the governments have completely changed. Both economies operate under highly centralized control and with a minimum of private enterprise. Furthermore, the Russian-Chinese model is frequently offered as the answer to the question of how best to ameliorate poverty in the world. Wrongly so, this book holds, for although accurate information is lacking for the Chinese Republic, even Russia's remarkable progress in the heavy production industries does not compensate for the fact that Russia has fallen far behind free Europe and the United States in its production of food and other consumer goods. Centralized government planning is not the answer. This brings us to one of the central issues in the book at hand—an issue that Professor Friedman further discusses in "Myths That Keep People Hungry" (Chapter 5)—to the decision between: Private Enterprise Versus Centralized Control—Free Europe and the United States Versus Russia.

The issue of private enterprise versus centralized control is the issue to which the last few pages have been pointing and for which the readings mentioned have their greatest relevance. The "Introduction" affords an opportunity to compare the success of these conflicting economic ideologies by comparing some economic measures from countries that function by these ideologies. The two major world powers are the United States and Russia. In the United States, and in free Europe, the major part of production and distribution of goods and services is now done by private enterprise; the Russian economy is dominated by centralized government control. A comparison of these economies shows that the greatest achievement in Russia has been in its heavy goods industries, including steel, space exploration, and military equipment. Because of this, Russia ranks second only to the United States in the world of nations. But while Russia has made some progress in improving its agriculture, year by year it is falling further behind free Europe and the United States in the efficiency of its agricultural production and distribution. Because of this, the high proportion of its people required to produce and distribute food, the standard of living in Russia is far below that of most of the industrial nations of the world.

Steel and Heavy Production Industries

Fifty years of centralized state control in Russia show a wide contrast in achievements. In contrast to its failure to keep up with other industrial nations in the production of food and other consumer goods, Russia has had a most phenomenal growth in steel production. In 1914, before the revolution, Russia produced 4.7 million tons of steel, ranking fourth in world production (see Table 2). A half century later, in 1965, Russian steel production had increased to 91 million tons, 20.5 percent of world production, and ranked second only to the United States. This remarkable increase took place under centralized state control, as did the production of Sputnik and other outerspace explorations and the building of a huge military force. In the heavy production industries as a whole, Russia ranks second only to the United States.

Agriculture and Food Expenditures

In 1865, a century ago, three of every four people in Russia were engaged in agriculture (see Table 3). The same proportion held in 1913, nearly half a century later. By 1965, only one out of every three Russians was farming. This was a great improvement in the efficiency of Russian agriculture since the revolution. But despite this progress made under its system of collective and state farming, Russia has been falling behind in agricultural efficiency as compared with the United States and free Europe. In 1940, about one of every four people (23.4 percent) in the United States was engaged in agriculture, approximately half the proportion in Russia (50 percent). By 1965, only one of every 16 (6 percent) in the United States was producing food, less than one-fifth the proportion in Russia of almost one in 3 (32.7 percent. In the countries of free Europe, excluding the United Kingdom, only one of seven (14 percent) was in agriculture, less than half that in Russia. Including the United Kingdom with the other countries reduced this proportion to one of 10 (10 percent), less than a third of Russia's.

Table 2. Steel Production, Selected Countries and Years, 1865-1965[1]

	1865	*1914*	*1929*	*1932*	*1938*	*1948*	*1955*	*1965*
	millions of metric tons [percent of world production that year]							
United States	.014	23.9[39.0%]	57.3	13.9	28.8	80.4	106.2	119.3[26.9%]
USSR	.004	4.7[7.7%]	5.0[2]	5.9[2]	18.0[2]	......	45.3	91.0[20.5%]
Austria	.005	2.2[3.6%]	0.6	0.2	0.7	0.6	1.8	3.2[.7%]
Belgium	.003	1.4[2.3%]	4.1	2.8	2.3	3.9	5.9	9.2[2.1%]
Czechoslovakia	......	....	2.2	0.7	1.9	2.7	4.5	8.6[1.9%]
Denmark	......	....	......	......	......	0.7	0.2	0.4[.1%]
France	.042	2.6[4.2%]	9.7	5.6	6.1	7.2	12.6	19.6[4.4%]
Germany (East)	......	....	......	......	......	......	2.5	3.9[.9%]
Germany (West)	.098	15.6[25.5%]	16.2	5.8	22.7	5.6	21.3	36.8[8.3%]
Hungary	......	....	0.5	0.2	0.6	0.8	1.6	2.6[.6%]
India	......	....	0.6	0.6	1.1	1.3	1.7	6.4[1.4%]
Italy	......	0.8[1.3%]	2.1	1.4	2.3	2.1	5.4	12.7[2.9%]
Japan	......	....	2.3	2.4	6.5	1.7	9.4	41.2[9.3%]
Netherlands	......	....	......	......	......	0.3	1.0	3.1[.7%]
Norway	......	....	......	......	......	0.1	0.2	0.7[.2%]
Spain	......	0.4[.7%]	1.0	0.5	0.6	0.6	1.2	3.5[.8%]
Sweden	.005	0.5[.8%]	0.7	0.5	1.0	1.3	2.2	4.7[1.1%]
United Kingdom	.225	7.9[12.9%]	9.8	5.3	10.6	15.1	20.1	27.4[6.2%]
Yugoslavia	......	....	......	......	0.2	0.4	0.9	1.8[.4%]
Other	.024	1.2[2.0%]	8.7	5.0	6.5	11.7	25.3	47.2[10.6%]
World total	.420	61.2[100.0%]	120.8	50.8	109.9	136.5	269.3	443.3[100.0%]

[1] 1865-1914, *The Mineral Industry: Its Statistics, Technology and Trade*, New York, 1892 and 1922; 1929-1965, *United Nations Statistical Yearbook*, 1948, 1952, 1964, 1966.
[2] Estimated.

Table 3. Population Engaged in Agriculture, Selected Countries and Years, 1865-1965[1]

	About 1865	*About 1914*	*About 1929-1932*	*About 1938*	*About 1948*	*About 1955*	*1965*[2]
	percent of total male population [actual year of census]						
United States	59.0[1860][3]	31.0[1910][3]	21.4[1930][3]	23.4[1940]	15.4[1950]	......	6.0
USSR	75.2[1897][3]	74.8[1913][3]	82.2[1926]	50.0[1940][3]	......	34.3[1959]	32.7
Austria	......	......	31.1[1934]	......	25.0[1951]	18.0[1961]	20.2
Belgium	39.1[1866]	23.9[1910]	17.7[1930]	......	13.6[1947]	......	6.0
Czechoslovakia	44.5[1900][3]	40.5[1910][3]	32.3[1930]	......	29.6[1947]	......	16.1
Denmark	38.7[1901][3]	36.2[1911][3]	28.9[1930][3]	33.8[1940]	20.9[1950][3]	26.2[1955]	15.1
France	62.1[1861]	40.9[1911]	33.6[1931]	33.1[1936]	33.3[1946]	25.2[1957]	18.0
Germany (East)	......	......	......	16.4[1939]	23.4[1946]	......	19.2
Germany (West)	......	......	......	18.1[1939]	16.4[1950]	12.0[1957]	11.0
Hungary	64.8[1850][3]	52.1[1910][3]	54.7[1930]	47.8[1941][3]	52.4[1949]	......	31.2
India	......	......	70.1[1931]	......	69.4[1951]	68.6[1961]	70.0
Italy	58.6[1871]	54.3[1911]	49.4[1931]	49.0[1936]	40.3[1951]	31.3[1957][4]	23.7
Japan	79.6[1875]	51.8[1910]	41.2[1930]	35.4[1940]	40.2[1950]	33.5[1957]	27.0
Netherlands	35.0[1889]	26.3[1920]	22.6[1930]	......	19.8[1947]	......	9.0
Norway	64.1[1865][3]	43.4[1910][3]	43.7[1930]	......	31.4[1950]	......	17.5
Spain	......	71.6[1910]	50.6[1930]	55.6[1940]	53.4[1950]	49.7[1958]	34.7
Sweden	72.4[1870][3]	48.8[1910][3]	35.5[1930]	31.9[1940][3]	25.3[1950]	......	12.0
United Kingdom	22.2[1861][5]	11.5[1911][5]	8.0[1931][5]	......	6.4[1951][6]	......	3.7
Yugoslavia	......	......	74.2[1931]	......	......	60.1[1953]	53.4

[1] Part of the data (particularly that for before 1930) obtained through the courtesy of Professor Folke Dovring, Department of Agricultural Economics, University of Illinois. Other data came from the *FAO Production Yearbooks* for 1958-1962, 1965-1966.

[2] FAO estimates for "economically active" population in agriculture.

[3] Data for total population, both sexes, in agriculture. Used only when data for males was unavailable. It is generally somewhat higher and less reliable for intercountry comparisons.

[4] Sample survey of the labor force.

[5] England, Wales, and Scotland only.

[6] England, Wales, Scotland, and Isle of Man.

An even larger proportion of Russia's population would be required to produce food were it not for the fact that the state permits private enterprise to operate on a small part of the land. According to various studies, about 33 percent of the total farm production in Russia comes from 3 percent of the land, where workers are free to produce and sell on the open market.[2] Private enterprise accounts for 42 percent of Russia's milk supplies, 70 percent of the eggs, and over 20 percent of the wool. This high production is a portent of what would happen if all agricultural production in Russia were on the same basis.

Another measure of the efficiency of an economy is the proportion of private consumption expenditures required for food. For nine countries in free Europe, food expenditures in 1965 averaged 29 percent of total private expenditures as compared with approximately 40 percent for Russia and 19.5 percent for the United States (see Table 4). Obviously, if two-fifths of the total income of a family is required for food, this results in a lower standard of living than when food costs take less of the budget and leave more money to buy other things.

Centralized Control and Standards of Living

Because of the failure of state and collective farms in Russia to attain an efficiency comparable to that in the countries of free Europe and in the United States, the Russian standard of living based on GNP is substantially lower (see Table 5). In 1967, the purchasing power of GNP in the 13 countries of the European Common Market and the European Free Trade Area averaged $2,076 per person, 42 percent above the $1,461 per person in Russia.[3] Purchasing power of

[2]D. Gale Johnson, *Bulletin of the Atomic Scientists,* January, 1964, pp. 11: "Estimates for 1959, based upon official Soviet data of output and its distribution by sectors, indicate that about 33% of gross agricultural output is produced on the private plots of collective farm members and of rural and urban workers and employers. While these plots occupy only 3% of total sown area, they produce almost 16% of the total crop output. Almost half of all livestock products is produced in the private sector, though an unknown amount of feed comes from the socialized and the privately owned livestock graze on public land...."

[3]According to the *United Nations Monthly Bulletin of Statistics,* September, 1968, the National Marketable Product (NMP) of the Union of Soviet Socialist Republics in 1965 was 193.31 billion rubles, and the exchange rate .90 rubles equals one dollar. 193.5 divided by .90 = $214.79 billion, or NMP for 1965 in dollars.

According to the *U.S. News & World Report* of January 31, 1966 (pages 76–77), the gross national product (GNP) for the USSR based upon estimates of the International Monetary Fund was $300 billion in 1965, or a purchasing power of 39.5 percent above the 1965 NMP in the USSR for 1965.

The estimated NMP in Russia for 1967 was $246.7 billion. Assuming the same proportion that GNP exceeded NMP in the USSR in 1967, as in 1965, the estimated GNP in 1967 would be $246.7 billion x 1.395, or $344.15 billion. The reported

Table 4. Expenditures for Food, Selected Countries, 1955 and 1966[1]

	1955	*1965*
	percent of total private consumption expenditures	
United States[2]	22.5	19.5
USSR[3]	50.1	40.3[1963]
Austria	38.5	30.4
Belgium	29.1	
Czechoslovakia	N.A.[4]	N.A.[4]
Denmark	27.6	21.9
France	34.0[5]	29.3
Germany (East)	N.A.[4]	N.A.[4]
Germany (West)[6]	40.7	34.6
Hungary	38.9[1960]	36.6
India	N.A.[4]	N.A.[4]
Italy	41.0	38.9
Japan[6]	51.6	38.5
Netherlands	33.7	29.1
Norway	31.6	28.5
Spain	34.3	36.5[1964]
Sweden	30.0	25.5
United Kingdom	31.3	23.6
Yugoslavia	53.2	46.4[1964]

[1] *UN Yearbook National Accounts Statistics*, 1966. Shown at current market prices. With thanks to the *USDA National Food Situation*, February 1967, Table 13, p. 31.
[2] Includes nonalcoholic beverages.
[3] Includes all beverages.
[4] Not available.
[5] Not strictly comparable to later years.
[6] Includes beverages and tobacco.

GNP in the United States averaged $4,037 per person, 276 percent of that in Russia. Joseph Fromm's articles from Moscow (Chapter 4) illustrate this sharp contrast between the U. S. and Russian standards of living and discuss the difficulties this implies.

The Role of Labor Unions in a Competitive Economy

Among the reasons for the success of modern private enterprise in the United States are its labor unions. One might demur. A reader of newspapers, a watcher of television, or a listener to the radio gets almost hourly reports every time there is a labor strike in the American economy. Based on the attention given each strike, one would think that the whole field of industry was in an uproar and that work stoppages were seriously crippling the total output of our

population in the USSR in 1967 was 235.5 million people (*United Nations Monthly Bulletin of Statistics*, October, 1968).
$344.15 billion divided by 235.5 million = $1,461, or estimated purchasing power of GNP per person in the USSR in 1967.

Table 5. Changes in the Purchasing Power of the Gross National Product of the Countries in the European Economic Community and the European Free Trade Area, 1948-1967[1]

	GNP purchasing power in dollars: 1967 = 100									
	1948		1953		1958		1963		1967	
	Total (billions)	*Per person*	*Total (billions)*	*Per person*	*Total (billions)*	*Per person*	*Total (billions)*	*Per person*	*Total (billions)*	*Per person*
I. European Economic Community										
Belgium	8.27	967	11.07	1,261	13.54	1,4[illegible]6	17.92	1,929	23.50	2,444
France	27.06	659	40.17	942	58.01	1,295	80.15	1,675	103.27	2,063
Italy	15.46	336	23.82	501	32.55	664	48.65	961	65.70	1,251
Luxembourg	0.33	1,178	0.47	1,541	0.63	2,019	0.80	2,454	1.03	3,046
Netherlands	7.85	801	10.28	980	13.92	1,245	19.48	1,628	26.63	2,106
West Germany	20.78	431	48.88	952	77.13	1,421	120.35	2,090	149.24	2,483
EEC	79.75	518	134.69	836	195.78	1,174	287.35	1,617	369.37	2,001
II. European Free Trade Area										
Austria	4.19	603	6.56	942	10.25	1,462	13.94	1,944	17.79	2,420
Denmark	4.04	963	5.51	1,261	6.71	1,485	9.32	1,990	12.49	2,576
Norway	2.80	875	3.82	1,136	4.86	1,380	6.31	1,720	8.55	2,258
Portugal	2.61	316	3.57	418	4.67	535	6.55	694	9.47	1,003
Sweden	7.36	1,069	9.70	1,353	12.32	1,661	16.80	2,209	22.92	2,912
Switzerland	4.80	1,045	6.19	1,269	8.23	1,583	12.61	2,186	16.21	2,669
United Kingdom	53.10	1,061	65.24	1,282	80.20	1,546	100.97	1,877	122.22	2,206
EFTA	78.90	938	100.59	1,167	127.24	1,442	166.50	1,815	209.65	2,219
III. United States	299.36	2,042	423.81	2,655	525.12	3,003	690.68	3,646	803.90	4,037

[1] Data for 1948, 1953 and 1958 from *General Statistics*, OECD, November, 1956, and November, 1964. Data for 1963 and 1967 from *Main Economic Indicators*, OECD, July, 1968. The official exchange rate for the mid-point of 1958 for each national currency was used to convert to dollars. For method used for each country, see *Illinois Agricultural Economics*, July, 1967, p. 7, Table 3.

economy. In fact, however, the image created by our news media is inaccurate. In 1968, for example, when there were several most thoroughly reported, the amount of time lost by the 82,000,000 workers in our total labor force was about one-half of 1 percent of the total manhours worked.[4] On an overall basis, one of the underlying reasons for the high productivity of the American economy is the efficiency of labor. Nowhere in the world does a worker have as much freedom as in the United States; in no major country in the world is the average worker as productive as in this country.[5]

The union movement in the United States was founded on the principles that Louis Brandeis, former Associate Justice of the United States Supreme Court, set forth so well almost half a century ago that they are generally accepted today. Many of the most pertinent of these are quoted in Chapter 6. Bolstered by such supporters as Brandeis, the labor unions have grown greatly. In 1900 only one of every 30 wage-earners was a union member. By 1944 about one of every four belonged to some type of labor union, and by 1968 more than one of every three had union affiliations. If it is true that leaders of labor unions frequently attempt to get unreasonable concessions from management, it is still true that in the long run progressive labor unions serve as part of the system of checks and balances that is necessary to keep an economy productive. In his discussion of "Realities of Union Power" (Chapter 7), Professor Benjamin M. Selekman explains the power that unions have and argues for the necessity of close working relationships between unions and management. One of the more recent philosophers of the place of labor unions in the American economy is Eric Hoffer, whose education includes a short time in school, his experiences as a longshoreman on the West Coast, and his extensive reading. In "Some

---

[4]*Monthly Labor Reviews,* Bureau of Labor Statistics, U. S. Department of Labor, 1968. Currently, the greatest increase in union membership is taking place among public employees and white-collar workers.

[5]Unions have been a power both for increased productivity on the one hand and brakes in the path of economic progress on the other. For example, in the mining industry, between 1949 and 1959, automation replaced two out of every three miners, the average wage doubled and unit costs of labor declined 31 percent. Automation was favored by John L. Lewis who was then the most influential union leader in the mining industry. As a result of his philosophy and liberal use of their pension fund, the adjustment for miners was attained with the minimum of trouble. By keeping costs competitive, the industry is still a viable one and American coal is now being exported to many foreign countries.

On the other hand, in some industries labor unions have been a deterrent to economic progress. Pressure for higher wages frequently has pushed wage rates upward faster than increases in productivity thereby forcing higher prices. Also, in some unions, such as in the construction industry in several cities, union rules have prevented the introduction of new low-cost methods, thus indirectly contributing to perpetuation of slums in these cities.

Thoughts on the Present" (Chapter 8), Mr. Hoffer gives us a clear picture of his viewpoint of the place of a workingman in a democracy, as compared with a totalitarian state. His paper is, in essence, a tribute to the system of private enterprise in which the workingman plays a key role.

The Role of Cooperatives in a Competitive Economy

In 1937 the United States Steel Corporation officially recognized the right of labor to bargain collectively with them through their labor union, the Congress of Industrial Organizations. Prior to this, unions of unskilled workers usually were viewed with suspicion and were not permitted by many firms. Today labor unions of both skilled and unskilled workers in industry are recognized as an integral part of our competitive economy. And an increasingly greater recognition is being given labor organizations of the white-collar workers in professional and service industries.

In contrast to the widespread acceptance of labor unions in industrial economy by employers generally, cooperatives in the business arena, though operating under state or federal laws, are still suspect by some firms who must meet their competition as well as by some students of business.

Concerning cooperatives, Dr. Raymond W. Miller has stated:[6]

> The nonprofit corporation falls into various categories from giant insurance companies, commonly spoken of as mutuals, to small associations of individual taxicab owners with a dozen members. These mutual or cooperative corporations all have one thing in common—to perform a service for their members at cost.
>
> Cooperatives are a part of our enlightened twentieth-century Service Capitalism. I believe that 90 percent or more of all Americans are part of one or more cooperatives. I believe that within their structure lies a legal device that the rest of the world can and will increasingly use. This nonprofit segment of the capitalistic field has no quarrel with the profit section. In some areas the one is more appropriate, and in other areas the other—but they both are capitalistic.

From the point of view of membership, credit unions are probably the largest type of nonprofit organization in the business field. Currently there are some 24,000 cooperative credit unions in the United

---

[6]From his book *A Conservative Looks at Cooperatives,* Ohio University Press, 1964. p. 71. Used by permission of the author.

States with a total membership of over 20 million. In their service to the American people, however, farmer cooperatives have made as much if not a greater contribution than credit unions to the welfare of both farmers and consumers. Hence, attention in this book is centered upon the role of farmer cooperatives in a competitive economy.

Farmer Cooperatives

In 1860, a little over a century ago, it took 59 percent of the people in the United States to produce enough food to feed its population. By 1914, the proportion had dropped to 31 percent, and by 1965 to only 6 percent. Today American farmers not only produce enough food to feed the United States but also have substantial surpluses available for export. American agriculture, largely under private enterprise, today is the most efficient in the world. This remarkable record has resulted not only from the application of modern technology by individual farm operators but also from the growth of farmer cooperatives which have been pacesetters in the efficient purchase of farm supplies and marketing of farm products. In a highly competitive world, farmer cooperatives, which are definitely a part of our system of private enterprise, have aided more efficient production and distribution and have given farmers a voice in legislative halls as well as in the marketplace. This is another of the checks and balances needed in a democracy.

At an annual meeting of the American Institute of Cooperation, M. J. Briggs, General Manager of the Indiana Farm Bureau Cooperative Association, gave a talk on the objectives of farmer cooperatives (Chapter 9). This clearly sets forth what these cooperatives are and how they fit into a competitive economy. At another meeting of the Institute, H. E. Babcock, General Manager of the Grange League Federation Exchange and then President of the Institute, gave a paper on "Scope of the Cooperative Movement" (Chapter 10), explaining the opportunities and limitations of farmer cooperatives. Both these papers give us another insight into the reasons for the success of modern private enterprise in the United States.

The Role of Government in a Competitive Economy

The complexity of our modern civilization is such that even an economy dominated by private enterprise must have many governmental regulations if it is to operate in the public welfare. In fact, one of the biggest problems of mankind is to use the wisdom and knowledge of the ages for the public good without curbing the initiative and creative efforts of each succeeding generation. In our economic organization, the main problem is one of balancing competition, which permits freedom of opportunity and individual initiative, with such state regulation as has proved desirable to protect public health and safety and to increase productivity.[7] The desirability of regulation has generally been accepted in these areas:

Public health and safety: protection of human life and health through the prevention of contagious disease and the control of drugs; prevention of adulteration of water, milk, meat, and so forth; prevention of unsanitary conditions; prevention of exploitation of children and of improper working conditions of labor; action against pollution of streams and air.

Education: provision of public schools, land-grant colleges, state teachers colleges, city colleges.

Resources: conservation of soil, water, minerals, forests.

Banking: protection against misuse of funds; guaranteed deposits.

Roads and bridges: provision of these for the convenience and benefit of the people.

Securities: protection against fraud.

Franchises: safeguarding of community interests.

Natural monopolies: governmental control of enterprises such as the telephone and natural gas, where it is impractical to have competition. (The telephone system for the urban areas in the United States and pipe-line distribution of natural gas operate on a very efficient basis.)

Economic security: protection of opportunity to make a living; maintenance of high and steady rate of employment.

Most of these functions of government have been accepted and in operation for many years. The last, the philosophy that government should function to maintain economic security, namely, to exert some degree of control while retaining the benefits of private initiative, is, however, a relatively new concept of government responsibility. The history of private business enterprise and the theory of national planning by government to provide a more stable environment in which this private enterprise can operate, are ably discussed by Dr. Edwin G. Nourse in "Economic Enterprise and National Planning" (Chapter 11). As the first chairman of the Council of Economic Advisers to the President, Dr. Nourse writes with authority.

In some areas of our competitive economies, especially in those

---

[7]Roland, W. Bartlett, *Trade Barriers in Milk Distribution,* University of Illinois Agricultural Economics Bulletin (June 1960), pp. 32-33.

areas with high risks, private enterprise has failed to give people needed goods and services. Furthermore, in many of the developing countries, there is no backlog of private capital which can be used to develop new industries or to provide essential services. In such situations, government can again step in, to help local groups to help themselves by means of self-liquidating government loans which the local groups can pay for as they use the new facilities. A good example of this is rural electrification in the United States, much of which is due to the government's establishment, under the Rural Electrification Act of 1936, of a system of providing loans for generating, transmitting, and distributing electricity to rural areas. With governmental information on engineering standards such as tensile strength of wire, poles per mile, and customers needed per mile of wire, local groups of farmers (usually sponsored by the Farm Bureau, the Grange, or the Farmers Union) got together and got government loans to set up cooperative systems for transmitting and distributing electricity. In some areas, local cooperatives set up generating plants with self-liquidating government loans payable in 25 or 40 years. When the cooperatives repaid the loans, the government pulled out and the electric cooperative became part of the system of private enterprise owned and operated by the users of the electricity. As officials of the Rural Electrification Administration (REA) point out in Chapter 12, REA loans have furnished electricity to about 20,000,000 people, largely through the 930 local cooperatives whose members use the electricity. Since its inception, REA has advanced about $6.3 billion to its borrowers, who have repaid $1.4 billion on principal and over $809 million on interest. The soundness of the loans is attested by the fact that less than 1/100 of 1 percent of the payments due REA have been delinquent.

The Federal Land Banks and the Banks for Cooperatives are other examples of the use of self-liquidating government loans to provide for the people's necessities. Since 1933 more than $5 billion have been loaned to farmers through the 12 Federal Land Banks. All of these loans have been repaid, and the Land Banks are now the property of the farmers to whom the loans are made. Similarly, by the summer of 1968, 6 of the 13 Banks for Cooperatives had repaid their government capital and were completely farmer-owned. Many governments—state, municipal, as well as federal—use self-liquidating loans for the public welfare. Thus, universities throughout the United States build dormitories with loans guaranteed by the state. Such loans are amortized over a period, usually of 25 years, after which the buildings become the property of the university. The principle of self-liquidating, government-guaranteed loans is also being used by the developing countries. For example, Kuwait, which has an excess of capital, has loaned money to several adjacent countries. One loan for $10 million was made to pay the cost of transmitting and distributing electricity for Amann, Jordan, and the loan is being amortized from income received from the electrical service.

The Role of Private Enterprise in Solving Public Problems

The evidence of the past two decades shows conclusively that the productivity of those countries whose economies are based on private enterprise has been substantially greater than the productivity of those countries whose economies are under centralized state control. This efficiency makes it reasonable that private enterprise should also assume a major responsibility in the attempt to solve public problems.

Currently the racial problem is one which needs the attention of the best brains in the United States. As an example of the part that private enterprise can play in solving this problem, the activities of the Los Angeles Management Council during the past few years merit special attention. After the Watts riot in 1965, a group of businessmen under the leadership of H. C. McClellan organized to provide jobs and job-training for those in Watts. According to the Council's third progress report, over 18,000 of the unemployed or underemployed now have jobs at wages substantially above any they had ever before received (Chapter 13). A study of their employers, a study written by Professor William H. Reynolds (Chapter 14), shows that management has benefited too. These efforts may well serve as a pattern of what can be done, without large government expenditures, to work toward a solution of racial inequities in employment. Housing in the slum areas of the United States is another problem, to which major attention is directed by George Champion in Chapter 15. He discusses a project to renovate tenements in the Harlem area of New York and suggests that this may be a practical way to quickly change a slum, by imaginative use of available technology.

Thus returning to the point from which we began, hunger is a problem facing large areas of the world, as Duncan Norton-Taylor's article "World Hunger" (Chapter 16) shows. Exemplifying the approach basic to this book of readings is the practical approach by which private enterprise has helped toward a solution of this problem of hunger in at least one area. Mr. Lee Morgan of the Caterpillar Company, in "Changes and Challenges" (Chapter 17), discusses an experiment in which his company, working in cooperation with government, used the most advanced technology to clear land, at a relatively low cost, in the Costa Rican jungle in the hopes of making it productive and enabling its people to live and work on their own farms insured against the specter of hunger and with hope for the future.

The Future of Private Enterprise and Centralized Control

The underlying purpose of this book is to explore in breadth and depth the thesis that private enterprise is far more effective a means than centralized state control to improve the living standards of the people in the many countries of the world. Too often, those in responsible positions have failed to consider this thesis—and the evidence for its accuracy—in making their decisions. By bringing together in one volume the philosophies defining modern private enterprise and the examples of its successes, as both have been set forth by some outstanding spokesmen, it is hoped that the vision of the decision-makers may be broadened, if only to a small degree.

Some principal points may be summarized. (1) *The colonial, "robber baron," and other types of exploitative capitalism which, historically, were characteristic of private enterprise have, in large part, been replaced by a system of private enterprise centered upon efficient production and distribution of the goods and services wanted by consumers. The monopolies which once flourished in a system of exploitative capitalism have been largely replaced by competition in the major industrial countries of the world.*

(2) *During the past two decades the greatest economic progress has been made in the countries dominated by private enterprise, not in countries with centralized planning.* The sharp contrast between monopolistic private capitalism which existed before World War I and competitive private capitalism now prevailing, is well illustrated in West Germany. In the early part of the twentieth century under the German Empire, a substantial part of industry was dominated by huge cartels such as Krupp and I. G. Farben. In large part these monopolies have been displaced by firms which are highly competitive. As stated, the revival of private enterprise in West Germany following the devastation of World War II has been one of the marvels of the twentieth century.

Despite substantial economic gains, particularly in the heavy-goods industries, after 50 years of state control in Russia, living standards there are considerably lower than those in the United States and in most of the countries of free Europe where the principal incentive to innovation and improvement has been private enterprise. *The greatest failure of central planning has been in the production of agricultural products and other consumer goods. The proportion of Russian workers required to feed the country's population is more than double the proportion in free Europe and over five times that in the United States.*

(3) *Labor's efficiency under modern private enterprise is directly related to efficiency by consent.* This is in sharp contrast to the situation in countries with centralized planning. Labor unions in the United States have played an important part in attaining efficiency and have made possible high wages by helping to attain high productivity.

(4) Non-profit cooperatives, though differing in structure from profit-making corporations, are an integral part of our competitive enterprise system. Ranging from giant insurance companies commonly called mutuals to small associations with a few members, probably the best-known are the cooperative credit unions and farmer-owned marketing and purchasing cooperatives.

(5) The role of government should be three-fold. In the first place it should provide an environment in which modern private enterprise can operate efficiently. Some specific things included under this are public safety, protection of health, economic security, guaranteed bank deposits, conservation of resources, regulation of transportation, and security regulation.

In the second place, the government should provide for the distribution of wealth created by private enterprise so that it will contribute to the long-run benefit of all the people as well as those in charge of its creation. Education ranks first in the benefits of a productive economy. Exemplifying this is the fact that two out of every five individuals of college age in the United States are now in college. Along with this, an expanding economy makes it possible for the mass of people to be better-fed, better-clothed, and better-housed, and better able to afford education, medical care, and recreation. The graduated income tax and the property tax are probably the two most important factors in making the benefits of a free enterprise system available for all the people.

Finally, the key to resolving problems such as hunger, poverty, disease, racial inequalities, slums, riots, crime, and other problems lies in bringing to bear in an imaginative way the vast resourcefulness of private enterprise working with government. Rural electrification, financed by the government and now serving over 20,000,000 people, is a good example of this. Establishing self-liquidating loans has made possible a gradual withdrawal of government leaving eventual control and operation in the hands of private enterprise cooperatives being served with electricity.

One of the outstanding thinkers of our present age is Professor Kenneth E. Boulding, of the University of Colorado, and President (1968) of the American Economic Association. In his discussion of "Symbols for Capitalism," he has explored in depth the realities of private enterprise as compared with centralized planning by the state and evaluated these ideologies for the future (Chapter 18). His conclusion is that while much can be done to improve it, private enterprise is more likely to survive the forces of dissent than centralized planning. His article is a fitting summary and projection of the articles and ideas that precede it.

Part II

PRIVATE ENTERPRISE VERSUS CENTRALIZED CONTROL

Chapter 1

Too many people still speak of American capitalism in terms of the era of the "robber baron," the era which prevailed during the latter part of the nineteenth century and the early part of the twentieth century. In fact, however, the modern private enterprise which has prevailed since World War II is not, for the most part, of the exploitative type which once existed. Indeed, most of the monopolies in American business during the early twentieth century have been facing increasing competition in the past two decades. In his book *Can Capitalism Compete?* my friend of some 30 years, Dr. Raymond W. Miller, clearly states the difference between modern capitalism and the old, exploitative type. As he defines it, this new capitalism is "private enterprise with a conscience." I am in complete agreement with the philosophy Dr. Miller sets forth. His argument speaks for itself, and its approach is a good one with which to begin the search for the answers to the questions we have posed.

CAN CAPITALISM COMPETE?*

Raymond W. Miller**

What Does Modern American Capitalism Offer?

What, then, is this "capitalism" which the Marxists and Communists are seeking to destroy, and yet which we Americans (and others) feel is the servant of all mankind?

Capitalism has been defined as follows:

> . . . an economic system in which capital and capitalists play the principal part; specifically, one in which the ownership of land and natural wealth, the production, distribution, and exchange of goods, and the operation of the system itself, are effected by private enterprise and control under competitive conditions.[1]

With this I would not quarrel—insofar as it goes. But it carries little hint of the philosophies, attitudes, and the democratic framework which in the United States and Canada have produced a dynamic North American capitalism which is unique in its functioning. There is no one definition of American capitalism. It is of necessity a definition that varies with experience and viewpoint. American capitalism is evolving and therefore has to be defined in its condition at a particular time; but it is the North Star of hope for mankind if it is to find a way out of the morass caused by exploitative capitalism—the very morass which prompts the Marxists to condemn all capitalism. Its essential characteristic is that *mid-twentieth-century American capitalism participates in producing economic progress through social justice by democratic means.*

In contrast to socialism or communism, under capitalism the basic economic decisions are determined by the sum of countless individual decisions of all the people, rather than by the state. Under North American capitalism the ultimate consumer, in the long run, determines the types of goods that are to be made and sold. The previously

---

*Taken from Chapter III, "American Service Capitalism," of the book ***Can Capitalism Compete? A Campaign for American Free Enterprise*** (New York: Ronald Press), 1959; reproduced by permission of Dr. Miller.

**President of World Trade Relations, Inc., and former lecturer in the Harvard Graduate School of Business.

[1] *Webster's New Collegiate Dictionary* (Springfield, Mass.: G & C Merriam Co., 1956).

mentioned study made by the Council for Advancement of Secondary Education, of which the author is a trustee, points out: "Free enterprise assumes that individuals are in the long run the best judges of their own interests, and that an economic system that makes it possible for them to pursue those interests will achieve the greatest welfare for all."[2] The basic foundations of the system are *private property, profit motivation, competition, and economic freedom.* Further definition of the latter develops particular economic freedoms:

> *Freedom of enterprise* is the right of the individual businessman to decide what business to enter, and what goods to produce or what services to render. Once his business is established, it is his right to conduct his enterprise responsibly in pursuit of profits. His decisions, of course, are guided by market conditions; they are not arbitrary ones.
>
> *Freedom of choice* assures a person the right to live where he pleases, work at what he can do best, and to buy the goods and services he prefers. Many believe this to be the most fundamental economic freedom—the one that especially distinguishes a free-enterprise economy from others and that is most essential to a democracy.
>
> *Freedom of contract* means the right of consumers, producers, workers, land owners of property to bargain with one another, and to exchange goods and services on terms acceptable to all concerned.[2]

Noting that certain modifications of free enterprise have been developed in this country the study describes the foundations of American capitalism as follows:

> (1) Its property and enterprises are *predominantly* privately owned. (2) The Profit motive provides a *major* incentive for its operation. (3) Active and *substantially* free competition exists. (4) The maximum *desirable* economic freedom is assured.[2]

These four foundations support our market economy in which individual decisions and initiative determine what consumer or capital goods are to be created—where, how many, and at what price—how to organize for the most effective production and distribution, and who should receive the products.

The italicized words in the definitions of the four foundations of American capitalism are indicative of the developments by which we

---

[2]These quotes are taken from Council for Advancement of Secondary Education, *American Capitalism, An Introduction for Young Citizens* (Washington, D. C.: The Council, 1958), pp. 21, 22, 23.

have moved away from exploitative capitalism. Underlying the changes is the basic philosophy that business should serve as well as get. To this end it should be subject to reasonable regulation by the state when the people through their freely chosen representatives determine that the public interest so requires. In speeches in Congress, Senator Ralph E. Flanders of Vermont has recognized this situation several times. He sent me the following statement during the Suez crisis:

> This closing off of Western Europe's supply of oil has brought problems to this country. The oil companies have raised the price of oil and its products to American customers. On the basis of free enterprise of which I am an ardent supporter, it can be argued that they can and may charge all that the market will bear. This, however, is not in the long-range self-interest of the oil companies. If they continue to take advantage of a foreign situation when their stocks are high and their production capable of great expansion, they may look for legislation in the near future which will declare the oil industry to be a public utility in which prices will be determined by the government instead of competitively. The principle of free enterprise is best served when the free enterprisers regard their long-range interests instead of looking for immediate profit.

If a job is too big for private enterprise, or if private business has failed to perform a necessary service for a reasonable price, the people should and do determine by their individual votes or by the votes of their representatives whether they wish the state or the community to assume some function normally performed by private capitalism. Congressman Brooks Hays of Arkansas, until 1959 a member of the House Foreign Affairs Committee, in a statement prepared for inclusion in this study, sums up what I believe is a cross-section of Congressional opinion in regard to capitalism, as follows:

> Capitalism is private enterprise with a conscience. If the conscience is lacking, then no amount of technical proficiency or managerial genius can prevent the breakdown of the system. Where there is no self-imposed moral discipline, government will inevitably take notice of the problems created. The breakdown thus leads to some form of statism which marks the end of industrial freedom.

Under the modern Sino-Soviet system, state capitalism is blended with a political oligarchy.[3] The net result is that the beneficence of

[3]Under the system of free enterprise capital is owned largely by individuals. The open market determines the value of goods and services. The law of supply

service capitalism is something that does not need to be taken into consideration by those operating the state organizations, because they are responsible only to the political arm of government for the operation of an economic function. In North America where the government, either federal or local, enters into the operation of a business, the officials are directly or indirectly responsible to the voters.

To appreciate the changes that have taken place in this century, one should read *The Age of the Moguls*,[4] which is not a muck-raking document per se but does point out the general failure to recognize social responsibility as part of the role of capitalists during the era when the United States became materially great. The revolt of the American conscience and some of the subsequent reforms in our economic society have been well presented in *The Big Change*.[5]

Can Capitalism Compete?

Due to the constant discovery by scientists and engineers of new products, and the development of means to manufacture and distribute them by fabricators and distributors, modern business manufactures many products that are obsolescent when put on the market; there is often a better one on blueprints or in the initial stages of manufacture. These dynamics of business are largely impossible where the supply and demand is regulated by the all-powerful state.

As material products become obsolescent, similarly many of the old concepts of capitalistic business have become obsolete. Some of the changes have been reflected in legislation. When exploitative monopolistic corporations were concentrating economic control in the hands of a few to the detriment of the many, Congress passed the Sherman Anti-Trust Act and Canada legislated its Combines Investigation Act. These acts, with their amendments and regulations, established the principle that every North American should have the opportunity to become a capitalist. Today's corporations largely not only accepted

---

and demand acts as a regulator of values, with the government providing the rules of "fair play."

Under the Communist system the state becomes the sole owner of working capital, and most personal possessions are taken over by the state. Capital is used both at home and internationally by the state. Prices are determined not by the rules of the ordinary buyer-and-seller transaction but by the determination of policy in line with the objectives of the state. Capital remains as an indispensable ingredient in life, but its use and values are determined by political as well as economic considerations.

[4] Stewart H. Holbrook, *The Age of the Moguls* (Garden City, N.Y.: Doubleday & Co., Inc., 1953).

[5] Frederick Lewis Allen, *The Big Change, American Transforms Itself, 1900-1950* (New York: Harper & Bros., 1952).

this principle but as a whole actively encourage individual capitalism in another sense—through widespread ownership of their stocks—by employee purchase plans and by offerings to the public. Over 8 million families are stockholders in the United States today. Many millions more are capitalists through their interests in savings, life insurance, pensions, and so forth. These funds are managed by privately operated institutions which in turn lend to or invest in private enterprise. A significant proportion of North Americans are capitalists via their ownership of farms and real estate.

For centuries, the doctrine of *caveat emptor* (Let the buyer beware) was the rule of trade. Under it, wooden nutmegs were sold to unsuspecting "natives," and dangerous medicines and adulterated foods sent many a person to an untimely grave. So extensive were these evil practices of "exploitative capitalism" that Congress saw fit to pass the Pure Food and Drug Act of 1905. Equally strict are the regulations under Canada's Food and Drug Act. However, during the last half-century North American capitalism with enlightened management has largely removed the fear of *caveat emptor* from the mind of the purchaser. The overwhelming majority of goods and services are today guaranteed to satisfy the customer. Some stores even advertise that they will refund the money for a roast if the housewife is not satisfied with its tenderness! This is a distinct step ahead from the "Let-the-public-be-damned" attitude of the later nineteenth century.

Times are changing in the direction of fair dealings in the public interest. Many an innocent investor used to be fleeced through shady practices by issuers or sellers of stocks and bonds. But the principle of *caveat venditor* (Let the seller beware) has been legislated into most of the state and provincial acts regulating securities, and particularly into the U. S. Securities Exchange Act of 1934 and amendments thereto. The latter makes subject to civil suit and criminal penalties individuals who violate its provisions, for instance, by failure to give adequate information about a company whose securities are to be issued, or taking advantage of inside knowledge, or manipulating the market. The operations of dealers and of securities exchanges can incur severe administrative penalties if they do not comply with standards set up under the act.

American Capitalism Is Responsible

North American capitalism has worked out other concepts unrelated to any compulsion of law. One of those is to help people help themselves. Just two illustrations. Within a business organization there is usually the opportunity for an individual to advance to the extent of his ability. Even more, many enterprises, recognizing latent abilities in their employees, enable them to develop their potentialities through training programs either within or outside the company. Business, as a matter of course, applies the same concept to its customers and suppliers by encouraging them to develop products which will enhance the growth of those outside enterprises.

A fundamental attribute of mid-century American capitalism is equality of respect. The patronizing attitude of the proprietor or manager in the 1890's has largely disappeared, and the man who works at the bench, or drives a truck, or sells behind the counter receives as his human due approximately the same amount of respect and consideration as does the white-collar man, or proprietor, customer, stockholder; in fact, he is often a stockholder himself. This is so far from the old concept of business that it is very hard for people in other parts of the world to understand. Largely a thing of the past is the situation where an employee would come into an office and bow as though he were appearing before a lord of the realm, or would come in "with his cap in his hand," as the old expression went. One finds in most of private business in America a fraternal relationship that is unique.

Closely related but going beyond all these is the essential ingredient of today's American capitalism—the matter of business responsibility, human or public relations, human engineering, or whatever you want to call it. The American industrialist has learned to put fellowship, truth, and honesty into business. Practically unknown until a few years ago, this philosophy is perhaps the greatest development of the genius of America in the field of economics—the discovery that business can function and still be friendly; that the businessman does not have to tell the truth to a few and some prepared story to the many; that goods can be honestly made, distributed, and sold to the consumer at a fair profit. The extent to which these ideas go beyond any legal requirements is reflected in the emphasis which today's industrialist places on the brand name he gives his products. He holds out his brand as a hallmark of integrity and of a certain quality at a suitable price, and he is careful so to design and make each item as to support the brand's reputation.

We have developed a capitalist enterprise system that has made it possible for men of all strata of society to enjoy the benefits of industry in a way that just a generation ago was the goal of the radical "soap box" orator. This is not solely due to the techniques of mass production, for the needed increase in markets to support mass production depended on concepts unrecognized by exploitative capitalism. American businessmen have learned that when they set prices at a low enough level to allow more people to buy their products, the resulting increase in the market for most goods returns an increased total profit; that the new income of the additional workers needed for the increased production again increases the market potential; and that wages which reflect a sharing of the cost savings from increasing productivity enable workers to enter the market for goods which in their grandparents' day would have been the privilege of the wealthy. The woman on Main Street can wear the same fashion in clothes as the woman on Fifth Avenue. The farmer from out where the creek forks, when he gets into the city, is hard to differentiate in appearance from the businessman. And if one were to call at their homes he would find labor-saving devices, luxuries, and evidences of culture that would make him realize that in its own way American capitalism has gone a long distance toward a classless society.

Present-day responsible American capitalism looks upon community and civic projects as something in which it should take an active part. Just a generation or so ago, it was rather uncommon for a company to understand that its employees owed any other duty during their waking hours except to the corporation. Today, this is very largely reversed, and increasing numbers of American businesses recognize that the employee who takes an interest in community development in his off-duty hours—and sometimes during working hours as well—can and does perform a service not only for himself and his company, but for democracy itself.

This same thinking prompts business leaders to accept the call of the government to fill responsible posts despite the financial sacrifice to themselves and the loss of their leadership to their companies. Private enterprise as a responsible force in our society has set up, or contributed substantially to, many foundations for research in medicine, education, and other social areas.

Modern Capitalism Outshines "Socialism of the Chair"

In the late nineteenth century there developed in Germany a concept known as "Socialism of the Chair." The term was applied, at first in ridicule, to the doctrines of a group of economists who advocated state aid for the betterment of the working class. In America our sense of responsibility has led us to take the very principles which Germany enunciated in "Socialism of the Chair" and make them a large part of the basic economic practices of our land. We have enacted laws first proposed by the socialists, among which are workmen's compensation, unemployment insurance, wage and hour laws, and veterans' insurance and health services. An increasing number of people are coming under Social Security, to which few object; we do not allow the poor to suffer at home and alone—we hospitalize them at public expense and see that they receive adequate medical service. The costs of many of these benefits are borne completely by industry; of others, business enterprises pay a significant share through their taxes. No political party in North America has made any serious attempt to undo any of the social or welfare legislation enacted under preceding administrations. This fact was illustrated by the 1957 election in Canada.[6]

In 1953, after Norman Thomas had retired as active head of the Socialist Party (having been its Presidential nominee six times), I sent him a copy of a speech I had made before the Third Annual Conference on Constitutional Relations, at the University of Utah, November 28-29, 1952. It was entitled "Dynamic Capitalism." In this speech I had said:

> ... The study of despotic materialism is interesting. Norman Thomas, the leader of the Socialist Party, was one of the first to denounce it. He was, perhaps, the first leader of consequence in the United States to expose the men of the Kremlin as being opposed to human liberty in the Twentieth Century. He said that the world has its choice of being free or slave. Many of our politicians didn't see it that way. Many of those who thought so didn't have "nerve" to say the things that they knew were right. No one will ever successfully attack you if you say the thing you know is right. "Truth though crushed to the earth will rise again." Norman Thomas had the nerve to do it. A few months ago when he retired as leader of the Socialist Party, a big banquet was given *for Norman Thomas.* A thousand business, religious, political and industrial leaders came to pay their respects to him as *a man.* Mr. Thomas, following the simple rule of integrity, had said the things in which he believed and had often been called a radical. Today, many of his ideas are in the Democratic and Republican party platforms—this is a demonstration of how democracy works in the U.S.A., and this is as it should be.

In a letter to me, dated June 23, 1953, Mr. Thomas wrote:

[6]*Time* magazine reported: "Triumphant Tory "Leader of Canada's Progressive Conservative (Tory) Party, which last week downed the powerful Liberals: John George Diefenbaker.

"... Politics: Accents the 'progressive' in his party's official name, Progressive Conservative. Backs flexible farm supports, social security and health measures, more federal aid to penniless Atlantic provinces. Shunning a doctrinaire stand, he goes along with Canada's pattern of government competition with private enterprise in rails, airlines, hotels, T.V. ..."—*Time* (June 24, 1957).

> Thank you for your pamphlet, "Dynamic Capitalism." In these days when obviously so much rethinking is necessary, the old division lines aren't what they were. It may be that "dynamic capitalism" and democratic socialism are growing nearer and nearer together. Anyway more forthright discussion is in order. I appreciate your references to me which were, if anything, too complimentary.

In a succinct way this states the whole case of the changing status of capitalism from the laissez faire to the dynamic.

Yes, "Socialism of the Chair" and a lot more "socialistic" ideas unconsciously became a fundamental part of the American social economic and financial system; but American business has very slowly begun to realize the fact that it is living in a new and fast changing world, and that it has a chance to penetrate that new world and work cooperatively with it for mutual benefit and universal peace and prosperity. A "creeping socialism" has understandably accompanied a "creeping" (or galloping) capitalism, but it has not seriously impaired the capitalistic nature of our economy.

Definitions of Capitalism Are Many and Varied

"What is capitalism?" is a question that I have asked citizens of most of the free nations of the earth, ranging from rulers in high places to students in the classroom, farmers in the field, managers in their offices, and laborers at the bench. No two definitions were the same. The great majority of answers of persons not living in America included some form of statements or prophecy to the effect that the welfare state will be an integral part of modern life—usually with an approving reference to the Scandinavian use of capital. I have asked this same question of a cross-section of North Americans, both citizens of Canada and of the United States, and find much the same answer, except with an almost universal appreciation of the fact that business now represents a great improvement over the concept of business in 1900. The belief of most people in and out of business seems to be that had not business recognized the responsibility of capitalism within a responsible society, organized business in America would have been inextricably enmeshed in the toils of state control or ownership.

The definitions of some observers of the American scene seem particularly worthy of inclusion here. Dr. Tojuro Murai, Chief Editorial Writer of the *Hokkahu Shimbun,* as well as lecturer at Toyama University and Kanazawa Women's College in Japan, had been told that our capitalism was still of the exploitative type. But because he is an astute, natural researcher, he wanted to base his opinions upon his own observations. Dr. Francis Brown of the American Council on Education arranged for him to spend a few days with us at the Harvard Business School in 1956. We made for him many other contacts, among them John Kenneth Galbraith, Professor of Economics at Harvard, with whom he developed a warm and close friendship. Dr. Murai proved to be an intense, interesting man, and his questioning about our new capitalism was among the most searching I have encountered. Dr. Murai's definition of capitalism as he found it here is included in a round-table discussion he had with other educators upon his return to Japan. Below are some direct quotes translated from this discussion, published under the title *Capitalism Is Already Exceeding Itself*:

> [Preface:] Capitalism already appears to have changed into something completely different. Capitalism is difficult to understand unless it is understood as something dynamic and different from what Marx defined. Particularly, in the changing American society, it appears that a firm, new trend is being worked out by management executives, labor union leaders, and a number of leading scholars. This trend is to discover within capitalism itself a public-ness, and to further and develop this public-ness.[7]
>
> [Kobayashi:]... Today it is already a question whether we should badly say, "Choose capitalism" or "Choose communism." How has capitalism as represented by the United States today changed? Can capitalism progress further? If it can, what kind of labor-management relations will be born? As a matter of fact, already in America a new labor-management relationship may be a-borning.
>
> If there is indeed something new in American capitalism, the big question is how to adapt it and use it in Japan. I would like all of you to give us your opinions with this background in mind. First of all, I shall call on Mr. Murai, in order to have him indicate the direction in which we should take our discussion.
>
> [Murai:] ... I was first struck by his [Mr. Raymond W. Miller's] contention of the dynamic nature of American capitalism. The question is, of course, practically speaking, how did capitalism come to take a course different from that prescribed by Marx? Well, it seems to me that, first of all, in regard to labor, capital, management—all these important production factors in the capitalistic structure—an atitude of, what shall I say, a kind of social responsibility has been very strongly developed.

[7]Public-ness (kokyo-sei) is a coined word derived from kokyo, or public, as used in such terms as the public welfare, the public good (but not the general/or public opinion) and sei, or nature-ness.

> Specifically, capital, for instance, is not looked upon as one form of the right of absolute possession by an individual. It is looked upon as a wealth shared by society as a whole. Of course the starting point was the formation of an organization through which the individual would seek to gain profits. But as this concept progressed, it was looked upon simply as one factor within a common society. The main factor then came to be regarded as a whole. Management, for instance, in its relations with labor, came to look upon its ultimate aim as that of dealing with good citizens. I feel that America is proceeding and will proceed in that general direction. This is what will make capitalism dynamic, I feel.

Dr. Dale Yoder, then Professor of Economics and Director, Industrial Relations Center, University of Minnesota, now of Stanford University, participated with me and others in an Executive Development Program in Utah, in June, 1958. This program was sponsored by the Institute of Industrial Relations and the College of Business of the University of Utah. The thirty executives in attendance gave freely of their time and thought in discussing many of the ideas expressed in this book, and Dr. Yoder added greatly to a stimulating and exhaustive examination of the whole subject of twentieth-century capitalism. During these seminars he made the vital statement:

> As managers of American industries have faced the growing relative scarcity of manpower and as competition for available labor supplies has become sharper, we seem to be developing a new type of economy that might be called *capitalistic socialism*. The basic Marxian precept—to each according to his needs—is increasingly implemented through our expanding program of employer-financed employee benefits and services. These "fringe benefits" provide many of the objectives, advocated by Marxists, at the same time that they preserve the incentives, motivations, and freedoms that have been the distinctive contribution of the private capitalistic system. This development is a part of the emerging theory of agency management, in which managers propose to act as the agent of employee team-members. As agents, they promise to encourage the continuing personal development of their worker clients, to maximize their contributions and rewards, to coach them in their work, and thus to develop each team-member as an All-American worker.

A most significant analysis of the genius of North American freedom in developing the most highly productive economy in the world was made by Herbert Hoover before he became President of the United States. In defining the American social system he says:

> We have, in fact, a special social system of our own. We have made it ourselves from materials brought in revolt from

conditions in Europe. We have lived it; we constantly improve it; we have seldom tried to define it. It abhors autocracy and does not argue with it, but fights it. It is not capitalism, or socialism, or syndicalism, nor a cross breed of them. Like most Americans, I refuse to be damned by anybody's "word-classification" of it, such as "capitalism," "plutocracy," "proletariat" or "middle class", or any other, or to any kind of compartment that is based on the assumption of some group dominating somebody else.

The social force in which I am interested is far higher and far more precious a thing than all these. It springs from something infinitely more enduring; it springs from the one source of human progress—that each individual shall be given the chance and stimulation for development of the best with which he has been endowed in heart and mind; it is the sole source of progress; it is American individualism.

The rightfulness of our individualism can rest either on philosophic, politicial, economic, or spiritual grounds. It can rest on the ground of being the only safe avenue to further human progress.[8]

Col. Richard P. Crenshaw, Jr., a fellow-member of the Bar who has long been familiar with national and international affairs, has sent me the following thought-provoking paragraph regarding the value of the new capitalism:

The competitive North American free enterprise system (modern "capitalism") is absolutely indispensable to human freedom and the inevitable future world-wide system, since no other system both (1) gives the individual full incentive to work and thus throw off the bondage of want, and (2) splits up economic and thus political power, and prevents its concentration by providing many bosses and alternatives instead of (as in the Soviet) only one. A man given too much power will always abuse it and competitive free enterprise alone sees that no one man gets too much power.

Sylvia and Benjamin Selekman, authors of *Power and Morality in a Business Society,* explore how the various centers of power in our society interoperate, and come up with a research concept of our American capitalism. They say:

These critics [of capitalism] assume that, with the abolition of private property, materialistically motivated business managers will be replaced by dedicated, selfless servants of the state. Events have by now clearly demonstrated that before very long the selfless servant, in fact, turns into an ab-

[8]From *American Individualism,* by Herbert Hoover, pp. 12-13. Copyright 1952 by Doubleday & Co., Inc. Reprinted by permission of the publishers.

> solutist commissar. Such is the logic of power. The gradual gains growing out of the exchanges of negotiation in our capitalist democracy, on the other hand, furnish convincing evidence of steady advance toward social goals without the risk of enthroning commissars. For capitalism, as it has evolved in the West, is a decentralized form of power–in contradiction to Marxian theory–with negotiation as the strategic form of administration.[9]

The Structure of the North American Economy

With the growth of large business enterprises for production, transportation, and distribution of goods, there gradually emerged the general use of the capitalistic corporation—a legal device seldom needed or used until mass production made posssible wide use of products. Many of these corporations, as in the automotive, electrical, steel and telephone industries, are of truly massive size. Most large businesses, either directly or through subsidiaries or affiliates, perform in varying degree a wide variety of functions. In manufacturing, these may range from extraction of raw materials to franchising dealers in the finished products; in insurance, from selling and servicing the insured to the development and management of residential or commercial buildings in which some of their funds are invested. Perhaps size and integration are the most widely known aspects of our economic structure.

Less widely understood and deserving of emphasis is the place of small business. For despite giant corporations there is room and need for enterprises on a scale that could be duplicated in almost any part of the world. Of all retail establishments in the United States, for instance, over one-third are run by the proprietor, with no paid employees. Over another third have five or fewer employees. Together their sales volume is over one-third of all retail sales, including those of large retail chains. Even more surprising to many, perhaps, is the degree to which manufacturing offers an opportunity to the man who desires to create goods for others while making a profit for himself. There are over 100,000 manufacturing enterprises in the United States—nearly 40 per cent of all manufacturers—with fewer than five workers. Nearly 240,000 or over 80 per cent of all manufacturers, employ fewer than fifty.[10] Some of the smaller enterprises serve local needs; others have found a wider niche. Many have found a sure

---

[9]By permission from *Power and Morality in a Business Society,* by Sylvia Kopald Selekman and Benjamin M. Selekman, p. 172. Copyright, 1956, McGraw-Hill Book Company, Inc., New York.

[10]The figures cited are based on the latest available U. S. Census of Business, for 1954.

place for themselves simply because their very smallness allows them quick flexibility in adjusting to the changing needs or desires of those whom they would service.

The nonprofit cooperative enterprise is a fundamental part of the American business scene, recognized and respected throughout the nation. To quote the National Association of Manufacturers:

> A "cooperative" is a form of business enterprise that enables a group of individuals, partnerships, or corporations, to combine together for the purpose of producing or buying or selling a commodity or service. City consumers have gotten together to buy goods and sell them. Businessmen have formed mutual fire insurance companies. Individuals join together to buy life insurance through a mutual insurance company or merchandise through a mutual wholesale purchasing association. People who save money put their funds in a mutual savings bank. Farmers join together to buy goods they use in production or to sell the things they grow. All of these are "cooperatives." They are also legitimate forms of private enterprise.[11]

One of the fields in North America in which cooperatives are most active is agriculture. The Railway Express Agency, shipping packages of a size comparable to or larger than those the Post Office accepts, is a nonprofit cooperative corporation owned by about seventy-four railroads using it as a service agency.[12] Several million American families living in small towns and rural communities secure their electric service through private cooperatively owned power companies (R.E.A.), whose original capital was borrowed from the government, and which is being repaid ahead of schedule. Every bank clearing-house, rural telephone and electric cooperative, mutual building and loan association, mutual insurance company, mutual savings bank, credit union, and cooperative apartment are sign posts pointing to the fact that people in a free society demand and have achieved freedom to organize for their own best economic interests.[13]

The area where the people choose to have enterprise owned and

---

[11]National Association of Manufacturers, *NAM and Cooperatives* (privately published in New York, 1946), p. 7.

[12]"...Express companies...have handled small packages for 118 years, even though the competition of the subsidized parcel-post service has, since 1913, been almost insurmountable.

"...The Express Agency conducts the express business for substantially all the express-carrying railroads of the country, in effect serving as the express department of each railroad. The Express Agency collects the express revenues, pays its own operating expenses and taxes, and turns the balance over to the express-carrying roads." *U. S. News & World Report* (June 21, 1957).

[13]See Joseph G. Knapp, "Are Cooperatives Good Business?" *Harvard Business Review* (January-February, 1957).

operated by local or federal government is not clearly defined. There is the government-owned Post Office which is universally accepted as a public business operation. Even this, however, is sometimes challenged.[14] We have a dynamic economy, in which functions change from the public to the private sectors and vice versa as serious need may arise. As an example, there are in the United States today something over 2,000 municipally owned electric services providing power and light for communities that have decided to create or take over such functions rather than have private enterprise own and operate them. Many cities own and operate their own water supply. On the other hand, there are the facilities and services in government-owned national parks which are provided by private enterprises operating under a government franchise. There are hundreds of municipally owned airports where the state or municipality charges a fee for the use of the field or its terminals. There are wholly owned federal projects, such as the Tennessee Valley Authority, which has been one of the most controversial of all national projects, and at the same time one of the most widely heralded abroad as an American triumph.

Many of our early highways and country roads in the United States were largely privately owned toll roads at one time. Later, under the post road provision of the federal Constitution and the taxing power of the states, nearly all of them were thrown open to public use. Recently, however, there has developed a trend to special high-speed toll roads, with the state acting as operator, and borrowing the money to build them from the general public through the means of bonds, the income from which is nontaxable.

In the United States, rail and truck transportation systems are owned by profit- entity corporations highly regulated by government-city, county, state and federal. In Canada, a major part of the public transportation systems—air, rail, and water—is conducted by government-owned corporations. Canada prides itself on an excellent system of hotels owned and operated by its government-owned railways, but these are in direct competition in many places with hotels which are the property of the privately owned competing railway.

Banking and credit are largely in the private enterprise sector. Canada has its government-owned Bank of Canada along with the other independent banks. In both countries there are a number of

[14]"*Private Mail Contract Suggested by President*—Apparently annoyed at the all-out pay raise fight being made by the postal employee unions, President Eisenhower is reported to have told a group of Republican Congressmen that a lot of the Nation's postal problems could be solved by the Government turning over its postal operations to a private firm . . ." Joseph Young, *The Evening Star* (Washington, D. C., June 18, 1957).

federal credit agencies which lend capital to risks which private banking does not care to undertake.

Labor is organized into trade unions when the workers themselves choose to do so. Some of these organizations draw their membership from individual crafts, others represent all categories of workers in a particular industry. When a labor union is certified as representing a majority of the workers in its field within a plant or company, the employer must bargain with it regarding wages, hours, and working conditions. While organized labor's primary activity is to serve the interests of its membership through negotiation with employers, it is also active in the political sphere—primarily by endorsing or opposing either individual candidates for political office or proposed legislation which is of interest to labor. Officials of organized labor frequently serve on governmental or independent boards or agencies which are concerned with matters of public interest.

Employers, too, voluntarily organize into trade associations which without indulging in monopolistic practices serve the interests of their memberships. Some of their activities are pooling knowledge of their markets; collecting, computing, and publishing average operating figures so that individual members may judge and improve their own performance; citing individual experiences in overcoming some particular problem; and representing to the public and to the government the interests of their own group and the ways in which their industry serves society.

While not immediately a part of business, there are hundreds of organizations by which business is informally linked to the community. Among them are the Chamber of Commerce, trade associations, and service clubs. These are composed of business and professional men who as individuals bring their knowledge and their leadership to the finding of voluntary solutions to community social and economic problems. In this same category might also be included the large foundations which are set up for social purposes and whose funds originally come from corporate or individual enterprise.

I would not wish anyone to think that we in America have reached the millennium. We, too, are human. We make mistakes. Not every businessman appreciates all the values which underlay the transition from exploitative capitalism. But I do believe that in American service capitalism we have found one of the roads toward the optimum material condition of man: economic power used for profit and social justice with the government as a referee and umpire, with freedom of conscience introduced into material well-being as business tries to serve as well as to get.

Chapter 2

Another basic misconception about the modern American economy is that competition is gradually diminishing in vigor and is being supplanted in many industries by various forms of monopoly. Probably no single belief has done more to undermine public confidence and convince people that socialism or central planning is inevitable. Through close contact with the rough and tumble of American business over several decades, however, I personally know that competition is not dying out but is taking new forms and growing in vigor. In fact, not only in America but throughout the industrial world, we are now in the midst of an industrial revolution in which competition is the pacesetter of our modern private enterprise.

It was my privilege years ago when I was at Cornell University to have had Professor Sumner Slichter as my instructor in economics. Shortly before, Professor Slichter, the son of a midwestern university dean, had spent two years in a coal mine so that he would know first-hand what it meant to be a worker. Over a long productive career, Professor Slichter, a leader in economics, continued to impress both his students and his business associates with the breadth and depth of his knowledge. His article on "The Growth of Competition," which was written in the early 1950's, is a classic well worth the reading of everyone interested in knowing how our American economy is working.

THE GROWTH OF COMPETITION*

Sumner H. Slichter**

One of the most widely held misconceptions about the American economy is the belief that competition is gradually diminishing in vigor and is being supplanted in many industries by various forms of monopoly. The belief that competition is dying is probably accepted by a majority of economists and certainly by a large part of the general public. Probably no single belief has done more to undermine confidence in the future of the economy and to convince many people that socialism or central planning is inevitable.

If competition in fact were dying out, the matter would be most serious. Competition quickly and severely punishes managements that are stupid or lazy or that get out of touch with conditions. In the rough struggle between Communism and private enterprise, business needs the spur and the discipline of stiff competition to keep it dynamic and well managed.

But as inquiry will show, competition is not dying out, it is steadily spreading, taking new forms, and growing in vigor. Granted that in some industries it is not as strong or as pervasive as it should be. Granted that the business world is full of groups that wish strong competition for the other fellow but desire restraints on rivalry among their own members. Granted that some of the groups wishing to limit competition (the high tariff advocates and the "fair trade" advocates) have strong influence within Congress, and that there is danger that this businessman's Administration may weaken the foundations of private enterprise by supporting curbs on competition. But the fact which overshadows all others in significance is that competition over the years has been gaining, not losing, in vigor, and there is good reason to expect it to continue to grow. What steps can we take to encourage it?

The belief that competition is dying owes its broad acceptance mainly to the rise of big business. People quite understandably but wrongly confused big business with monopoly. It was discovered that

---

*Published in *Altantic Monthly,* Vol. 192, No. 5, November 1953, pp. 66-70; reproduced by permission of the trustees of the literary estate of Professor Slichter to whom the editors of *Atlantic Monthly* had turned over the copyright of this article.

**Dr. Slichter was Lamont Professor of Economics at Harvard University.

in most industries half to three fourths of the output was concentrated in the hands of four or five firms or less. The conspicuous growth of large companies led to the belief that concentration of economic power was growing. Books expounding this theme were widely read, and one by Berle and Means became famous. The Roosevelt Administration appointed a special commission to study the alleged concentration of economic power.

Within the last few years, however, it has become clear that the public's ideas about the concentration of economic power were wrong. Two facts in particular stand out. One is that a considerable degree of concentration is found in many forms of activity. For example, more than half of the members of Protestant churches are found in 5 denominations out of more than 220; half of the candidates for Ph.D. in economics are found in four institutions, and half of the physicists with Ph.D.'s received their degrees in one of ten large institutions. Similar concentration occurs in other fields of learning—though the institutions that give the most degrees vary. Consequently, when consumers concentrate their buying of cars or cigarettes or soap, they are behaving in a normal fashion—in the same way that people do in selecting their churches or schools. Hence, concentration of production does not mean that sellers are dominating buyers. It simply reflects the fact that there is frequently a great concentration of people's choices.

The second fact is that the degree of concentration of production has not appreciably changed in the last fifty years. Measurement of concentration is difficult—some studies show some increase, others show some decrease in recent decades. The only safe conclusion is that there has been little change in the degree of concentration. In so far as the belief that competition is declining rests upon the assumption that concentration of production is growing, it rests upon a fictitious foundation. Incidentally, even a growth in the concentration of production is not conclusive evidence that competition is becoming less vigorous, because a few large concerns may battle strenuously for larger shares of the market.

The evidence that competition has been spreading, taking new forms, and growing in vigor is abundant. This evidence falls into five principal parts: 1) the disappearance of various conditions that have limited competition; 2) the rise of new business methods and new types of business organizations that increase competition; 3) the increase in the number of products, services, and processes, broadening the range of buyers' choices and intensifying the struggle for the buyers' trade; 4) changes in conditions which intensify old forms of competition; and

5) the growing efforts of business to improve its products and to meet the desires of consumers.

The disappearance of various conditions that have limited competition. The holders of the belief that competition is declining look back to an imaginary age when the country was made up of many thousands of small concerns all vigorously competing with one another. As a matter of fact, these conditions never existed. Population was sparse and transportation was poor and expensive. Most communities could afford few business concerns and were pretty completely cut off from other places by the poorness of roads. It is plain that such conditions limited competition.

What a transformation has occurred! The growth of population has made possible several competing stores or dealers in many places where formerly there was room for only one. Far more important has been the effect of better transportation. The automobile and good roads have given extraordinary mobility to consumers. With two out of three families owning cars and with good roads covering the land, buyers are able to switch their custom from one seller to another, indeed from one town to another, to take advantage of any attractive buying opportunities within a radius of fifty miles or more. Never in the history of the world has such a large body of consumers been so well provided with good transportation and thus been so independent of the merchants of any particular town or place.

Improved transportation has also stimulated competition by exposing producers to competition from new and distant sources of supply. Of special interest are refrigeration and pipe lines. Refrigeration in vessels and railroad cars has put the winter fruits and vegetables of the South and the tropics in competition with the canned and preserved fruits and vegetables of the North; coal from West Virginia and Pennsylvania must compete in the East with gas piped halfway across the continent from Oklahoma and Texas.

The rise of new business methods and new types of business organizations that increase competition. One of the most stimulating competitive developments of the last century has been the rise of mail-order selling, because it has brought vigorous competition into thousands of communities, no matter how isolated. Mail-order selling has been a fairly recent growth. Back in the days of Adam Smith—a time when many people uncritically assume that competition was more pervasive than it is today—there was no selling by mail. The great mail-order houses got their start in the last quarter of the nineteenth century. But mail-order selling is by no means confined to the mail-order houses, and it is constantly being extended to new products. One may buy by mail, not only any article of apparel or food or furniture, but trailers, boats, insurance, and prefabricated houses.

Mail-order selling was soon followed by two other types of distributor—the chain store and the supermarket. Each is based on the discovery that cutting traditional retail mark-ups produces rapid turnover of stocks and good profits. The grocery chains and supermarkets have little respect for the conventional boundary lines of business and are selling cigarettes, toys, phonograph records, hardware, underwear. Today about half of the supermarkets are carrying nylon hosiery. A year ago the proportion was one out of four. Three out of four supermarkets now handle houseware items such as cutlery, cake pans, butter dishes, and many others, and their sales of these items are estimated at more than $135 million a year. The supermarkets are even invading the fields of the drug store, the great disregarder of business boundary lines. In many communities more tooth paste and shaving cream are sold in supermarkets than in drug stores. But the drug stores have retaliated by selling groceries, so that in some places more coffee is sold in drug stores than in grocery stores.

New kinds of business are constantly arising to threaten the markets of old businesses. The motel competes with the hotel, the drivur-self companies with taxis and even with owning one's own car, the outdoor movie with the motion picture theater, the book clubs with the retail bookstores, the vending machine with the retail store. Self-service drug stores have recently come into existence. Another new type of business is the renting of tools to persons who wish to build their own houses or to do other construction work for themselves. Savings banks, within the last fifty years, have had to meet stiff competition for the savings of individuals from life insurance salesmen, credit unions, mutual funds, and even government savings bonds; in some states savings bank life insurance competes with the ordinary life companies. Of particular importance in increasing the competitiveness of the economy are the recently developed venture-capital companies. These concerns help promising new companies get started in business by putting capital into them and in some cases giving them managerial assistance.

The increase in the number of products, services, and processes. The competitiveness of the economy is constantly being intensified by new products, services, and processes. It is true, of course, that the making of new products (and the plant and equipment to produce them) increases the demand for goods as well as the supply of goods because it brings into existence jobs and incomes. But the new products can get a share of the expanding market which they create only by competing vigorously with old products for the incomes of consumers.

In the period 1940-1951, when the output of the economy as a whole increased by about 5 per cent a year (faster than the long-trend growth) and population was growing less than 1 per cent a year, output and sales of television sets grew 113 per cent a year, freezers 71 per cent, dishwashers 21 per cent, frozen foods 19 per cent, kitchen cabinets nearly 15 per cent, water heaters 14 per cent, electric shavers 8.5 per cent, cigarettes 7.6 per cent, washing machines 7.5 per cent. Unfortunately two of the fastest-growing industries have been pari-mutuel betting, on which people spent over $269 million in 1952—thirty-three times as much as in 1929—and the gambling coin-machines, on which $150 million was spent in 1952—nineteen times as much as in 1929. New industries which grow faster than the average are a constant threat to the established industries. The new industries force the old ones to keep prices down and values up in order to retain their share of the market and to keep their sales from shrinking.

Many new commodities and services meet essentially the same need as some old product or service. When this happens, two or more products or services battle for the same market. The advance of technology is constantly increasing the number of commodities and services that are in direct competition with each other. Consider some of the many cases of intercommodity competition that have developed during the last fifty years. Today oil competes with coal, and gas in turn competes with oil. Cotton and wool meet the evergrowing competition of artificial fibers, paper competes with glass and cloth, the bus and the privately owned automobile with the railroad, frozen food with canned food, the telephone with the telegraph, the movies with the legitimate theater, and television with the movies, the radio with the newspaper, oleomargarine with butter, the trailer with the apartment or dwelling house. Five years ago the volume of detergents sold was one-eighth the volume of soap. Today sales of detergents by weight exceed the sale of soap.

Changes in conditions that intensify old forms of competition. Competition is being stimulated by the growth of leisure and by the fact that people own much larger stocks of goods than they formerly possessed. Within the last fifteen years the five-day week has become fairly universal outside of agriculture. The spread of the five-day week has intensified the ancient competition between home work and industry and has caused the home to win back part of the lost ground. Largely because Saturday is no longer a workday in industry, people are painting and papering their own houses, even building their own houses in all or part, and are making increasing quantities of furniture and clothing. In one community the building of additional bedrooms in attics is so great that a course in night school instruction is offered to help owners do a better job. The result has been a rapid growth in sales of paints, patterns, hand tools, and semiprefabricated houses to individuals. Industry, of course, continues to strive for work that might be done in the home. One of the most interesting recent efforts of industry to compete with the home is the launderette—the self-service laundry.

The great increase in personal possessions in itself intensifies competition between the new and the old. In the early days of the automobile industry, for example, there was little competition between new cars and old ones—nearly all of the cars purchased were new ones. Today, most prospective buyers have the choice of buying either a good secondhand car or a new one. Indeed, the purchases of old cars in 1952 were considerably more than half again as large as the purchases of new cars. That means that unless the new cars are sufficiently more attractive than the old, the owners will use their old cars a year or two longer. Despite this, about three out of five purchasers of new cars trade in a car that is less than five years old.

What is true of automobiles is true of other forms of durable goods—refrigerators, vacuum cleaners, radios, even television sets. A large proportion of the possible buyers of new articles already possesses an earlier model which serves the essential purpose and is not discarded until the new models are sufficiently superior. The secondhand market flourishes. The fact that American families are already well stocked with a wide variety of durable consumer goods is additional reason why producers place so much emphasis upon improving the quality of their goods rather than simply reducing the price.

The expansion of technological research. The expenditure of huge sums on improving old products and developing new products is a recent change in industry which has attracted surprisingly little attention. Half a century ago industry depended for inventions and discoveries largely upon enterprising and daring individuals (a Morse, McCormick, Bell, Goodyear, Edison, Marconi, or Ford) who went ahead on their own with such resources as they had or could beg or borrow.

During the last thirty years (and especially the last twenty) a revolutionary change has occurred. The search for new and better products and for better methods in many enterprises is becoming a normal part of business operations and is being financed out of the current revenues of business concerns. The result has been a startling growth in the scale of research and the support given to it. In 1950, private industry spent about $1.1 billion on technological research—nine times as much as in 1930. More than four times as many scientists were employed in industrial laboratories in 1950 as were employed twenty years before.

Industrial research is competition at its best, because it means that the producer is making systematic efforts to reduce his costs or to improve his product. Hence, the spectacular growth of research and the huge sums now spent every year on improving products and cutting costs refute effectively the assertion of those who argue that the economy is becoming less competitive. Never in the world's history have existing products and methods encountered a greater challenge from new products and better methods. Better fabrics, better methods of insulation, better methods of preserving food are among the many changes that will soon be ready. Furthermore, the kind of competition represented by research tends to spread and to grow more intense. The very fact that one enterprise is using research to cut its costs or to improve its products means its rivals must do the same thing or be left behind. One laboratory leads to others and to further competition. Although industrial research has been spreading rapidly, even today only a few managements appreciate its possibilities. Hence there is room for an enormous expansion of research during the next few years.

Even though the economy has been growing more competitive, the country would be wise to encourage competition still further. So important is keen business rivalry that we should not trust to chance that it will continue to gain in vigor. There are a number of ways in which it could be encouraged:—

Avoid reimposing the excess profits tax except in time of war. This tax hits hardest the very person who needs to be encouraged—the successful innovator. He will become a more formidable and effective competitor if he is permitted to plow back a large part of the profits of his successful innovation instead of turning most of them over to the government.

Forbid agreements by which manufacturers control the prices which retailers charge for the manufacturer's product. Such agreements prevent the more efficient retailers from attempting to gain volume by underselling their less efficient rivals and thereby limit competition. Experience proves that the margins which manufacturers give to retailers are far greater than efficient retailers require.

Encourage enterprises to install new and better equipment by giving managements greater discretion over the rate at which they are permitted to charge depreciation for tax purposes. More rapid replacement of equipment would be encouraged by permitting larger write-offs in the first several years of the life of an asset.

Withdraw undue protection to American industries against foreign competition. A large part of American manufacturing industries are protected by such high duties that they have virtually no foreign competition. Although they are exposed to all kinds of competition in the American economy, some direct competition from abroad would be stimulating.

Encourage able young executives to go into business for themselves. This is a difficult and complicated problem. Many thousands of new enterprises are started in the United States each year, but about half of them are sold or liquidated within two years. One of the difficulties is that the persons best qualified to start new enterprises—namely, successful young executives in established concerns—usually have such good prospects for advancement with their present employers that they are little inclined to take the enormous risks inherent in striking out on their own or in accepting an offer from a struggling new company.

The venture-capital companies that have come into existence within the last few years are an important step in the direction of encouraging able executives to start out on their own. These concerns, as I have pointed out, are especially important because they put capital into new enterprises—enterprises which have no earnings record but which appear to be promising. Thus the venture-capital companies help able men obtain much-needed funds.

Changes could be made in the corporate income tax laws that would make working for a new and struggling concern a more attractive gamble for executives than it is today. An executive who gives up a secure job with an established enterprise is now compelled to sacrifice the pension rights he has earned during his service. This is unfair and, in addition, it is bad for the economy as a whole. When an executive who shifts from one company to another sacrifices his pension rights, pension rights become a form of industrial serfdom and discourage competition among concerns for executives. Company contributions to pension plans should not be permitted to be counted as an expense in computing tax liability unless the plan vests with any employee of, say, ten years service or more the right to claim all premium payments made on his behalf.

Help small companies with an earnings record obtain the capital needed for growth. Next to the scarcity of capital for new companies, the most serious lack in the capital market is the scarcity of funds for small but growing companies—companies which need medium-term or long-term loans but which are too small to go to the bond market and which represent too great a risk for life insurance companies and other institutional investors. Hence there is need for more venture-capital companies and also for more of the similar industrial development companies, such as the Industrial Development Bank of Canada and the Maine Development Corporation. If small concerns find it easier to grow, competition is bound to be brisker.

Expand the government's support of research. There are limits on the kind of research that private industry can support, because the results of much research soon become available to everyone. Therefore, much of the support of research should come from the government. There has been an enormous increase in government support in the last fifteen years, and the Federal government is spending over $1.3 billion on research. Unfortunately the availability of the results of much government-supported work is unduly restricted by sincere but ill-conceived efforts to protect national security, and the government is now disposed to cut instead of increasing its grants for research. But government support of research not only aids defense but helps make the national economy both more productive and more competitive.

The growing competitiveness of the economy causes one to be confident that industry will continue to be progressive and that it will adapt itself successfully to changing conditions. The development that gives most reason for confidence is that the support of invention and discovery has become a normal part of business operations. There is, however, a paradox about competition in the making of innovations. Each innovator is attempting to discover something unique—in other words, to become a sort of monopolist. But the public need not fear this sort of monopoly. Each of the would-be monopolists is limited in his power by the fact that he has many rivals who are also attempting to discover acceptable innovations. America is fortunate that its economy in the last generation or so has developed to such an unprecedented degree this best of all kinds of competition. Rivalry in efforts to discover new products and to improve old ones assures us that our fund of technical knowledge will grow rapidly and that the economy will be tough, adaptable, and pretty well prepared for any emergency. The daily necessity of meeting new threats to their markets will keep managements keen and alert and will assure that only the most resourceful and progressive managements will survive.

Chapter 3

The revival of West Germany since World War II is one of the most outstanding examples of the vigor of private capitalism as opposed to socialism or central planning. In 1946 when food rations fell below 1,500 calories per person per day, the German people were frustrated, not only by the prevailing conditions of devastation, exhaustion, and disruption, but also by the supposed experts, in and outside Germany, who were clinging tenaciously to their reliance upon state controls. Despite all this, the people worked on doggedly, tormented by hunger and exasperated by zonal restrictions, corruptions, and the black market. During this period, Dr. Ludwig Erhard, who was then Honorary Professor in the Department of Political Science of Munich University and who later became Minister of Economics under Prime Minister Adenauer, was the most vigorous proponent of the philosophy of private enterprise.

Between 1946 and 1963 Dr. Erhard brilliantly defended his position against socialism and central planning in over 50 papers assembled in his book *The Economics of Success*. The two papers presented here are typical of those included in the book, and the relevance of their arguments is attested by the later show of success of private enterprise in West Germany, which can be measured by the increase in purchasing power of the gross national product. This rose from $431 in 1948 to $2,483 per person in 1967, a six-fold increase in this nineteen-year period (Table 5).

Japan was the only major country in the world in which industrial expansion during this period was as rapid. These early articles by Erhard foreshadowed, and, indeed, helped lead to the success story of how private enterprise combined with Marshall plan aid and the will of its people, restored West Germany to its place in the industrial world.

FREE ECONOMY VERSUS PLANNED ECONOMY*

Ludwig Erhard**

Local government elections in the Länder *demonstrated the German people's will to live, to turn away from despair, and to shun both nationalism and communism, and this in spite of the fact that food rations still fell short of 1,500 calories a day per head of the population. All attempts at mending matters were frustrated, not only by the prevailing conditions of devastation, exhaustion and disruption, but also by the supposed experts, in and outside Germany, clinging tenaciously to their reliance on controls. The people worked on doggedly, tormented by hunger and exasperated by zonal restrictions, corruption and the black market. The outlines of a new approach emerge in the following article, the title of which at once indicates the dividing line along which the intellectual and political arguments of those days were ranged.*

In the work of threshing out the *Länder* constitutions, discussion of what shape the future economic order should take naturally occupied an important place. I shall attempt in this article to disentangle the specific problems of the moment from the web of polemics and to make a sober assessment of our position by formulating what is common to all the proposals that have so far emerged. It is typical of our present situation that these conflicting views should invariably be pushed to extremes terminating on opposite sides of a supposedly unbridgeable gulf—on one side free economy, on the other planned economy, here socialism, there capitalism—although the economic developments actually taking place should rather make us ask ourselves whether influences are not in fact emanating from both fronts and tending to bridge the gap between conflicting viewpoints. To imagine, for instance, that any free economy must exhibit symptoms of the uninhibited exploitation associated with the early days of capitalism is to misunderstand the dynamism of the advanced economies of today as completely as does the detached individualist for whom any kind of economic planning is tantamount to the life-destroying

*From Chapter 3 of the book *The Economics of Success* (New York: D. Van Nostrand Company, Inc.); reproduced by permission of Thames and Hudson Ltd., London. This article was originally published in *Die Neue Zeitung*, October 14, 1946.

**Dr. Erhard is well known as past Vice-Chancellor and Minister for Economic Affairs of the German Federal Republic.

levelling of a soulless bureaucracy. And the same applies in regard to the concepts of capitalism and socialism. Today it is just as hopelessly biased to think that capitalism means exploitation of the workers as it is to think that socialism means the ruthless denial of the last trace of freedom. If, for example, the main characteristic of a capitalist economy is taken to be merely the capitalist mode of production involving the large-scale investment of capital formed within the national economy, then there is no difference between it and a socialist economy. Conversely, a free economy, which simply because it is free is commonly dubbed 'capitalist', need not preclude full regard for the social needs of the day. And whereas in capitalist countries with a free market economy the accumulation of capital is often violently criticized, the formation and use of capital in socialist countries are often not subjected to such effective public scrutiny and criticism. In other words, catch-phrase criteria are no longer applicable in appraising an economic system, least of all its social aspects. When it is remembered that a capitalist and socialist economy are equally compelled to make provision for the building up of capital resources, and at the same time it is agreed that this can only be done, whatever the shape of the economic structure may be, by saving and consumer restraint, then it looks very much as if the systems are not so irreconcilable after all.

It is indeed true that a socialist economy cannot do without planning on an extensive scale, but this does not mean that a free economy—or, to be more precise, a market economy—can be written off as aimless or anarchical. The fact is that it uses the highly developed methods of market research so extensively for the systematic recording of economic data and the evaluation of trends, that with this type of economic order there is a very strong and growing tendency to put plans first. In an earlier article I pointed out that between an economy which embraces many plans and a fully planned economy there are any number of possible systems, varying according to the particular kind or degree of influence or guidance brought to bear on the functions of the economy, and that it is therefore wrong and dishonest in this connection to play around with absolutes.

The real contradistinction is not between free and planned economic systems, nor between capitalist and socialist economic systems, but between a market economy with free price-level adjustment on the one hand and an authoritarian economy with state controls extending into the sphere of distribution on the other. In the last analysis it is simply a question of whether the market as the voice of the economic society as a whole or, alternatively, the state or some other collective entity is better able to decide what is conducive to the common good or the well-being of all. It is still a widely held fallacy that the outcome of free competition is to arrest movement and change within the social structure or at least to set up economic strains and stresses. In actual fact, all liberal-minded experts with a sound knowledge of the social organisms are agreed that it is precisely the other way round, that it is the limiting of freedom of movement that throws the economy out of balance and produces crisis after crisis, each more unmanageable than the last. Provided in future the state sees to it that neither social privileges nor artificial monopolies impede the natural process by which economic forces reach and maintain a state of equilibrium, and that the operation of supply and demand is allowed free play, the market will adjust the total input of economic forces so as to create optimum running conditions and to compensate any mistakes made at the controls. Anyone who wishes is welcome to believe that a planning and regulating economic authority might be a better judge of the economic intentions and wishes of society; but just let him try to prove it. What can be said is that in a free market economy mistakes of judgment in the management of affairs automatically produce price changes with all their attendant repercussions, whereas in a state-directed economy there is always the danger that equally serious mistakes can be covered up and left to fester until they ultimately erupt with elemental force. We have had experience in recent years of how easily a state-directed economy can deteriorate, by imperceptible stages, into a travesty of what an economy should be.

Our criticism is thus not directed against the planned economy *per se,* whose manifold forms can be variously interpreted, but most definitely against the state-controlled authoritarian economy, which if carried to its logical conclusion wipes out the market and robs the consumer of all freedom of choice. On the other hand, a collectively managed economy responsive to market reactions is a contradiction in terms and therefore unthinkable; disregard for the wishes of the consumer as reflected in market reactions is bound to destroy freedom of action and stems from the fallacy that human happiness can be secured by maximum satisfaction of statistically measurable needs. So, even assuming that the authority wielding economic control had no other motive than to serve the good of the community—and this not even the socialist state guarantees—it is still open to doubt whether the people as a whole would prefer any form of collective economy to the free market economy.

As things are today, the state must provide the economy with the principles and broad lines of a policy and with objectives designed to guide and regulate its functioning. In this respect the state indisputably has and should have the initiative. But to go further and reduce the independent businessman to the status of a mere puppet or servant of the authority's will would be to destroy all the values derived from personality and to rob the economy of its most precious source of inspiration and strength. Now, if ever, is the time to realize that the economy is not opposed to social progress but, on the contrary, treats it as a yardstick. All steps capable of contributing to a fair distribution of the national product, and with it of the national income, deserve our most careful consideration. But then we have the chance to do this through the very act of honouring the obligations arising from our country's distress, if only we put actuality before dogma.

I am convinced that the tasks of today call for the full participation of the individual. We shall be doing our country a real and lasting service if we establish an economic order which is purged of the theorizing and bureaucratic spirit that everyone hates and which enables people to act freely in response to a sense of their social responsibilities.

CONFUSION OF TONGUES ON THE QUESTION OF THE ECONOMIC ORDER*

Ludwig Erhard

On June 5, 1947, the US Secretary of State, George Marshall, outlined his far-reaching plan for aid to stricken Europe and its vanquished peoples, and for European co-operation. While controversy was still raging behind the scenes in Germany as well as in Allied circles, Ludwig Erhard—then Honorary Professor in the Department of Political Science of Munich University—threw himself into the general discussion of what had to be done and of what could be done towards reconstruction and recovery.

The purpose of all economic activity is to meet consumer needs and thus to contribute to the well-being of the community. Since this purpose is inalienable and independent of passing phenomena and theories, it is only the means and methods to be used to this end that should really be discussed. Yet it is extremely difficult today to conduct a sober discussion of any one specific problem. The reason for this is that the political parties insist on making acceptance or rejection of particular economic systems a matter of policy, even of dogma. Another reason is that a low standard of living tends to magnify the importance of economic as compared with all other considerations both social and political.

Any attempt to lift the discussion of economic affairs out of the turmoil of party strife comes up against the blind credulity with which large bodies of the electorate or significant social groups cling to political beliefs put out by individual prophets as if they were immutable and absolute truths, making it utterly impossible for them to appreciate the complexity of most economic and sociological problems. It is widely held, for instance, that anyone who has socialist leanings must be in favour of a planned economy, and anyone in favour of the market economy must be a capitalist at heart—a completely mistaken view. Another mistake is to try to bring moral judgments to bear. Or, again, to identify any totalitarian system, whether fascist or bolshevist, with a planned economy in order to disparage planning *per se*. Equally, opponents of capitalism ought not to use the

*From Chapter 4 of *The Economics of Success;* originally published in *Die Neue Zeitung,* June 23, 1947.

admitted faults of this system as an excuse for condemning the market economy. From the point of view of economic development, fascism and bolshevism on the one hand and capitalism on the other are in reality merely historically delimited phases in the fluctuating development of the two basic or generic types of economy, namely the planned economy and the market economy.

The present author, who has never made any secret of his liberal outlook, is at any rate very far removed from the slightest intention of supporting one-sided capitalist interests, and is indeed far rather inclined to charge capitalism with progressively betraying the basic principles of the market economy, namely competition and price freedom, and becoming itself *dirigiste* by assuming one collectivist attribute after another. Looking back, it was surely tragic aberration on the part of the socialists to deprecate competition, thereby playing into the hands of the cartels and other economic monsters, instead of realizing that competition was the very giant-killer they were looking for. It is sheer economic muddle-headedness to go on imagining, as people now commonly do, that capitalism can be fought by obstinately trying to arrest competition, for if they succeed they would paralyze the mainspring of the market economy.

If the idea behind this form of attack is by any chance the Marxist idea of "expropriating the expropriators", to compel strongholds of private power to give way to strongholds of public or state power and to set up a centralized, in place of a ramified and more or less privately controlled, type of planned economy, then it is indeed time to point out to those who think on these lines that in any decently run state there are, after all, limits to the power of private institutions, and that, furthermore, the various group interests tend to counterbalance each other, whereas the power of the state must of necessity be absolute, so that (as indeed history proves) the danger of arbitrary and wrongful use of power is then immeasurably increased.

May I therefore say to non-doctrinaire socialists, who are prepared to draw lessons from experience, that the accepted tenets of socialism do not tie them down in this way. Liberal socialism, for example, is unequivocally in favour of the free market economy and of freedom of action for the individual and recognizes in legalistic and artificial monopolies the real evils of capitalism. It is not the market as an institution, but the misuse of power, invariably preceded by suppression of the free market, that is responsible for robbing the economy of its capacity to respond to the will of the public, so that it goes further and further downhill and finishes up by clamouring for one piece of planning after another.

What we are up against here is a plain case of confusing cause and effect, with disastrous results. The social strains and stresses generated by capitalism in the early stages were concomitants of a technological revolution and of misinterpreting the so-called liberal freedoms, and not effects of the market economy principle as such. What posterity will blame us for is that the state was so rooted in class prejudice that it failed to apply the force of law to deal with the evils that had grown up. Yet the functioning of the market economy did not become vitiated—one has but to remember the delicate and finely poised mechanism of the world economy in those days—until the capitalist system itself began to break the rules and to assume more and more of the attributes of a planned economy by allowing the individual to be replaced by collective agencies or entities in the performance of economic functions. One is surely entitled to speak of a Babel of voices, a confusion of tongues, when in certain quarters capitalism in its most advanced and orthodox form is condemned because by eliminating competition it has become in effect a planned system, while elsewhere people attack it because they regard the market economy itself as a bad thing and merely want a different kind of planned economy. Economic mismanagement and malfunctioning cannot be ruled out by replacing a privately controlled planned economy by one operated by the state or any other collective agency. It is not between the thinking of the advocates of a planned economy as against that of the advocates of a collectivist version of it that the gulf is fixed, for, however much they may differ in their social and economic aims and ideals, they are at one in believing in the complete accountability of all economic phenomena; no, the real cleavage is between reliance on planning of any kind and belief in the truly free market economy kept in rein by the rule of law, or in other words between collectivist and individualist-libertarian modes of thinking and living.

The preconditions for the successful application of the planning principle simply do not exist in the world as it is, however much one may delude oneself into imagining that they could be artificially established by some systematic authoritarian limitation of man's freedom of action in the decisive areas of economic life and by instituting some form of regimentation. In modern times planned intervention has invariably upset the economy. The planners are in a logically weak but tactically strong position. Except for the fact that a disrupted fiscal system makes a free market economy unworkable without overt inflation, it has to be admitted that the transition from a market economy to a planned economy is easily effected whereas the converse process is immensely difficult. This is because it is easy to act freely, and therefore foolishly as well as wisely, on the basis of an economy having an inherent tendency to maintain itself in a state of equilibrium, but difficult to restore at one stroke the workings of a free market in an economy that has been thrown out of a naturally balanced state. The great opportunity that will undoubtedly accrue to us in the foreseeable future as a result of the currency reform will be of regaining, through this operation on the living organism of our economy, the ability to decide, freely and in full awareness of what we are doing, which road we shall take.

And there is one other point to bear in mind: at a time of dire stringency it is not possible to say anything conclusive about the quality and workability of a planned economy. When the consumer will accept anything and everything the market has to offer there is no risk of off-target production, and there is nothing to prevent the planners from cherishing the illusion that they are on the right lines. But if the planned economy is to be accepted as the pattern of the future, it must stand the test under very different conditions, that is to say when the producer has to work hard to sell and cannot rely on coercing the consumer. Its inferiority to the market economy will then be shown up clearly enough. Here again the confusion of tongues is reflected in the attitudes of the political parties, although there is in fact no point on which it is more important that there should be clarity and full understanding of the implications. The advocates of economic planning elevate it to the status of a dogma yet remain unaware of the inconsistency involved in going on to promise that it can provide full scope for freedom of action and initiative. Others again put the accent on these very freedoms yet feel obliged to make a half-hearted semiconfession of belief in a planned economy. Of course all the parties would like to see the economy so constituted that it was no danger to peace at home or abroad, yet they apparently do not realize that the strains and stresses involved in getting collective economies to deal with national economies can be far greater than those engendered when individuals everywhere are allowed to conduct international trade; and in my opinion they will make a better job of it, by looking after their own interests in their own limited spheres without regard for the balance of trade and payments between the countries.

It is not a case of deciding between socialism and capitalism, both of which have undergone change under the stress of social and economic development. And, above all, there is no kind of correspondence between the two commonly "bracketed" pairs of concepts: socialism and capitalism on the one hand, and planned economy and market economy on the other. If it is true that socialists work for fair distribution of the social product, then it is equally true that supporters of the market economy can whole-heartedly subscribe to the same aim, since this is implicit in the principle of order to which they are committed. When capitalism misguidedly calls for still more privately controlled collective agencies, determined liberal opposition is certain to be aroused. Modern liberalism does not seek freedom to exploit, but combats intolerance and the denial of freedom in any sphere of life. True liberalism fights the dragooning of the spirit—begetter of every political tyranny—wherever it may appear.

Chapter 4

In Part I was discussed the fact that while in its highly centralized heavy production industries, including steel, Russia is now one of the leading nations in the world, in its agricultural production it is still the most backward compared with the other industrial nations in free Europe and with other industrial nations of the free world. Developing countries may wonder, why, after 50 years of communist rule, 33 out of every 100 workers are required to feed Russia's population, and why in a bad crop year, Russia must still import food from other countries, when, on the average, other European countries need less than half of this number to feed their people. The Russian collective and state farms with all their engineers, craftsmen, and scientists under centralized control have failed to attain the productivity of countries such as France, where under private enterprise, less than 18 percent of the workers produce more than enough food to meet the needs of its own population. A release of a large number of farm workers as well as other workers in Russia for other jobs is necessary before their living standards can be increased comparable to those in other European countries or approach those in the United States. The recent articles from Moscow by Joseph Fromm, a Senior European Editor of *U. S. News & World Report,* show how living standards of the ordinary people in Russia compare with those in other countries. His reports are valuable at this time when all countries, but particularly the developing countries, are taking steps to improve their standards of living.

LATEST FROM INSIDE RUSSIA*

Joseph Fromm**

Moscow

Changes, now showing up here in Russia, could mark the beginning of the end of the Communist system as it has operated in this country for nearly 50 years.

The most striking changes are these:

Kremlin leaders—particularly Premier Alexei Kosygin—now concede that the Soviet Union cannot build a modern economy with the system of total centralized planning imposed by Joseph Stalin.

No longer do you hear in Moscow the boast that Russia will overtake the United States economically by 1970, 1980 or any other target date in the foreseeable future.

A Frank Confession

Instead what you hear from Russian economists is the frank confession that, despite its spectacular achievements in space, the Soviet Union is still the most backward of the industrialized nations.

The far-reaching reforms of the Communist economic system are accepted as imperative by top Soviet leaders if this country hopes to compete in the same league with the United States and other advanced industrial nations of the non-Communist world.

The first steps toward overhauling this system now are being taken.

These steps are aimed at reducing the power of the central planners, increasing the autonomy of individual factory managers and offering greater material rewards to induce workers and farmers to toil harder and more efficiently.

But the most experienced Western economic observers in Moscow are unanimous on this verdict:

The changes now being started, while rational and realistic, fall very far short of what is needed if the Soviet Union expects to develop and run a modern economy comparable to that of the United States.

"Communism in Russia is at a crossroads," says the leading

---

*Reprinted from *U. S. News & World Report,* March 28, 1966, and **July 1, 1968.**
**Senior European Editor of *U. S. News & World Report.*

Western economic expert in the Soviet capital. "If Soviet leaders do not carry through fundamental changes in the system, this country in 50 years' time still will have an economy producing shoddy, second-rate goods and importing technology from the West."

Why It Doesn't Work

What is forcing Soviet leaders to face the fact that the present Communist system no longer works?

For part of the answer, visit the new housing estates and the shops in Moscow and talk to the customers.

What you quickly discover is that Communism, as it has been known in the Soviet Union for nearly half a century, is unable to deliver the goods that the Russian people now expect.

The Russian people, particularly in the cities, have had a small taste of the comforts of an affluent society—better-made and better-designed shoes and clothing, television, washing machines, vacuum sweepers and electric shavers. They like it and want more. What they want now are refrigerators, bigger and better flats, smart and stylish clothes and the prospect of cars without long waits.

An American reporter, returning to the Soviet Union after an absence of seven years, notices a striking change in the attitude of the people. No longer do they believe the Communist propaganda that workers in Russia are moving into paradise, while those in the "capitalist" West are being crushed into impoverishment.

They are able to judge for themselves. Western films and Western radio broadcasts, now authorized by the Kremlin, are seen and heard by millions. The impact shows up in the fact that American music and dancing and Western fashions—male and female—are the rage.

No longer are urban dwellers prepared to accept supinely what bureaucrats order in the way of shoddy, ugly clothing and trashy trinkets. There is evidence of a "pocketbook revolt" by consumers against centralized planning.

The Consumers' Revolt

Russian economists estimate that stocks of unsalable goods now total between 2 billion and 3 billion dollars. One Soviet economist points out that this is more than the unsold stocks that accumulated in America during the depression of the '30s when people could not afford to buy what was available. But in Russia today the huge stocks of unsalable merchandise are building up, not because consumers lack the money to buy them, but simply because they will not accept what is offered.

Rather than buy the inferior or defective goods on sale, more and more people are saving money. Last year personal savings in Government banks jumped by 19 per cent.

Besides the trashy quality of much of the consumer goods on sale in Russian shops, the erratic central-planning system produces wasteful swings from scarcity to surpluses.

For example, several years ago the planners decided to tackle the acute shortage of sewing machines. And this equipment started to pour out of factories. So many were produced that sewing machines are being sold now for use as tables.

Another example: Something as obviously essential as nipples for baby bottles are almost impossible to find. The reason: The planners in fixing production targets didn't take into account the fact that they and their fellow bureaucrats use nipples on their glue pots.

Flashlight batteries, another obvious essential, are unavailable in Moscow shops, but they can be found in cities in Central Asia. In a Moscow toy store, electric trains are on sale. But the transformers needed to operate the trains are not available.

Fashion Shows, but—

Attractive frocks, copying Western styles, are displayed by models at a new "house of fashions" in downtown Moscow. Every performance is packed. But the dresses are not on sale. Many women buy the patterns to make the dresses themselves or to have them made by professional dressmakers, now having a booming business. But the necessary material and the accessories often are unavailable. An example: Recently a frock with metal buttons was modeled. Many women bought the pattern. But they found that no metal buttons are on sale.

For Russian women, shopping under the system of centralized planning is a time-consuming, endless and frustrating search. That's why the shopping bag is called a "perhaps bag"—perhaps you find what you're looking for and perhaps you don't. And perhaps it may even turn up in a shop when you are not looking for it.

By Western standards, Moscow shops, with few exceptions, can be compared only with the general stores in remote country villages in the U. S. or Western Europe, or with the discount "junk" shops in slum and semislum districts of big cities.

For the things that Russian consumers really want, exorbitant prices are fixed arbitrarily by the planners.

A medium-sized refrigerator, widely coveted by Russian house wives, is priced at approximately $400 (between 350 and 400 rubles). Even at that price there is a waiting list of nearly one year in Moscow.

For 1,000 Persons, 3 Cars

What this means is that a lot of Russians are willing to spend for a refrigerator the equivalent of more than four months' average wages. The average monthly money income of nonfarm workers in Russia is 95 rubles. Cars, considered a necessity, not a luxury, by workers in the U.S. and many non-Communist industrial countries, still are an impossible dream here in the "workers' paradise." As compared with 344 cars in use for every 1,000 people in the United States and 90 in Western Europe, there are only 3 cars per 1,000 persons in Russia. And almost all of those are Government-owned.

Only a small proportion of the 200,000 passenger cars produced last year were offered for sale to private individuals. Several years ago, more than 120,000 people had paid the full price for a car with the prospect of delivery in a matter of years.

To deter car buying and cut the waiting list, the planners several years ago boosted car prices by 25 to 35 per cent. Now the most popular model, the five-passenger Volga, which is about the same size as a Ford Falcon, is offered at 5,602 rubles—nearly six years' average income of nonfarm workers. And there's a one-year waiting list.

At one of the few state car-sales offices in Moscow, this reporter was approached by a Russian who asked wistfully: "Do you have to wait so long to get a car in Britain?" He was incredulous when I told him that I had bought a car before leaving London and had gotten delivery in a few days.

But even if a Russian has the money, the patience and the luck to acquire a car, his troubles are only beginning. In all of Moscow there are only nine garages that handle maintenance and repairs. If a car breaks down on the road, it may take a day or two to get a tow-truck—unless you can use "blat." "Blat" is the Russian equivalent of special influence or pull. But one Russian car owner says that if you aren't an amateur mechanic it is hardly worth owning a car.

Housing Desperately Short

In the great new housing developments around Moscow and other cities you find further evidence of the failure of the rigid Soviet system of centralized planning.

Despite a massive building program, there still is a desperate shortage of housing. Rent is exceedingly low. For a flat in a state housing project, rent is 8 to 11 rubles a month, including utilities. But thousands of families still are compelled to double up, with young married couples sharing small flats with their parents. Also, it is virtually impossible to get a bigger apartment as your family grows.

Even by minimum health standards set by the Russian Government itself, the average family lives in unhealthfully crowded conditions.

A unique Soviet process of "instant antiquity" seems to be used in the construction of these state housing projects. Doors and windows often do not fit and cracks appear in the walls before work is completed. Within a year the interior of many of these buildings looks 20 years old or more. Around one big project in Moscow built 10 years ago a safety net has been erected to catch falling bricks.

"Anything can be said about the Russian housing program," says a Western expert in Moscow. "It's the biggest in the world but it's still terribly inadequate. Buildings go up faster than anywhere else and fall down faster."

The Government now is bending Communist principles of egalitarianism in an effort to deal with the mounting disgruntlement with housing conditions among the "elite" and to reduce the financial burden of housing on the state. Cooperative apartments are being authorized for factory groups and various professional unions. Employes and members are allowed to buy co-op apartments and actually to own these as a form of private property.

The cost of a two or three room flat is $10,000 to $12,000. Applicants are required to pay $3,000 to $4,000 down and then monthly payments of $40 to $50.

Some More Equal Than Others

Thus, if you have money and the right connections you have a chance of buying your way around the housing shortage in Communist Russia. In this, as in many other fields, you find that in Russia everyone is equal—but some are much more equal than others.

What all this adds up to, in the opinion of veteran observers in the Soviet capital, is this conclusion: The Soviet system of comprehensive centralized planning by bureaucrats is unable any longer to satisfy the increasingly sophisticated tastes and variegated demands of Russian consumers. And as "consumer politics" grows in the Soviet Union, the Kremlin leaders are under mounting political and economic pressure to do more to satisfy these consumer demands.

Look at Russia's collective farms and you will find further evidence of the pressures that are forcing Kremlin leaders to face up to the failure of their Communist system to meet the changing needs of this country.

Nearly 50 years after the Communist Revolution, agriculture in the Soviet Union is the most backward and inefficient of any industrialized country in the world. Yields on collective farms are very low by comparison with yields in the non-Communist West.

For example: The grain yield per acre in the U. S. is three times as much as that in Russia. The sugar-beet yield is almost three times as large in the United States while the potato yield is 2.5 times as large.

The failure of Communist agriculture, Western experts in Moscow say, is partly due to inadequate investment. Per acre, American farmers have five tractors for every one in Russia and five combines for every two in the Soviet Union. And American farmers use four times as much fertilizer.

Planning at Fault

But Western experts stress that the Communist system of centralized planning itself is a major factor behind the failure of agriculture. In the past, bureaucrats remote from the scene have told collective farms what to plant, how much and when, and when to harvest. This still is the practice in wide areas, despite efforts to give farm managers greater autonomy.

The stress is on maximum production each year to meet current targets regardless of the destructive effect on the soil. The result is widespread erosion and frequent disasters.

Bad farming techniques, not inadequate investment, are blamed for the recurrent disasters in the "virgin lands" that Nikita Khrushchev opened 10 years ago with an enormous investment of equipment and manpower. Three out of the 10 harvests have been good. Three have been mediocre. Four have been disastrous. In 1963 and 1965, it is reported authoritatively that virgin-land farmers barely got back their seed.

But the failure of Communist agriculture is not confined to the virgin lands. Even in the exceedingly fertile farm lands of the Ukraine, collective farms produce miserable results by comparison with American farms.

An American agriculture expert who has traveled thousands of miles through Russian farm lands says: "There is no reason in theory why big corporate farms should not be successful in Russia. After all, they're highly successful in America. When I travel through the lovely farming country of the Ukraine, I can't help but imagine what American farmers would do with that soil. If Americans were farming it, the Ukraine alone could almost support this country.

"What constantly amazes me are the primitive farming methods that still are used here and the fact that infrastructure of agriculture is still nineteenth century. The waste and cost involved in getting things from country to town and back again are fantastic."

Failure of Collective Farming

Although Russia has 42 per cent of its working population laboring on farms, it still cannot feed itself. In recent years it has had to import millions of tons of grain from the West, and experts say these imports probably will have to continue indefinitely.

But the failure of collective farming tells only half of the story. The other half is the success of farming on the private plots that collective farmers are allowed to cultivate. They are allowed to sell the produce from these plots to the state at premium prices or in free markets in Moscow and other cities.

These private plots comprise only 3 per cent of the cultivated land in the Soviet Union. Yet they account for more than 34 per cent of the total agricultural production. They produce 42 per cent of Russia's milk supplies, 70 per cent of the eggs and over 20 per cent of the wool. Moreover, the yields are materially greater than on collective farms.

Why Russian farmers work so much harder on their private plots than on collective farms is easy to understand on the basis of information from a leading Soviet economist. He reveals a farmer can earn 1.5 rubles a day on the collective farm and 3.5 rubles on his private plot. This economist adds:

"Is it to his advantage to work on the collective farm? No. In the present state of affairs, if people were permitted to leave the countryside, there would be almost nobody left there."

The Kremlin leaders who get advice from this economist have been forced to the conclusion that Communism on the farms, as it has been practiced for decades, is a failure. They also have been forced to acknowledge in their latest reforms and Five-Year Plan that material rewards, not Communist slogans, are what makes Russian farmers work hard and produce big yields.

Disillusionment with the centralized, planned system of collective farming has reached the point where an official Soviet publication recommends that it be abandoned.

The publication, "Komsomolskaya Pravda," says the present system is leading the countryside to ruin. It recommends that collective farms be broken up and juridical ownership of land be turned over to groups of five or six peasants.

Muddle in Planning

In industry, too, the Soviet leaders are told by their economists that the Communist system of centralized planning has created a real mess.

Under this system, the central planners in Moscow send out detailed "norms" to control every aspect of industry—production targets, the size of the labor force, and the wage bill, among others. The emphasis has been on quantity production. That worked adequately when the build-up of coal, iron, steel and heavy industry was the paramount objective. But it is written off now as a dismal failure as a system for managing a more sophisticated industrial economy which must become increasingly consumer-oriented.

For under that system factory managers have been rewarded for meeting quantity targets regardless of the quality or salability of their products.

Thus: A shoe factory produced only small shoes and no big ones in order to fulfill its quota. A lampshade manufacturer produced only orange shades to keep production uncomplicated. A washing-machine factory met its production target, but all the machines turned out in one month were defective.

Innovation in industry has been stifled by Communist planning. It is also now conceded by Soviet leaders that this system has stifled modernization and technological progress and has encouraged massive waste and inefficiency.

Industrial System: "Most Backward"

This indictment was voiced by a Soviet economist at a private conference of industrialists and planners in Moscow:

"Among all the developed countries, we have the worst and most backward structure of production.

"We have as many machine tools as the United States, but only half of our tools are working while the remainder are either not utilized or in the repair shop. More of our workers are engaged in repair work than in the production of new machines.

"At the present moment the problem of unemployment is an acute one. In the coming five years we shall have to find work for an army of 10 million young people new to the labor force. In the last two years there has been a significant rise in unemployment, particularly in medium-sized and small towns.

"Our trade with other countries is chronically unfavorable. We export mainly raw materials since many countries, including even the Socialist countries, do not want to buy finished goods from us because of their low quality.

"But the external causes are not the main ones which lead to our difficult economic situation. The primary causes are internal. First, the incorrect direction of the economic development of our country. Second, the inadequacy of our system of planning, incentives and economic administration in relation to the demands of practical life."

Under this system, the planners have demanded maximum production, and plant managers resist technological change that might temporarily disrupt production.

The result is that great sectors of Russian industry use obsolescent equipment. Another result is great resistance to the development of new products because this, too, disrupts production temporarily. Flexibility to adjust to changing consumer demands is penalized under this system—even if there were some way of ascertaining what these demands were without a market mechanism.

For an insight into the way this system discourages technological innovation and practical development of new products, look at the experience of a British firm that found in Russia a new counting device. The British company signed a licensing agreement, almost unique, to produce this Russian invention. A year later the equipment was in full production in Britain. But the Russians who had developed it had not moved beyond the design stage. The result: The British company applied for a further license to market the device in Eastern Europe, Russia's special market.

Slow Rate of Growth

A sharp slowdown in the rate of industrial and over-all economic growth in recent years is what finally is forcing Soviet leaders to face the fact that something is wrong with their system.

Russia's gross national product is now growing at a slower rate than that of most of the industrialized countries of the West. The growth rates of the United States, Japan, West Germany and Italy—all basically free-enterprise countries—are appreciably higher than that of the Soviet Union, with its centrally planned economy.

The United States, with a gross national product more than twice as big as that of Russia, actually is now widening that gap. Russia's leaders have had to admit that their system, far from overtaking the U. S., actually is falling further behind. And a prominent Soviet economist now asserts that the Central Intelligence Agency assessment last year of the Soviet economy and its slow rate of growth was "embarrassingly correct," while the rejoinder by Soviet spokesman was an attempt to "prove the impossible."

Reforms on the Way

Far-reaching reforms of the Soviet system are now being introduced in an effort to cope with the Communist-made crisis.

Central planning is to continue, but not in the detailed way it has operated in the past. Instead of getting 30 or 40 "plan indicators" controlling every aspect of their enterprise, plant managers are to get only about half a dozen. Thus, control is to be less comprehensive, less detailed. Responsibility of the enterprise managers is to be increased.

But more important is a change in priorities. Under the reformed system, the profit motive is being introduced. Bonuses for managers and their workers are to be increased and are to be based not on the quantity of production they achieve, but on the level of sales and level of profits. It is hoped that this will encourage not just maximum production, but production of the kinds of goods that people will buy, and efficiency in order to maximize profits. Plant managers and workers are to receive a share of the profits.

Furthermore, industrial managers are to be allowed to negotiate directly with their customers—industrial consumers and retail outlets—about details of the product they manufacture. Central planners still will issue production targets for each enterprise, but in terms of value rather than weight or quantity.

For example, the manager of a shoe plant now will be permitted to work out with retail outlets the styles and kinds of shoes that his factory should produce for them, and the assortment of sizes. Presumably the retail sales managers, in placing orders, will attempt to reflect the tastes of their customers rather than risk being stuck with big unsold stocks and loss of the potential profits.

Another major reform abolishes the authority of the central planners to dictate the size of the labor force in each enterprise. Now, as the new system is introduced, managers are to be free to determine the number of workers they require to run their enterprise most efficiently, and to get rid of surplus workers.

Individual enterprises are to be allowed to retain a bigger share of the profits for reinvestment. The hope is that this will encourage the purchase of new, modern equipment and technical innovation.

Bureaucrats Resist

These reforms are seen as a historic departure from nearly 50 years of dogma. Already there are rapidly growing signs of sabotage and resistance by the bureaucrats whose powers are to be curtailed if the reforms are carried out.

Veteran diplomatic observers are skeptical about how far and how fast Soviet leaders will move in the face of enormous inertia, bureaucratic resistance and political dangers.

It is emphasized that the top leadership of the party itself was sharply split over the reforms. According to Russian sources, the reforms were accepted largely due to the efforts of Premier Alexei Kosygin, who is said to have offered to retire if his colleagues in the Communist Party Central Committee thought they had a better way to deal with Russia's economic crisis.

But Western experts say that even if the reforms are made, they don't go far enough. One of the best-informed observers says that the reforms, if carried through, would increase the efficiency of individual enterprises. But they would have a minimum effect on the efficiency of the economy as a whole.

What to Do About Prices?

In the opinion of these experts, a crucial element is missing. That element is a rational price policy. Russian economists and political leaders concede that something must be done about prices, but they have repeatedly deferred decisions.

They are now considering fixing prices based on average costs in various industries. This, it is pointed out, would mean that the few most efficient enterprises in each industry would show enormous profits. But the inefficient enterprises—and there are many of these—would register big losses.

What would happen to these inefficient enterprises running at a loss?

In the West, under ordinary circumstances, they would go bankrupt. But not in Russia—at least, now on the basis of the present plans. It is proposed that they should be allowed a form of bookkeeping which would conceal their losses and their inefficiency.

For example, if a price of 100 rubles were fixed for a certain product, efficient plants would sell the product at that price, show it that way in their books and make a big profit. Inefficient firms, however, would sell the product for 100 rubles but would be allowed to enter the sale in their books at 125 rubles.

Western economic experts say that under a price system of this sort, inefficiency, obsolescence and waste will still be built into the Soviet economic system.

Some Russian economists who share this judgment are arguing for the introduction of a system of marginal prices in some industries to kill off, for example, coal mines showing highest costs and least efficiency. They contend that Russia cannot overcome her problems without some rational price system.

Kremlin More Realistic

But the thing that impresses you most forcefully in the Soviet Union today is this: The Russian economic system is in deep trouble —and Kremlin leaders no longer are kidding themselves about it.

A new sense of realism is now apparent among the top leaders. They realize that, the way things have been going, they face the danger that Russia will drift toward economic stagnation and fall further and further behind the United States, and that Russian Communism will be associated with austerity, shortages and a backward economy.

As a further concession to realism as opposed to dogma, Soviet leaders in their new Five-Year Plan offer the first glimmering of a new deal for the downtrodden Russian peasant and the frustrated consumer.

For the consumers, there is the promise of narrowing the gap between investment in heavy industry and in light industry. There also is the promise of a steady increase in production of refrigerators and cars and in the quality of consumer goods.

For the collective farmers an even more important new deal is promised. One Western expert says that the old Stalinist policy of squeezing the farmers in order to finance heavy industry is being abolished. Investment and price policies are being aimed at reducing the great gap between the standard of living of farmers and that of industrial workers, and of giving collective farmers a material incentive to work harder, and more ably.

The reforms of the Communist system that these leaders now are introducing are seen as the first steps down a path that could lead gradually over the years toward a market economy. It will still be called Communism—as it is now in Yugoslavia—but it will bear no resemblance to the system of detailed centralized planning that Russia has known for nearly 50 years.

The consensus of Western economic experts you meet in Moscow is that the alternative facing Soviet leaders is a drift toward economic stagnation. For, it is pointed out, these leaders themselves now concede that the Communist system that has operated in Russia for nearly half a century is incapable of developing and running a modern economy.*

NEW WORRY IN THE KREMLIN: WHY RED LEADERS ARE SCARED

Joseph Fromm

Moscow

This is a time of rising danger and deepening crisis for Russia's aging and conservative Communist leaders.

To an outsider, returning after an absence of just a few years, it is clear the men who rule from the Kremlin now see their system of Communist control and planning gravely threatened at home and abroad:

- The ideas of Czechoslovakia's "quiet revolution"—promising more freedom of expression and greater political liberty—are crossing frontiers into Russia. Such ideas threaten the Communist Party's traditional monopoly of political power.
- The economic "reforms," introduced here nearly three years ago to put new vitality into a sagging economy, have reached the stage where Soviet planners are face to face with this dilemma:

Continuing the reforms will in time create a market economy such as exists in Communist-ruled Yugoslavia. As in Yugoslavia, the result would be drastic curtailment of the Communist Party's role in managing Soviet affairs.

The Consequences

Abandoning the reforms will almost certainly slow down what progress has been made and could lead gradually to economic stagnation. Russia then would fall even further behind the U. S. and other Western countries in technological progress, industrial efficiency and living standards.

What are Russia's leaders doing to meet the threat to their system of Communism based on a centralized control over the economy? The answer, given by qualified diplomats: Nothing decisive, so far.

Comments an experienced political observer of Moscow:

"The Soviet Union is ruled now by a leaderless oligarchy, and rather than face difficult decisions that might split the collective leadership, they sweep them under the rug."

Active Police

Decisions or no, the Kremlin's anxiety about the future is clearly seen in activities of the secret police. They are in charge of a severe crackdown that reminds many foreigners of the worst days of Stalin's reign. The "ideological freeze" is setting in hard.

Selective terror is being practiced against intellectuals to crush even the slightest sign of dissidence and drown out demands for greater freedom of expression.

Modern art and controversial literature, flourishing for a while, are once again banned.

Not long ago an estimated 150 to 300 professors, students, poets and editors who had participated in discussion groups were arrested in Leningrad. Some were charged with conspiracy to commit armed rebellion.

Those convicted were given long prison sentences.

Soviet intellectuals until recently mingled fairly freely with Westerners. Some of the intellectuals have dropped out of sight; others ignore their former friends at casual meetings.

Housing areas inhabited exclusively by Moscow's 2,000 foreigners are now surrounded by high wire fences, erected in recent months to prevent Russians from visiting foreign friends without first checking in at the main gate's police post.

The "freeze" is also reflected in revival of the campaign to vilify the U. S. accompanied by a new emphasis on Communist ideology in official policy and propaganda. All talk of "liberal" reforms, fashionable in recent years, is officially frowned on.

Target Is Youth

Main target of this Kremlin propaganda is Soviet youth—castigated by party elders as "negative, nihilistic and apolitical" despite years of heavy Communist indoctrination.

The elderly Bolsheviks who still rule this country are dismayed and worried by the cynicism and materialism so prevalent among the young people. Yet much blame for this rests on the party's official history that describes Russia's rulers for nearly 40 of the last 50 years as either a madman—Stalin—or a dangerous bumpkin—Nikita Khrushchev.

Western expert comments:

"Young people now enjoying their new five-day workweek and first fruits of affluence find it difficult to show any enthusiasm or idealism for a political movement that officially admits a record of that sort."

Things, Not Politics

You find this apathy to the party and its ideology cutting across almost all segments of Soviet society. The reason is clear: Consumers are earning more and buying more. But with living standards lower than in any other modern industrialized state, expectations are at the same time steadily rising higher. Most Russians are far more interested in what they can get to eat and wear than they are in Communist Party affairs.

Visit Moscow's markets and shops, and this is what you see:

A Georgian peasant, colorfully garbed, sells fresh tomatoes for $2 a pound. Apples from other parts of the South sell for $1.60 a pound. Growers earn enough to pay their round-trip fare between home and Moscow and still pocket a sizable profit.

Oranges are available throughout the year. So are fresh vegetables and other fruit. But out-of-season produce comes from private plots that account for a third of Russia's agricultural output. This is capitalism, not Communism, in action.

All of the better quality shoes come from foreign countries. Women willingly spend $45—equivalent to two weeks' pay—for shoes from Holland.

In a department store, more than 100 women fight to buy imported sweaters selling for $19 each.

A young woman interpreter asked to name the product that delighted her most in recent years, says; "Hair spray from Poland."

Delights of Affluence

Russian consumers see "significant improvements" in their living standards. A TV set with 17-inch screen sells for about $400, equivalent to four months' wages for the average worker. Such sets are readily available to all comers.

Waiting time for delivery of a new refrigerator has been cut from two years to six months or less.

A Russian with $4,200 in cash can buy an apartment in a privately financed cooperative and pay off the remaining $6,000 indebtedness over a period of 15 years. But those with small savings may wait years for apartments in Moscow's new, prefabricated buildings owned by the state.

A car is still little more than a dream to most Russians. A Moskvich sells for $5,000, and prospective buyers must wait years for delivery. Most of Russia's current output of about 200,000 automobiles a year goes to the Government.

Many Russians are far from being shy of cash with which to buy even the most expensive products. A recent survey discloses there are 61 million savings accounts with deposits averaging more than $400 each.

But rather than buy shoddy goods, the Russians save their money —waiting for imported products to arrive, or until the quality of domestic goods improves.

Hopes are slender that there will be vast improvement in quality soon.

The economic "reforms" initiated in 1965 were aimed at encouraging industry to produce efficiently by eliminating a staggering waste of labor, materials and equipment. Another idea was that industry would become profitable because it would turn out goods really acceptable to consumers.

The power of the centralized planners to dictate every detail of economic activity was to be curtailed. Industrial managers were to be given wide powers in planning, production and marketing. A rational price system was to replace the one dictated from the center.

Bumbling Bureaucrats

The reforms, applied first to Russia's most efficient factories, started off smoothly. Labor productivity rose. So did profits.

But Communist Party and Government bureaucrats fought the reforms, continue even now to interfere with management. Planners at the center retain the right to decide the range of products to be turned out by individual enterprises. Plant managers still lack full freedom to rid themselves of surplus workers.

Slow-moving bureaucrats control and allocate raw materials. When bottlenecks develop, enterprises send their "tolkachi"—pushers—about the country to make private, technically illegal deals for materials essential to keep the plants operating.

All prices—millions of them—are arbitrarily set by the planners. Managers complain that some prices are too low to earn profits for reinvestment in new technology. Economists say other prices are so high they encourage continued production of obsolescent products.

A dress manufacturer remarks that by the time the price of a new model is approved by central planners, the dress is already out of fashion.

This view of the system comes from a Western economic expert:

"The administered, inflexible prices do not tell the enterprise manager what he should produce to earn a profit, or of what quality and at what cost he should produce to satisfy the consumer."

High Industrial Needs

More than any other industrialized country, Russia desperately needs high investments for modernization and renovation. Much of its industrial plant is obsolescent. Automation by Western standards is relatively primitive. Sophisticated computers are used in the space program, but Soviet industry as a whole leans on the abacus.

Russia's investment needs are obvious but are lagging under the strain of meeting other immense commitments: high and rising defense spending for nuclear-powered submarines, more and better missiles and an antiballistic-missile system; billions of dollars for aid to North Vietnam, Egypt and Cuba; promises to satisfy the unsatiable demands of Russia's consumers.

Says an economist in Moscow:

"The Kremlin's policy seems to be guns and butter at the expense of capital investment."

New plant investment in 1967 was to go up 10 per cent but actually rose by about half that amount. Investment in 1968 was scheduled to increase about 5 per cent, but diplomats now believe there may be no increase at all.

Not only is the rate of investment falling off, but the return in terms of additional output produced by the new investment is declining. This is considered a sure-fire formula for slower economic expansion in the future.

Growth Gap

Russia's gross national product even now—after spectacular gains in recent years—is only about 46 per cent of the U. S. figure. No one in Moscow talks any more about this country's overtaking America. Some specialists say that in real terms of modern industrial power the gap between the two countries is widening, not narrowing.

An expert makes this comment:

"Whenever I return to Moscow from a trip to New York, I realize that Russia is in a different age from the United States. Russia thinks in terms of coal, iron and oil production. America is in an entirely new technological era."

And from a German economist:

"By 1970, more realistically 1972, the Fiat 124 will start rolling off the production lines in the factories being built here, and then Russia will enter the automobile age. But by then no one in Western Europe will be driving a Fiat 124. There will be three better models available."

Some experts believe Russia's technological backwardness was an important factor behind Czechoslovakia's "quiet revolution" and also played a role in the breakup of the Soviet empire in East Europe.

Russia was unable to provide modern plant equipment needed by its one-time satellites. So, much of East Europe is now looking to the West for machinery and the markets to finance the purchases. The view of Russia in the East is of a colossus assuming the role of a technologically backward raw-material supplier, not a modern industrial power in a class with the U. S.

Lost Opportunity

Three years ago, Russians might have been able to transform their Communist system and launch an "economic miracle" through reforms.

But Soviet leaders have been shocked by what they saw happening, first in Yugoslavia, and now in Czechoslovakia. For economic reforms of the kind being considered by the Kremlin led to democratization of the Communist Party and to a market economy.

Russia's leaders are not prepared to pay that price to overcome the monumental inefficiency and waste of their own system of centralized control.

Now Russia must pay a different price to preserve its system. The price is a closed society under the shadow of a powerful and ubiquitous secret police, and a living standard that may rise fast enough to avoid dangerous discontent but that will lag further and further behind the other industrialized nations.

That is the price which the Kremlin's aging and conservative collective leadership is clearly prepared to pay to preserve the system they have.*

Chapter 5

Two ideologies struggling for supremacy today are the private-market economy and the state-controlled economy. A bird's-eye view of the situation shows that for the ordinary man throughout the world, real progress and hope for further progress are to be found where the private market is the principal device used to organize economic activity. But where the private market is largely suppressed and the state has undertaken to control in detail the economic activity of its citizens, the ordinary man has a low standard of living and little or no way of controlling his own destiny. The sharp contrast of the two types of economies has recently been set forth by Dr. Milton Friedman who, with his wife, recently made a tour through Eastern Europe, the Middle East, and the Far East. In "Myths That Keep People Hungry" Dr. Friedman points out that the many similarities of history in East and West Germany provide an almost controlled scientific experiment. In the Middle East, Israel and Egypt offer the same contrast as East and West Germany; in the Far East, Malaya, Singapore, Thailand, Formosa, Hong Kong and Japan, all relying primarily on free markets, are thriving in contrast to India, Cambodia, Indonesia and Communist China all relying heavily on central planning. While it is possible that Dr. Friedman has somewhat overstated his case, there is substantial evidence of the underlying truths of what he has to say. His article deserves reading by all decision-makers in the countries he visited and in the developing countries throughout the world.

MYTHS THAT KEEP PEOPLE HUNGRY*

Milton Friedman**

Some time ago my wife and I spent a year traveling through Eastern Europe, the Middle East, and the Far East. In country after country we were deeply impressed by the striking contrast between the facts, as they appeared to us, and the ideas about the facts held by intellectuals.

Wherever we found any large element of individual freedom, some beauty in the ordinary life of the ordinary man, some measure of real progress in the material comforts at his disposal, and a live hope of further progress in the future—there we also found that the private market was the main device being used to organize economic activity. Wherever the private market was largely suppressed and the state undertook to control in detail the economic activities of its citizens (wherever, that is, detailed central economic planning reigned)—there the ordinary man was in political fetters, had a low standard of living, and was largely bereft of any conception of controlling his own destiny. The state might prosper and accomplish mighty material works. Privileged classes might enjoy a full measure of material comforts. But the ordinary man was an instrument to be used for the state's purpose, receiving no more than necessary to keep him docile and reasonably productive.

By contrast, the intellectuals everywhere took it for granted that capitalism and the market were devices for exploiting the masses, while central economic planning was the wave of the future that would set their countries on the road to rapid economic progress. I shall not soon forget the tongue-lashing I received from a prominent, highly successful, and extremely literate Indian manufacturer when I made remarks that he correctly interpreted as criticism of India's detailed central planning. Or the numerous discussions with professors at government-supported universities in India, where I was told

---

*From *Harper's* Magazine, CXXXIV, April, 1967; reproduced by permission of Professor Friedman.

**Professor of Economics at the University of Chicago and former President of the American Economic Association. In addition to teaching economics at the University of Chicago, Dr. Friedman serves on the research staff of the National Bureau of Economic Research. His best-known book is *Capitalism and Freedom.* This editorial is an expanded version of the preface to the Japanese translation of that book.

again and again that in a country as poor as India it was essential for the government to control imports, domestic production, and the allocation of investment in order to assure that *social* priorities and not the market demand for luxuries dominated. Many of these discussions took place in comfortable university guesthouses, or relatively luxurious seminar rooms or lounges, well shielded from the nearby hovels where the common people live. One even took place in the magnificent Ashoka Hotel in New Delhi, a showplace built by the government. Yet not once was any question raised about the appropriateness of the "social priorites" reflected in the allocation of governmental funds for these amenities.

I remember, also, the attitude of my audience at the University of Malaya in Kuala Lumpur. They listened politely, though with clear signs of rising hostility, as I expounded the merits of the market and the demerits of central planning for underdeveloped countries. The one remark that brought down the house was by the Malay chairman—the head of the economics department of the university. India's current difficulties, he instructed me, were not the result of central planning but rather of the suppression of India by colonialism (this nearly two decades after Indian independence).

"Don't Bother Me with Facts"

A few examples show how clear the facts are. East and West Germany provide almost a controlled scientific experiment. Here are people of the same blood, the same civilization, the same level of technical skill and knowledge, torn asunder by the accidents of warfare. On the one side of the frontier, communism, tyranny, and misery; on the other, capitalism, freedom, and affluence.

Even two communist countries, Russia and Yugoslavia, offer a similar contrast. Russia is far more closely controlled from the center; private property and a moderately free market have almost no scope. In agriculture only 3 per cent of the cultivated area is in private plots whose produce the owners are free to market privately—though this 3 per cent produces one-third of the total agricultural output of the Soviet Union. In industry there is no legal scope at all for private activity, though apparently there is substantial black-market activity. In Yugoslavia, on the other hand, the great bulk of agricultural land is privately owned, there are many private handicrafts, and a deliberate attempt has been made to decentralize industry. Yugoslavia is far from free and its ordinary people are far from affluent by Western standards. Yet it strikes the traveler as a paradise in both respects compared with Russia.

As it happened, we went from Russia directly to Yugoslavia, and both our departure from Russia and our arrival in Yugoslavia emphasized the contrast. On our way to the airport in Moscow, we had an Intourist guide assigned to us, as we had at every arrival and departure in Russia. This one turned out to be a young man who was in his final year of studies in American and English literature at the university. After desultory discussion of authors, I asked him what he was going to do after he finished school. "I do not know," he replied; "they haven't decided yet where I can be most useful"—no annoyance at having his career decided for him, simply a matter-of-fact statement. Three key questions were asked us as we went through the formalities for embarkation: "Are you taking any papers or letters out for any Russian?" "Do you have relatives in Russia?" "Did you visit anyone except as arranged by Intourist?" Having truthfully answered no, we were permitted to embark on a plane headed for Accra via Belgrade and carrying mostly Ghanaians returning home after an extended stay in Russia for military training. (To judge by the unrestrained comments of our seatmates, whatever the stay might have added to military effectiveness of the Ghanaians, it had certainly inspired strong hostility toward the Russians and a heightened admiration of the West.)

When we landed in Belgrade, questions by the authorities were strictly perfunctory. What surprised us even more, after our Russian experience, was the absence of any governmental official to meet and shepherd us. We were left on our own, much to our great delight. Without difficulty we were able to wangle, for a modest side payment, a ride into town on the one vehicle that was going there. The dinars for the payment were advanced to us at the hotel where we had privately made reservations. (In Russia, we had been required to pay in full in advance and did not know what hotel we were to stay in until informed by Intourist on arrival.)

In the Middle East, Israel and Egypt offer the same contrast as West and East Germany; in the Far East, Malaya, Singapore, Thailand, Formosa, Hong Kong, and Japan—all relying primarily on free markets—are thriving and their people full of hope, a far call from India, Cambodia, Indonesia, and Communist China—all relying heavily on central planning.

We were struck most forcibly by the contrast between facts and ideas in Malaysia. This country is a testimonial to the potentialities of competitive capitalism. Singapore, which was still part of Malaysia when we were there, was built on free trade. It has a vigorous industry and the standard of living of the ordinary Chinese or Malay citizen is many times higher than in neighboring Indonesia or nearby India. Malay itself was mostly an unsettled jungle three-quarters of a century ago. Today it is an attractive country with widespread cultivated areas. The standard of life of its citizens, though somewhat lower than that of Singapore, is much higher than that of its other neighbors. Rubber and tin are its main export crops. Yet rubber is not even native to Malaya. The rubber tree was imported by private enterprises from South America; the tin mines were developed entirely by private concerns.

Malaysia, now independent, is in the process of deciding what economic policy to follow. Its own past offers one example. Its populous neighbors, Indonesia and India, offer another. Both have embraced widespread and detailed central planning, with results that are as depressing as they are clear. In Indonesia, the standard of living and the condition of the ordinary man has clearly deteriorated in the nearly two decades since independence—a major factor in the recent political turmoil. In India, the situation is only a little better.

Which example does Malaysia propose to follow? If the intellectuals have their way, as it appears they will, the new nation will follow India and Indonesia. The chairman of my meeting at the university, his colleagues, and the civil servants had no doubt that it was they who should control the direction of investment and development. A central bank had been established and a government development agency was already making long-range plans. A World Bank mission, headed by Jacques Rueff of France, a liberal in the nineteenth-century sense, had nonetheless bowed sufficiently to the temper of the times to recommend tariff protection, government development subsidies, and other measures of central planning. How clear it is that the world is ruled by ideas—not facts—and that ideas can for long periods live a life of their own, little affected by the facts.

Japan offers another striking example of the importance of ideas and the intellectual climate—less present-day Japan than its experience a century ago. We were much impressed by modern Japan: by the high level of income, its wide distribution, and its rapid growth; the aesthetic content of everyday life and common household goods; the dignity of the Japanese people, and their courteous hospitality to the visitor.

A century ago, just prior to the Meiji restoration in 1868, the situation of Japan was very different. Japan had experienced centuries of deliberate and enforced isolation from the rest of the world. Though by no means completely stagnant, Japan's social and economic structure had altered little in that time, and it had fallen far behind the advanced Western countries in scientific knowledge and productive techniques.

Why the Japanese Succeeded

There is a remarkable parallel between Japan just after the Meiji restoration and India after it achieved independence eight decades later in 1948. In both cases a major political change permitted drastic alteration in economic arrangements and the rigid class relations among men. In both cases the political change placed in power a group of able and patriotic men determined to convert prior economic stagnation into rapid economic progress—though for somewhat different objectives. In both cases these events occurred in countries with ancient cultures and a high artistic and literary civilization. And in both cases the countries were technologically far behind the leading economic powers of the time. Both had an opportunity to make major economic gains by using techniques developed at great cost in the West.

There were also, of course, differences—mostly favoring India. India's physical resources are distinctly superior to Japan's—except only for the sea around Japan, with its easy transportation and potential supply of food. Japan had been almost completely out of touch with the rest of the world; India had had extensive and widespread contact. The British, moreover, left India an excellent railroad system, many factories, much physical equipment, and—even more important—functioning political institutions, numerous skilled administrators, and many men trained in modern industrial techniques. In my own contacts, the top Indian civil servants impressed me as man-for-man the ablest people in any civil service with which I have had experience—including the American. True, they are few and there is a tremendous gap between them and lower-level civil servants, but progress in any area has always depended on small numbers of people.

Finally, in the years since 1948, the rest of the world has made available to India—largely as gifts—an enormous volume of resources, roughly equal to a quarter of India's total capital formation. Japan had no comparable advantage. The closest parallel was the fortuitous failure of the European silk crops in the early years of the Meiji restoration, which enabled Japan to earn more foreign exchange by silk exports than she otherwise could have earned. Japan herself financed the training of Japanese abroad and the importation of foreigners with technical skills. During the whole of the first half-century after the Meiji restoration, Japan had not only no net grants from abroad but not even any net capital import; she provided the whole of her own capital from domestic sources.

There is a widespread tendency to attribute India's difficulties to its social institutions, the character of its people, and the climatic conditions under which they live. Religious taboos, the caste system, a fatalistic philosophy are said to imprison the society in a strait-jacket of tradition; the people are thought to be unenterprising and slothful. I find it impossible to accept any of these explanations. The Indians who have migrated to Africa or to Southeast Asia have in country after country formed a major part of the entrepreneurial class, and have often been the dynamic element initiating and promoting progress. In the Punjab, an industrial revolution is taking place in towns like Ludhiana with thousands of small and medium-size workshops, reproducing, or so it seemed to me, the experience of Manchester and Birmingham at the end of the eighteenth century. There is no shortage of enterprise, drive, or technical skill; on the contrary, there is a self-confident, strident capitalism bursting at the seams.

For a nation to progress, it is not necessary for every individual to be an enterprising, risk-taking economic man. The history of every developed nation shows that a tiny percentage of the community sets the pace, undertakes the path-breaking ventures, and coordinates the economic activity of hosts of others. Most people everywhere are hewers of wood and drawers of water. But their hewing of wood and drawing of water are made far more productive by the activities of the minority of industrial and commercial innovators, and the much larger but still small number of imitators. I have no doubt whatever that India has an adequate supply of potential entrepreneurs, both innovators and imitators. The appearance of sloth and lack of enterprise is surely a reflection of the absence of rewards for different behavior, not a reason; the fatalistic philosophy is more likely an accommodation to stagnation, not a cause.

Many early foreign residents in Japan reported similar impressions. Wrote one: "Wealthy we do not think it (Japan) will ever become: the advantages conferred by Nature, with the exception of the climate, and the love of indolence and pleasure of the people themselves forbid it. The Japanese are a happy race, and being content with little are not likely to achieve much." Wrote another: "In this part of the world principles, established and recognized in the West, appear to lose whatever virtue and vitality they originally possessed and to tend fatally towards weediness and corruption."

They were wrong and so too, in my opinion, are those who are similarly pessimistic about India.

Although the circumstances of Japan in 1868 and India in 1948 were highly similar and the opportunities much the same, yet the outcome was vastly different. In Japan there was a thorough dismantling of the feudal structure, a vast extension of social and economic opportunity, rapid economic growth, and widespread improvement in the lot of the ordinary man—though, unfortunately, nothing approaching real democracy in the political sphere. In India there was much lip service to the elimination of caste barriers yet shockingly little actual progress; differences in income and wealth between the few and the many have widened not narrowed; economic output per capita has been nearly stationary; and there has probably been an actual deterioration in the standard of life of the poorest third of the population. With all this has come a growing network of deadening and restrictive controls.

Why the difference in results? I believe the contrast between the two countries reflects primarily the difference in the techniques of economic organization adopted, though no doubt other factors played some part. Japan followed essentially a free-market policy, taking the Britain of its time as its model. True, the state intervened in many and diverse ways, and played a key role in the process of development. It subsidized the technical training of many Japanese and the importation of foreign experts, established pilot plants in many industries, and gave numerous subsidies.

Yet at no time did it ever try to control the total amount or direction of investment or the structure of output. It sold off most of its pilot plants to private firms within a few years. The state maintained a large interest only in shipbuilding and iron and steel, industries that it deemed necessary to build military power. It retained even these industries only because they were not attractive to private enterprise and required heavy government subsidies. These subsidies were a drain on Japanese resources. They impeded rather than stimulated Japanese economic progress. Finally, by international treaty, Japan was prohibited during the first three decades after the Meiji restoration from imposing tariffs higher than 5 per cent. This restriction was an unmitigated boon to Japan, though naturally it was resented at the time, and tariffs were imposed after the treaty prohibitions expired.

India has followed a very different policy. Its leaders, schooled in the doctrines of Fabian socialism and central planning, have regarded capitalism as synonymous with imperialism, to be avoided at all costs. They have taken Russia as their model and embarked on a series of five-year plans with detailed programs of investment allocated between government and private firms and among industries. Certain areas of production are reserved to government. Tariffs, quotas, and subsidies to exports are widely used to shape foreign trade. When exchange difficulties arose, detailed and extensive exchange control was imposed. The Indian government controls wages and prices, prohibits private enterprises from building factories or making other investments without government permits, and levies taxes that are highly graduated on paper though largely evaded in practice.

Reliance on the market in Japan released hidden and unsuspected resources of energy and ingenuity, prevented vested interests from blocking change, and forced development to conform to the harsh test of efficiency. Reliance on governmental controls in India frustrates initiative, or diverts it into wasteful channels, protects vested interests from the forces of change, and substitutes bureaucratic approval for market efficiency as the criterion of survival.

An instructive specific example is the different experience with homemade and factory-made textiles in the two countries. Both Japan and India had extensive production of textiles in the home at the outset of their development. In Japan home production of silk was for long little affected, but home spinning of cotton, and later, hand-loom weaving of cotton cloth, unable to meet the competition of foreign spun yarn and factory-made cloth, were all but wiped out. A Japanese factory industry developed, at first manufacturing only the coarsest and lowest-grade fabrics, but then moving on to higher and higher grades and ultimately becoming a major export industry. In India, hand-loom weaving was subsidized and guaranteed a market, allegedly to ease the transition to factory production. Factory production is growing gradually, yet there is no sign of an end to the subsidy. Indeed, hand-loom production is now larger than it was when the subsidy was introduced. Had Japan followed a similar policy, it still would have an extensive home cotton-textile industry—and a drastically lower level of living.

The most dramatic illustration of the waste that has been created by substituting government for market control in India is in automobile production. For some time now, the importing of both second-hand and new cars has been prohibited, supposedly to save foreign exchange by reducing "luxury" imports. Naturally the price of second-hand cars has skyrocketed. When I was in Bombay in 1963, a 1950 Buick—much like one I had sold in New Hampshire a few months earlier for $22—was selling for $1,500. The government has licensed the production of new cars, mostly copies of foreign makes. Their manufacture is proceeding in uneconomical small runs and at extremely high cost. India, its government apparently believes, is too poor to use secondhand cars; it must have new ones. I estimated in 1963 that about one-tenth of total American aid was being absorbed in the extra cost to India of getting motor vehicle transportation by building new cars instead of importing used ones—a glaring example of the wastes of conspicuous production.

The tragedy of the industrial revolution in the Punjab lies in this same waste and misdirection. Businessman after businessman told me that one-quarter of his time was usually devoted to getting around governmental restrictions—price control, rationing, and so on. Even more important, the distortion of prices and costs through governmental intervention means that the businessman's energy and ability are being directed toward doing the wrong things in the wrong ways.

An Erroneous Notion in the West

Ironically, the men who took charge of Japan in 1867 were dedicated principally to strengthening the power and glory of their country. They attached no special value to individual freedom or political liberty; on the contrary, they believed in aristocracy and political control by an elite. Their political ideas were the basis for later tragic totalitarian excesses. The men who took charge of India in 1948 had very different ideas. They were ardently devoted to political freedom, personal liberty, and democracy. Their aim was not national power, but improvement in the economic conditions of the masses. Yet it was the Japanese leaders who adopted a liberal economic policy that led to the widening of opportunities for the masses and, during the early decades, a great gain in their personal liberty. It was the Indian leaders who adopted a collectivist economic policy that hamstrings their people with restrictions and continues to undermine the large measure of individual freedom and political liberty encouraged by the British.

The difference in policies reflects faithfully the different intellectual climates of the two eras. In the mid-nineteenth century, liberalism (in its original, not its current American sense) was the dominant view. It was simply taken for granted that a modern economy should be conducted by free trade and private enterprise. It probably never occurred to the Japanese leaders to follow any other course. In the mid-twentieth century, collectivism was the dominant view. It was simply taken for granted that a modern economy should be conducted by centralized control and five-year plans. It probably never occurred to the Indian leaders to follow any other course.

Ideas can for a time lead a life of their own, independent of reality. But sooner or later they must meet the test of evidence. It may be crucial for the fate of mankind that they do so soon.

We, who are fortunate enough to live in the West, take for granted the freedom and affluence we enjoy and regard them as the natural lot of mankind. They are not. They have been achieved only for brief intervals in the long history of mankind. At no time, and certainly not now, have they been achieved by more than a small fraction of the world's population. We have been generous in our material aid to the less fortunate; we have given them a fine set of aspirations and an example of a free and affluent society. But we have also transmitted a climate of opinion hostile to the market arrangements that appear to be a necessary condition for both freedom and affluence.

We have a sufficient margin of protection to survive such ideas for a long time. The less-developed nations do not. In their failure, they may destroy us as well. The continuing ascendancy of such ideas may doom mankind to a renewed era of universal tyranny and misery.

Part III

THE ROLE OF LABOR UNIONS IN A COMPETITIVE ECONOMY

Chapter 6

Louis Dembitz Brandeis, formerly Associate Justice of the United States Supreme Court, was a generation ahead of his time in perceiving the importance of efficiency by consent as the basis of labor productivity in our economy. When recommended as an Associate Justice by President Woodrow Wilson, five past presidents of the American Bar Association testified that Mr. Brandeis was not qualified for this high position. Despite this, the Senate approved of the recommendation, and over a period of three decades, Justice Brandeis along with Oliver Wendell Holmes were the intellectual leaders of public policy as it related to Supreme Court decisions.

The basic philosophy of Justice Brandeis was to insure honesty in government, integrity in business and finance, and to attain an economic well-being for all people in line with the American principles of democracy. More than any other writer in the twentieth century, Justice Brandeis, has got on paper, in easy-to-understand language, some of the basic philosophies which have helped make America a great nation. Unfortunately for contemporary writers, his philosophies unfolded case by case, as he presented them, first to the courts in Massachusetts and later in the U. S. Supreme Court. In a tribute to Justice Brandeis, Rabbi Solomon Goldman's book *The Words of Justice Brandeis* sets down the principal ideas of this wise man, gathered from his many writings. For the book at hand, however, it seemed to make sense to regroup the writings of Justice Brandeis under four major headings. The first of these was designated "American Principles of Democracy," and it includes Justice Brandeis' emphasis that American ideals are the development of the individual for his own good through liberty and the attainment of the common good through democracy and social justice. "Business Competition in a Democracy" sets forth the second major part of Justice Brandeis' philosophies. He was a firm believer in competition as opposed to monopoly, and was a staunch supporter of the Sherman Anti-Trust Law. To him competition constituted a way of business helpful to both the individual and to the world. And although Justice Brandeis emphasized the virtues of competition, he also clearly set forth the need for government regulation to prevent destructive competition in the third grouping of his writings, "Balancing Competition with Necessary Regulation." In the fourth category, "Trade Unions in an Industrial Democracy," are Justice Brandeis' philosophies of the rights and the responsibilities of labor in our American economy.

THE WORDS OF JUSTICE BRANDEIS*

Solomon Goldman**

I. AMERICAN PRINCIPLES OF DEMOCRACY

Justice Brandeis set forth clearly what he believed to be the American principles of democracy. In the modern day confusion which now exists for many people, particularly for some of our minority leaders, his philosophies are well worth reviewing. These principles are set forth under four headings: democratic ideals, democracy versus aristocracy, education in a democracy and dangers in a democracy.

A. Democratic Ideals

The history of Anglo-Saxon and of American liberty rests upon that struggle to resist wrong—to resist it at any cost when first offered rather than to pay the penalty of ignominious surrender.

The liberty of each individual must be limited in such a way that it leaves to others the possibility of individual liberty; the right to develop must be subject to that limitation which gives everybody else the right to develop; the restriction is merely an adjustment of the relations of one individual to another.

Liberty means exercising one's rights consistently with a like exercise of rights by other people; . . . liberty is distinguished and that no one can expect to secure liberty in the sense in which we recognize it in America without having his rights curtailed in those respects in which it is necessary to limit them in the general public interest.

Liberty has come to mean the right to enjoy life, to acquire property, to pursue happiness, in such manner that the exercise of the right in each is consistent with the exercise of a like right by every other of our fellow citizens. Liberty thus defined underlies twentieth century democracy. Liberty thus defined exists in a large part of the western world. And even where this equal right of all has not yet been accepted as a political right, its ethical value is becoming recognized.

---

*Reproduced by permission Abelard-Schuman, Ltd.

**Formerly a Rabbi in a New York City synogog. The subheadings below are Rabbi Goldman's and serve to place the references to his alphabetically organized book.

Liberty is the greatest developer. Herodotus tells us that while the tyrants ruled, the Athenians were no better fighters than their neighbors; but when freed they immediately surpassed all others.

American Ideals

What are the American ideals? They are the development of the individual for his own and the common good; the development of the individual through liberty, and the attainment of the common good through democracy and social justice.

Manhood is what we are striving for in America. We are striving for democracy; we are striving for the development of men. It is absolutely essential in order that men may develop that they be properly fed and properly housed, and that they have proper opportunities of education and recreation. We cannot reach our goal without those things. But we may have all those things and have a nation of slaves.

We Americans are committed not only to social justice in the sense of avoiding things which bring suffering and harm, like unjust distribution of wealth; but we are committed primarily to democracy. The social justice for which we are striving is an incident of our democracy, not the main end. It is rather the result of democracy—perhaps its finest expression—but it rests upon democracy, which implies the rule by the people.

American Standard of Living

What does this standard imply: In substance, the exercise of those rights which our Constitution guarantees—the right to life, liberty and the pursuit of happiness. Life, in this connection, means living, not existing; liberty, freedom in things industrial as well as political; happiness includes, among other things, that satisfaction which can come only through the full development and utilization of one's faculties.

Americans

There is in most Americans some spark of idealism, which can be fanned into a flame. It takes sometimes a divining rod to find what it is; but when found, and that means often, when disclosed to the owners, the results are often most extraordinary.

B. Democratic Versus Aristocratic Principles

America, dedicated to liberty and the brotherhood of man, rejected the aristocratic principle of the superman as applied to peoples as it rejected the principle when applied to individuals. America has believed that each race has something of peculiar value which it can contribute to the attainment of those high ideals for which it is striving. America has believed that we must not only give to the immigrant the best that we have, but must preserve for America the good that is in the immigrant and develop in him the best of which he is capable. America has believed that in differentiation, not in uniformity, lies the path of progress. It acted on this belief; it has advanced human happiness, and it has prospered.

Democracy and Aristocracy

Democracy rests upon two pillars; one, the principle that all men are equally entitled to life, liberty and the pursuit of happiness; and the other, the conviction that such equal opportunity will most advance civilization. Aristocracy, on the other hand, denies both these postulates. It rests upon the principle of the superman. It willingly subordinates the many to the few, and seeks to justify sacrificing the individual by insisting that civilization will be advanced by such sacrifices.

Democracy

Democracy means not merely, I had almost said not so much, the rights of the whole people, as the duties of the whole people.

We need democracy at all times no matter what the system is under which we work.

Conservation

Conservation, in its very essence, is preserving things public for the people, preserving them so that the people may have them. To accomplish this is the aim of our Republic. It is the aim of our great democracy that men shall, so far as humanly possible, have equal opportunities, and that the differences in opportunities to which men have been subject elsewhere shall not prevail here.

C. Education in a Democracy

The early New Englanders appreciated fully that education is an essential of potential equality. The founding of their common school system was coincident with the founding of the colonies; and even the establishment of institutions for higher education did not lag far behind. Harvard College was founded but six years after the first settlement of Boston.

Industrial Democracy and Thinking

One hundred years ago the civilized world did not believe that it was possible that the people could rule themselves; they did not believe that it was possible to have government of the people, by the people, and for the people. America in the last century proved that democracy is a success.

Social Inventions

The reason why we have not made more progress in social matters is that these problems have not been tackled by the practical men of high ability, like those who have worked on industrial inventions and enterprises. We need social inventions, each of many able men adding his work until the invention is perfected.

Democratic Ideals

Democratic ideals cannot be attained by the mentally undeveloped. In a government where every one is part sovereign, every one should be competent, if not to govern at least to understand the problems of government; and to this end education is an essential.

Democratic ideals can be attained only where those who govern exercise their power not by alleged divine right or inheritance, but by force of character and intelligence.

Our great beneficent experiment in democracy will fail unless the people, our rulers, are developed in character and intelligence.

D. Dangers in a Democracy

We shall learn most by unprejudiced painstaking study of our own strengths and weaknesses; by inquiry into our own achievements and shortcomings. It is thus that we may best learn how great are the possibilities of high accomplishments in the future; what the real dangers are with which we shall be confronted.

America, which seeks "the greatest good of the greatest number," cannot be content with conditions that fit only the hero, the martyr or the slave.

America in the last century proved that democracy is a success.

Employer and Employee

Don't assume that the interests of employer and employee are necessarily hostile—that what is good for one is necessarily bad for the other. The opposite is more apt to be the case. While they have different interests, they are likely to prosper or suffer together.

Both labor and employers should bear constantly in mind that each is his brother's keeper; that every employer is injured by any single employer who does labor a wrong; and that every laboring man and every union is injured by every individual unionist who does an employer wrong. The influence of a single wrongful act by one who can be classified is tremendous. It affects every other member of the class. When an employer acts improperly toward his employees, it is the business of other employers to see that such conduct is prevented, for his wrong will injure them. And in the same way any lack of fairness and any act of lawlessness on the part of labor is certain to injure other workers and the unions as a whole, and the individual members of labor unions with employers.

Our employers can no more afford to be absolute masters of their employees than they could afford to submit to the mastery of their employees.

Nine-tenths of the serious controversies which arise in life result from misunderstanding, result from one man not knowing the facts which to the other man seem important, or otherwise failing to appreciate his point of view. A properly conducted conference involves a frank disclosure of such facts—patient, careful argument, willingness to listen and to consider.

Greatest Danger

There cannot be liberty without financial independence, and the greatest danger to the people of the United States today is in becoming, as they are gradually more and more, a class of employees.

Possibilities of Human Development

I believe that the possibilities of human advancement are unlimited. I believe that the resources of productive enterprise are almost untouched, and that the world will see a vastly increased supply of comforts, a tremendous social surplus out of which the great masses will be apportioned a degree of well-being that is now hardly dreamed of.

Betrayal of Our Great Heritage

We cannot afford to be represented by men who are dishonest and reckless to the great heritage of an honorable, glorious past, handed down to us by our fathers.

Liberty's Greatest Danger

The greatest dangers to liberty lurk in insidious encroachment by men of zeal, well-meaning but without understanding.

II. BUSINESS COMPETITION IN A DEMOCRACY

One may well raise the question: Why is competition important in a democracy? In a competitive economy, the entrepreneur enters into production in the high hopes that he will make a profit on the product which he sells consumers. If he satisfies consumer's wants and does a good business, he makes a profit. On the other hand if through incompetent management, he fails to make a profit, before long he must improve his management or go out of business. Hence competition is the key to success under a private enterprise system.

Three phases of business competition in a democracy as set forth by Justice Brandeis are included under competition in business, wastes of competition and scientific management.

A. Competition in Business

Business should be, and to some extent already is, one of the professions.

Why should not we recognize in the great realm of business those principles which have been common property of the most advanced thought? Every man in the medical world glories in having given to the world something which advances medical science. Every man in the field of architecture glories when he can give to the world something that advances architectural science. You will find exactly the same thing in almost every department of engineering. Why should it not be so in business? Is there any lack of opportunity for competition, honorable competition, in the field of engineering or of architecture or of medicine? They can play the game wherever a man can see it. There need be no secrets when it comes to the question of advancing the art to which man devotes himself. And the same is absolutely true of business and will be recognized as true of business as soon as men come to recognize that business is one of the noblest and most promising of all the professions.

The Sherman Law

The Sherman Law seeks to protect men in the right freely to compete and to prevent practices which must result in suppressing competition. It seeks to preserve to the individual both the opportunity and the incentive to create, it seeks to encourage individual effort; and the right of the individual manufacturer of a competitive business to market his goods in his own way, by fixing, if he desires, the selling price to the consumer, is in entire harmony with the underlying purposes of the Sherman Law. But when men combine to form a monopoly, or control a particular line or branch of trade, however good may be their intentions, they necessarily curb individual effort. Under the fundamental laws of human nature and of trade they withdraw incentive from those who enjoy the monopoly, and they narrow the field of human effort by confining leadership to a comparatively few individuals.

B. Wastes of Competition

Undoubtedly competition involves waste. What human activity does not? The wastes of democracy are among the greatest obvious wastes, but we have compensations in democracy which far outweigh that waste and make it more efficient than absolutism. So it is with competition. The waste is relatively insignificant. There are wastes of competition which do not develop, but kill. These the law can and should eliminate, by regulating competition.

The history of combinations has shown that what one may do with impunity, may have intolerable results when done by several in cooperation. Similarly what approximately equal individual traders may do in honorable rivalry may result in grave injustice and public injury, if done by a great corporation in a particular field of business which it is able to dominate. In other words, a method of competition fair among equals may be very unfair if applied where there is inequality of resources.

Unrestricted competition, with its abuses and excesses, leads to monopoly, because these abuses and excesses prevent competition from functioning properly as a regulator of business. Competition proper is beneficent, because it acts as an incentive to the securing of better quality or lower cost. It operates also as a repressive of greed, keeping within bounds the natural inclination to exact the largest profit obtainable. Unfair and oppressive competition defeats those purposes. It prevents the natural development which should attend rivalry and which gives success to those who contribute most to the community by their development of their own business and the exercise of moderation in the exaction of profits. It substitutes devious and corrupt methods for honest rivalry and seeks to win, not by superior methods, but by force. Its purpose is not to excel, but to destroy.

No system of regulation can safely be substituted for the operation of individual liberty as expressed in competition. It would be like attempting to substitute a regulated monarchy for a republic.

Cutthroat Competition

Monopoly is the natural outcome of cutthroat competition.

Competition from Within

Every business requires for its business health a memento mori of competition from without. It requires likewise a certain competition from within, which can exist only where the ownership and management, on the one hand, and the employees, on the other, shall each be alert, hopeful, self-respecting, and free to work out for themselves the best conceivable conditions.

Unemployment

Unemployment—perhaps the gravest and most difficult problem of modern industry.

Unemployment is as unnecessary as disease epidemics. One who says in this intelligent age that unemployment is necessary or unavoidable is like one a generation ago who would have continued to insist that epidemics were, if not necessary and divinely imposed, at least inevitable.

Democracy

The wastes of democracy are among the greatest obvious wastes, but we have compensations in democracy which far outweigh that waste, and make it more efficient than absolutism. So it is with competition. Incentive and development which are incident to the freer system of business result in so much greater achievement that the waste is relatively insignificant. The margin between that which men naturally do, and that which they can do, is so great that a system which urges men on to action and develops individual enterprise and initiative is preferable, in spite of the wastes that necessarily attend that process.

C. Scientific Management

Scientific management is merely an application to business of those methods which have been pursued in other branches of science, to discover the best and the most effective methods of accomplishing a result. Scientific management does not mean making men work harder. Its every effort is to make them work less hard; to accomplish more by the same amount of effort, and to eliminate all unnecessary motions; to educate them so as to make them more effective; to give special assistance to those who when entering upon their work are most in need of assistance, because they are least competent.

The great fact to remember is this: The coming science of management, in this century, marks an advance comparable only to that made by the coming of the machine in the last. The profits from the machine were absorbed by capital. But we have developed a social sense. And now of the profits that are to come from the new scientific management, the people are to have their share.

Business Success

In the field of modern business, so rich in opportunity for the exercise of man's finest and most varied mental facilities and moral qualities, mere money-making cannot be regarded as the legitimate end. Neither can mere growth in bulk or power be admitted as a worthy ambition. Nor can a man nobly mindful of his serious responsibilities to society, view business as a game; since with the conduct of business human happiness or misery is inextricably interwoven.

Real success in business is to be found in achievements comparable rather with those of the artist or the scientist, of the inventor or the statesman. And the joys sought in the profession of business must be like their joys and not the mere vulgar satisfaction which is experienced in the acquisition of money, in the exercise of power or in the frivolous pleasure of mere winning.

III. BALANCING COMPETITION WITH NECESSARY REGULATION

Justice Brandeis recognized that government guidelines were necessary to make sure that private firms operated in the public interest. Hence, long before the advent of Professor Slichter's definition of "government-guided private enterprise,"[1] Brandeis gave his blessings to the principle that government should set forth rules of the game under which business should operate. His philosophies are shown under the headings, regulated competition, government intrusion in business, and law and public opinion.

A. Regulated Competition

Shall we abandon as obsolete the long-cherished policy of competition, and accept in its place the long-detested policy of monopoly? The issue is not (as it is usually stated by advocates of monopoly), "Shall we have unrestricted competition or regulated monopoly?" It is "Shall we have regulated competition or regulated monopoly?"

Regulation is essential to the preservation and development of competition, just as it is necessary to the preservation and best development of liberty. We have long curbed the physically strong, to protect those physically weaker. More recently we have extended such prohibitions to business. We have restricted theoretical freedom of contract by factory laws. The liberty of the merchant and manufacturer to lie in trade, expressed in the fine phrase of caveat emptor, is yielding to the better conceptions of business ethics, before pure-food laws and postal fraud prosecutions. Similarly, the right to competition must be limited in order to preserve it. For excesses of competition lead to monopoly, as excesses of liberty lead to absolutism. The extremes meet.

The issue, therefore, is: Regulated competition versus regulated monopoly. The policy of regulated competition is distinctly a constructive policy. It is the policy of development as distinguished from the destructive policy of private monopoly.

Regulation

The policy of regulating public-service companies is sound, but it must not be overworked. The scope of any possible effective regulation of an interstate railroad, either by Federal or by State commissions, is limited to a relatively narrow sphere. Regulation may prevent positive abuses, like discriminations, or excessive rates. Regulation may prevent persistent disregard of definite public demands, like that for specific trains or for stops at certain stations. Regulation may compel the correction of definite evils, like the use of unsanitary

[1]Slichter, Sumner H., *Economic Growth in the United States,* Louisiana State Press, 1961. p. 166.

cars. But regulation cannot make inefficient business efficient. Regulation cannot convert a poorly managed railroad into a well-managed railroad. Regulation cannot supply initiative or energy. Regulation cannot infuse into railroad executives the will to please the people. Regulation cannot overcome the anaemia or wasting-sickness which attends monopoly. Regulation may curb, but it cannot develop the action of railroad officials.

Government Employees

We want men to think. We want every man in the service, of the three or four hundred thousand who are there, to recognize that he is a part of the governing body, and that on him rests responsibility within the limits of his employment just as much as upon the man on top. They cannot escape such responsibility.... They cannot be worthy of the respect and admiration of the people unless they add to the virtue of obedience some other virtues—the virtues of manliness, of truth, of courage, of willingness to risk positions, of the willingness to risk criticisms, of the willingness to risk the misunderstandings that so often come when people do the heroic thing.

B. Government Intrusion in Business

Experience should teach us to be most on our guard to protect liberty when the Government's purposes are beneficent. Men born to freedom are naturally alert to repel invasion of the liberty by evil-minded rulers. The greatest dangers to liberty lurk in insidious encroachment by men of zeal, well-meaning but without understanding.

The makers of our Constitution undertook to secure conditions favorable to the pursuit of happiness. They recognized the significance of man's spiritual nature, of his feelings, and of his intellect. They knew that only a part of the pain, pleasure, and satisfactions of life are to be found in material things. They sought to protect Americans in their beliefs, their thoughts, their emotions, and their sensations. They conferred, as against the Government, the right to be let alone—the most comprehensive of rights and the right most valued by civilized men. To protect that right, every unjustifiable intrusion by the Government upon the privacy of the individual, whatever the means employed, must be deemed a violation of the Fourth Amendment. And the use, as evidence in a criminal proceeding, of facts ascertained by such intrusion must be deemed a violation of the Fifth.

Government as Lawbreaker

Decency, security, and liberty alike demand that Government officials shall be subjected to the same rules of conduct that are commands to the citizen. In a government of law, existence of the government will be imperiled if it fails to observe the law scrupulously. Our Government is the potent, the omnipresent teacher. For good or for ill, it teaches the whole people by its example. Crime is contagious. If the Government becomes a lawbreaker, it breeds contempt for law; it invites every man to become a law unto himself; it invites anarchy. To declare that in the administration of the criminal law the end justifies the means—to declare that the Government may commit crimes in order to secure the conviction of a private criminal—would bring terrible retribution. Against that pernicious doctrine this Court should resolutely set its face.

C. Law and Public Opinion

Whether a law enacted in the exercise of the police power is just, subject to the charge of being unreasonable or arbitrary, can ordinarily be determined only by a consideration of the contemporary conditions, social, industrial, and political, of the community to be affected thereby. Resort to such facts is necessary, among other things, in order to appreciate the evils sought to be remedied and the possible effects of the remedy proposed. Nearly all legislation involves a weighing of public needs as against private desires, and likewise a weighing of relative social values. Since government is not an exact science, prevailing public opinion concerning the evils and the remedy is among the important facts deserving consideration, particularly when the public conviction is both deep-seated and widespread and has been reached after deliberation.

Remedial Institutions

Refuse to accept as inevitable any evil in business (i.e., irregularity of employment). Refuse to tolerate any immoral practice (e.g., espionage). But do not believe that you can find a universal remedy for evil conditions or immoral practices in effecting a fundamental change in society (as by State Socialism). And do not pin too much faith in legislation. Remedial institutions are apt to fall under the control of the enemy and to become instruments of oppression.

Government Control

I have no rigid social philosophy. I have been too intense on concrete problems of practical justice. And yet I can see that the tendency is steadily toward governmental control. The Government must keep order not only physically but socially. In old times the law was meant to protect each citizen from oppression by physical force. But we have passed to a subtler civilization; from oppression by force we have come to oppression in other ways. And the law must still protect a man from the things that rob him of his freedom, whether the oppressing force is by physical or of a subtler kind.

IV. TRADE UNIONS IN AN INDUSTRIAL DEMOCRACY

The strongest organized group of people in most industrial communities in the United States today is the trade union. During the early part of the twentieth century this was not true, and labor, particularly unskilled labor, was in dire need of getting changes which would improve their lot. Justice Brandeis was one of the pioneers for industrial democracy, and during most of his life was a staunch supporter of the trade union movement. His philosophies set forth about this are presented under four groupings, namely unions and collective bargaining, efficiency and the social ideal, control and co-operatives, and industrial democracy.

A. Unions and Collective Bargaining

Since the adoption of the federal constitution, and notably within the last fifty years, we have passed through an economic and social revolution which affected the life of the people more fundamentally than any political revolution known to history. Widespread substitution of machinery for hand labor (thus multiplying a hundredfold man's productivity), and the annihilation of space through steam and electricity, have wrought changes in the conditions of life which are in many respects greater than those which had occurred in civilized countires during thousands of years preceding. The end was put to legalized human slavery—an institution which had existed since the dawn of history. But of vastly greater influence upon the lives of the greater majority of all civilized peoples was the possibility which invention and discovery created of emancipating women and of liberating men called free from the excessive toil theretofore required to secure food, clothing and shelter. Yet, while invention and discovery created the possibility of releasing men and women from the thralldom of drudgery, there actually came, with the introduction of the factory system and the development of the business corporation, new dangers to liberty. Large publicly owned corporations replaced small privately owned concerns. Ownership of the instruments of production passed from the workman to the employer. Individual personal relations between the proprietor and his help ceased. The individual contract of service lost its character, because of the inequality in position between employer and employee. The group relation of employee to employer with collective bargaining became common, for it was essential to the workers' protection.

The question here is not so much the question whether the number of cents per hour that this miserable creature receives is a little more or a little less. Whether it is enough, none of us are competent to determine. What we are competent to determine, sitting right here, as American citizens, is whether any men in the United States, be they directors of the Steel Corporation or anyone else, are entitled and can safely determine the conditions under which a large portion of the American (workmen) shall live; whether it is not absolutely essential to fairness, for results in an American democracy, to say that the great mass of working people should have an opportunity to combine, and by their collective bargaining secure for themselves what may be a fair return for their labor. There is the fundamental question, and there is the question which is at the bottom of this situation. The denial of that right of collective bargaining is an explanation of the miserable condition of the workingmen in the steel industry.

Industrial Injustice

The real fight today is against the inhuman, relentless exercise of capitalistic power. First we had the struggle for independence, and the second great struggle in our history was to keep the nation whole and abolish slavery. The present struggle in which we are engaged is for social and industrial justice.

Industrial Liberty

Prolonged peace and prosperity can rest only upon the foundation of industrial liberty. The peace which employers should seek is not the peace of fifty years ago, when the employers were absolute masters of the situation. The peace which the employers should seek is not the peace of medieval guilds, with their numberless restrictions. Industrial liberty must attend political liberty. The lead which America takes in the industrial world is no doubt due to our unbounded resources; but of these resources none are so great as the spirit and the ability incident to a free people. We lead the world industrially, not so much because the resources of nature are unbounded, as because the facilities and aspirations of men are comparatively unfettered.

Unionism

The essence of unionism is collective bargaining; that is, instead of the employer dealing individually with each employee, he deals with a large body through their representatives, in respect to the rate of wages and the hours and conditions of employment.

Union Leaders

Abuses of the trade unions have been innumerable. Individuals of slight education, of slight training, are elevated many times by shallow popularity to positions which can be filled adequately only by men possessing great minds and great characters. No wonder, then, that these leaders make mistakes; make grievous errors. The extraordinary thing is that they have not made more mistakes. It is one of the most promising symptoms in American democracy that with all the difficulties attending such positions the labor leaders on the whole have done so little that is wrong.

Unions

The employer needs the unions "to stay him from the fall of vanity"; the employees need them for their own protection; the community needs them to raise the level of the citizen.

The (Unions) have been largely instrumental in securing reasonable hours of labor and proper conditions of work; in raising materially the scale of wages, and in protecting women and children from industrial oppression.

The trade unions have done this, not for the workingmen alone, but for all of us; since the conditions under which so large a part of our fellow citizens work and live will determine, in great measure, the future of our country for good or evil.

One reason why the trades union had to come into existence was because the law of supply and demand did not work properly between the opposing forces of the powerful employer and the individual worker.

Strong, responsible unions are essential to industrial fair play. Without them the labor bargain is wholly one-sided. The parties to the labor contract must be nearly equal in strength if justice is to be worked out, and this means that the workers must be organized and that their organizations must be recognized by employers as a condition precedent to industrial peace.

Employers and Unions

The employers' refusal to deal with a union is ordinarily due to erroneous reasoning or false sentiment. The man who refuses to deal with the union acts ordinarily from a good motive. He is impressed with "union dictation." He is apt to think "this is my business and the American has the right of liberty of contract." He honestly believes that he is standing up for a high principle and is willing often to run the risk of having his business ruined rather than abandon that principle. They have not thought out clearly enough that liberty means exercising one's rights consistently with a like exercise of rights by other people; that liberty is distinguished from license in that it is subject to certain restrictions and that no one can expect to secure liberty in the sense in which we recognize it in America without having his rights curtailed in those respects in which it is necessary to limit them in the general public interest. The failure of many employers to recognize these simple truths is a potent reason why employers have not been willing to deal with unions. I think our employers, as a rule, are kind-hearted; they mean to do right; they mean to be just; and there is no difference between the men who have fought the hardest against labor unions and those who have yielded to and dealt with labor unions in that respect, except that the former have not had that education which comes from actual active cooperation with unions in the solution of these problems.

I should say to those employers who stand for the open shop, that they ought to recognize that it is for their interests as well as that of the community that unions should be powerful and responsible; that it is to their interests to build up the unions, to aid as far as they can in making them stronger, and to create conditions under which the unions shall be led by the ablest and most experienced men. A large part of all union activity today, and in the past, has been devoted to the struggle for existence; and that fact accounts also for a large part of union excesses. As nearly as possible union existence should be assured so that the efforts of the leaders might be devoted to solving the fundamental and difficult problems of discipline and organization, and the working out of other problems of the trades.

B. Efficiency and Social Ideals

Efficiency is the hope of democracy. Efficiency means greater production with less effort and at less cost, through the elimination of unnecessary waste, human and material. How else can we hope to attain our social ideals?

The "right to life" guaranteed by our Constitution is now being interpreted according to demands of social justice and of democracy as the right to live, and not merely to exist. In order to live men must have the opportunity of developing their faculties; and they must live under conditions in which their faculties may develop naturally and healthily.

In the first place, there must be abolition of child labor, shorter hours of labor, and regular days of rest, so that men and women may conserve health, may fit themselves to be citizens of a free country, and may perform their duties as citizens. In other words, men and women must have leisure, which the Athenians called "freedom" or liberty. In the second place, the earnings of men and women must be greater, so that they may live under conditions conducive to health and to mental and moral development.

Our American ideals cannot be attained unless an end is put to the misery due to poverty.

These demands for shorter working time, for higher earnings and for better conditions cannot conceivably be met unless the productivity of man is increased. No mere redistribution of the profits of industry could greatly improve the condition of the working classes. Indeed, the principal gain that can be expected from any such redistribution of profits is that it may remove the existing sense of injustice and discontent, which are the greatest obstacles to efficiency.

Efficiency

Efficiency and economy imply employment of the right instrument and material as well as their use in the right manner. To use a machine, after a much better and more economical one has become available, is as inefficient as to use two men to operate an efficient machine when the work could be performed equally well by one at half the labor cost.

The world's demand for efficiency is so great and the supply so small, that the price of efficiency is high in every field of human activity.

Real efficiency in any business in which conditions are ever changing must ultimately depend, in large measure, upon the correctness of the judgment exercised, almost from day to day, on the important problems as they arise.

Elimination of Waste

I believe all intelligent and enlightened thinkers will recognize, that the only way permanently and appreciably to better the condition of labor, is to increase productivity and to eliminate the waste. That is what scientific management is. It means merely getting more with less effort. It means stopping all waste effort either in the exertion of the individuals or in goods. Just how you are going to apply the principle is a matter of detail. It is more important that it shall be applied democratically. It cannot be successfully applied otherwise in the long run; that is, both employer and employee must come to recognize the fact that the elimination of waste is beneficial to both sides and that they must cooperate to produce the best results and the most effective methods of production.

Demand

Many labor leaders have regarded demand as static, as something fixed. They have therefore assumed that if there is a hundred percent to divide, it will last longer if we each do less, and it will go further. That I believe to be absolutely unsound, as shown by experience. There is no fixed demand. Demand is capable of almost any degree of expansion. It is partly this unfortunate lack of confidence in employers, as a whole, and partly a failure to recognize the results of economic experience, to which the tendency of many labor leaders to restrict production by the individual worker is due.

Conservatism

True conservatism involves progress. . . . Unless our financial leaders are capable of progress, the institutions which they are trying to conserve will lose their foundation.

C. Leisure and Cooperatives

No people ever did or ever can attain a worthy civilization by the satisfaction merely of material needs, however high these needs are raised. The American standard of living demands not only a high minimum wage, but a high minimum of leisure, because we must meet also needs other than material ones.

Serfdom, slavery, peonage, sweatshops held back progress for centuries. By bread alone or labor alone man can barely exist. To live and make life worth living he must have leisure to enjoy the fruits of his labor.

Leisure does not imply idleness. It means ability to work not less but more, ability to work at something besides breadwinning, ability to work harder while working at breadwinning, and ability to work more years at breadwinning. Leisure, so defined, is an essential of successful democracy.

The art of using leisure time, like any other, must be learned; but it is certain that the proper use of leisure, as of liberty, can never be attained except by those who have the opportunity of leisure or of liberty.

We need leisure, among other reasons, because with us every man is of the ruling class. Our education and condition of life must be such as become a ruler. Our great beneficient experiment in democracy will fail unless the people, our rulers, are developed in character and intelligence.

Control and Cooperation

The citizen in a successful democracy must not only have education, he must be free. Men are not free if dependent industrially upon the arbitrary will of another. Industrial liberty on the part of the worker cannot, therefore, exist if there be overweening industrial power. Some curb must be placed upon capitalistic combination. Nor will even this curb be effective unless the workers cooperate, as in trade unions. Control and cooperation are both essential to industrial liberty.

Cooperative Movement

Farmers, workingmen, and clerks are learning to use their little capital and their savings to help one another instead of turning over their money to the great bankers for safekeeping, and to be themselves exploited. And may we not expect that when the cooperative movement develops in America, merchants and manufacturers will learn from farmers and workingmen how to help themselves by helping one another, and thus join in attaining the New Freedom for all? When merchants and manufacturers learn this lesson, money kings will lose subjects, and swollen fortunes may shrink; but industries will flourish, because the faculties of men will be liberated and developed.

Financial Independence

There is no such thing as freedom for a man who under normal conditions is not financially free. We must therefore find means to create in the individual financial independence against sickness, accidents, unemployment, old age, and the dread of leaving his family destitute, if he suffer premature death. For we have become practically a world of employees; and, if a man is to have real freedom of contract in dealing with his employer, he must be financially independent of these ordinary contingencies. Unless we protect him from this oppression, it is foolish to call him free.

If the American is to be fitted for his task as ruler, he must have besides education and industrial liberty also some degree of financial independence. Our existing industrial system is converting an ever increasing percentage of the population into wage-earners; and experience teaches us that a large part of these become at some time financial dependents, by reason of sickness, accident, invalidity, superannuation, unemployment, or premature death of the breadwinner of the family. Contingencies like these, which are generally referred to in the individual case as misfortunes, are now recognized as ordinary incidents in the life of the wage-earner. The need of providing indemnity against financial losses from such ordinary contingencies in the workingman's life has become apparent and is already being supplied in other countries.

D. Industrial Democracy

Unrest, to my mind, never can be removed—and fortunately never can be removed by mere improvement of the physical and material condition of the workingman. If it were possible we should run great risk of improving their material condition and reducing their manhood. We must bear in mind all the time that however much we may desire material improvement and must desire it for the comfort of the individual, that the United States is a democracy, and that we must have, above all things, men. It is the development of manhood to which any industrial and social system should be directed. We Americans are committed not only to social justice in the sense of avoiding things which bring suffering and harm, like unjust distribution of wealth; but we are committed primarily to democracy. The social justice for which we are striving is an incident of our democracy, not the main end. It is rather the result of democracy—perhaps its finest expression—but it rests upon democracy, which implies the rule by the people. And therefore the end for which we must strive is the attainment of rule by the people, and that involves industrial democracy as well as political democracy. That means that the problems of a trade should no longer be the problems of the employer alone. The problems of his business, and it is not the employer's business alone, are the problems of all in it. The union cannot shift upon the employer the responsibility for conditions, nor can the employer insist upon determining, according to his will the conditions which shall exist. The problems which exist are the problems of the trade; they are the problems of employer and employee. Profit sharing, however liberal, cannot meet the situation. That would merely mean dividing the profits of business. Such a division may do harm or it might do good, dependent on how it is applied.

There must be a division not only of profits, but a division also of responsibilities. The employees must have the opportunity of participating in the decisions as to what shall be their condition and how the business shall be run. They must learn also in sharing that responsibility that they must bear, too, the suffering arising from grave mistakes, just as the employer must. But the right to assist in making the decisions, the right of making their own mistakes, if mistakes there must be, is a privilege which should not be denied to labor. We must insist upon sharing the responsibility for the result of the business.

Chapter 7

With far-reaching vision, Professor Benjamin M. Selekman has eloquently argued the importance of self-interest and private initiative, and has also been a leading exponent of the necessity of a close working relationship between unions, management, and government. He was convinced that all these should understand that only through increased productivity is it possible to increase real wages. The high productivity of industry today has resulted, in no small part, from the acceptance of this principle by both labor and management. The depth and breadth of Professor Selekman's philosophy is illustrated by the following statements:

> The Year 1776 marked the emergence of three great events destined to determine the fate of the nation.
>
> First was the Declaration of Independence, which dedicated government to the freedom and welfare of man.
>
> Second was Watt's steam engine. It marked the beginning of modern technology and the substitution of machine power for human drudgery. It presaged ultimately automation, electronics, computers, increasing mastery of nature's power, and the realization of abundance instead of the scarcity which had always confronted society.
>
> Third was the publication of Adam Smith's *Wealth of Nations,* which raised self-interest and private initiative, as against government-dictated activity, to the highest pinnacle of legitimacy. It became the dominant economic philosophy of our nation during the nineteenth and early twentieth centuries.

It was my privilege in 1945, as a representative of the University of Illinois Committee on setting up its Institute of Labor and Industrial Relations, to visit Professor Selekman at Harvard University and to get his advice on what might be best to include in such an institute. His advice, and that of others, led to a program that, with the final blessing of the University of Illinois Trustees, made the Institute a reality in 1946. His advice then was excellent, as is the following article, in which he reviews some of the events of the past quarter of a century and makes a plea for all parties in the American industrial economy to throw aside vindictiveness and to work toward a peaceful and productive economy. Professor Selekman was a man dedicated to the objectives which he here sets forth. His discussion in the following paper is well worth reading by all students of the American economy.

REALITIES OF UNION POWER*

Benjamin M. Selekman**

Let us first try to grasp the simple fact that we are dealing with a major sector of the American community. With eighteen million breadwinners as actual members, perhaps forty to fifty million Americans are involved directly and indirectly in unions. We must assume they constitute a normal distribution—average people, some exceptional, some mediocre; a majority of them honest, a minority dishonest.

In other words, we must accept union members as typical Americans. We should not be surprised, then, if they behave within the framework of American values and goals.

Of course, not all unions are alike any more than all corporations are alike. They differ a great deal—depending on their history, the quality of their leadership, the origin and distribution of their members, the industry in which they operate, the type of corporations they deal with, and so forth. But, allowing for differences, what are their common characteristics? Perhaps the best way to approach this question is to see what a union is not:

1. A union though perhaps idealistic in origin, is a practical, usually hardboiled organization with its eye on securing material gains for its members and, at the same time, enhancing the prestige and power of its leaders.

2. A union is not a revolutionary organization. On the contrary, it belongs among the most conservative. Unions are in the forefront fighting communism; they are impatient even with socialism. The vast majority of leaders and members—perhaps as many as 95 per cent—vote the straight Democratic or even the Republican ticket.

3. A union is not a public-service organization. It is primarily interested in its own members and in its own leadership. Of course, like all economic and political groups, a union may well argue that to the extent it serves its members it also serves the public. Nevertheless, it is essentially a self-interest organization; its primary aim is to get the very best wages, hours, and working conditions for its members.

4. A union is not a democratic organization. Although virtually

---

*From *A Moral Philosophy for Management* by B. M. Selekman, 1959 by McGraw-Hill, Inc.; used by permission of McGraw-Hill Book Company.

**Formerly, Kirstein Professor of Labor Relations, Graduate School of Business Administration, Harvard University.

every union has a constitution, stemming from its early grass-roots character, which provides for the usual democratic procedures such as secret ballots, periodic elections of officers, and regular conventions made up of delegates from the respective locals to formulate and adopt policies, behind this democratic facade stands a political machine.

5. Trade unions are not polite or well mannered or even diplomatic in their dealings with corporation executives, or even with government officials. Indeed, they usually adopt a posture of hostility, at least publicly, as they organize pressure to attain their objectives.

Role of Power

All of these negative aspects stem from the fundamental nature of unions. A union is a power organization. Its positive role is to mobilize economic, political, and moral power to win objectives for members and leaders. To do so, it will even compete with other unions, as is evidenced by recurrent jurisdictional disputes, the most hardy perennial unsolved problem in the house of labor. Nor will any union sacrifice a possible gain so that members of another union may benefit, even though its standards may already be higher. The auto workers, or steel workers, or printers, for example, do not forego making demands for higher wages in order that the lower-paid workers in other industries may catch up to them.

But this does not mean that the unions do not serve a useful purpose. To illustrate by an admitted oversimplification of function: if corporations are placed on one side and unions on the other, the one to maximize profits, the other to maximize wages and working conditions—it may be seen at once that they complement each other. Both groups are given the right under law to withdraw from the market if they deem the price offered for their products or services inadequate, and the bargaining activity between them produces prices and wages that approximate a sort of practical justice. (Of course, the consumer also has the right to withdraw from the market if exorbitant prices reflect too large a profit or too high a wage; indeed, the consumer is the ultimate sovereign with veto power in a three-cornered bargaining process.)

Hence our disillusionment with unions for failure to fulfill our romantic vision of idealism and public service should not mislead us into thinking we can dispense with them. Without the pressure of unions, wages and working conditions would be depressed to subnormal levels. Sweatshops did not come into being because employers of their day were evil, but because in the absence of unions, there was no counter-pressure to keep wages up to certain levels, which all competitors had to meet if they were to attract and hold labor. And sweatshops could happen again, under the pressure of competition, even though the overwhelming sentiment of the community would be against them.

It is for this reason that both the Taft-Hartley Act and the Wagner Act, though differing fundamentally in their posture toward organized labor, gave as their objective, in their respective preambles, the establishment of equality of bargaining power as desirable from the viewpoint of the public welfare and made mandatory the recognition of unions as bargaining representatives if a majority of employees so vote.

As Marketing Agency

It is from the perspective of a power system that one can best understand the nature and function of trade unions. First and primarily, a union is a combination of a political and business organization. From the business point of view a union is primarily a marketing agency. Every union is essentially a collectivity for selling labor as a unit in the form of various skills. All its other activities are directed to making this selling function as effective as possible.

To be sure, unions do not think of themselves primarily as marketing agencies; they still harbor in their own minds the image derived from their origin, namely a social movement launched to wrest a fair break for themselves from reluctant owners. Although hardly a union president subscribes to the concept of a class struggle or the nationalization of the tools of production and distribution, nevertheless labor representatives talk as if they were in a permanent contest with capitalist employers. Such sentiments are invoked in during preparations for and actual negotiation with corporations.

If, however, we keep in mind the function of a union as a marketing agency, we see that what looks like political propaganda is in reality part of a merchandising campaign particularly suited to its purpose of exacting the price desired as wages for its membership. Thus, union leaders and the whole union apparatus drum up emotionalism, ring the charges on the injustice of Wall Street and the justice of their cause, hold special conventions, go on radio and television, threaten strikes, all to dramatize their cause. And since the strike is raw power, its potential use has to be justified in political and moral phraseology—the workers against capital. In other words, it has to be sold to the membership, so that they will be willing to undergo the sacrifices entailed, and to the community, so that it will be willing to suffer the inconveniences consequent on a strike.

Thus every major negotiation is launched by a large-scale promotional campaign in which union demands are projected in terms of a moral cause calling for a living wage; advancing standards of living; security against hazards of unemployment, sickness, and old age; and, in recent years, purchasing power necessary to keep the wheels of industry moving.

It may well be that if all this militant union activity during negotiations were understood as a sales promotion campaign with a political flavor, it would upset us less. We do not get upset when corporations or political parties put on their campaigns. We read or ignore the advertisements; we look at, or turn off, television plays and radio skits. On the whole, we maintain a skeptical attitude.

Of course, the possibility of a strike makes the union campaign more of a threat than either the usual sales or political campaigns. Strikes spell loss not only to employees but also to merchants, landlords, and all the other people dependent on the continuous functioning of the business. But strikes are legal in a democracy, and every once in a while we have to undergo the discomforts attending a shutdown. Indeed, if we learned to take a calmer, more naturalistic attitude toward strikes, unions might be more sober and restrained in using them. It is the threat of their use that causes fear and capitulation, even when management may be convinced that it is wiser to face a shutdown than to grant the price demanded by the unions and the workers.

Centralized Power

The trade union, then, is a power organization putting pressure on management for advancing wages and working conditions. From its nature as a power center stems the necessity for centralized administration. Since in the final analysis the threat of shutdown determines the price which a corporation will pay for labor, a union must be able to initiate and conduct strikes, and a well-organized strike is essentially an exercise in military strategy and tactics calling for highly centralized decision making. It is a form of blockade. Hence the weapons that trouble businessmen and the community in general come into play—the picket line and the boycott. But once we grant the legitimacy of a strike as a weapon in the negotiating process, then we must also grant the legitimacy of using the weapons which make the strike effective.

The tendency toward centralization in American trade unions is therefore rooted in their militant origin. From the beginnings until well into the 1930s, only by means of a miliatry strategy could the unions make any progress and hold on to any gains they might have made from time to time. Such strategy called for planning from the top—for deploying organizers, throwing up picket lines, establishing commissaries, providing legal assistance, and raising money to finance this widespread military activity. Unions had to "crash the gate," to force their way into industry. Such was the case with the old AFL unions, as with the younger CIO unions. The major difference was that, by the time the CIO got going, trade unionism and collective bargaining enjoyed legal backing.

It was his qualities as a military strategist that made John L. Lewis the natural leader of the CIO in its early days. By temperament he enjoyed the posture of a fighter, and by experience in the coal fields he had become adept at applying military tactics to enlisting union recruits in a hostile environment. He also had available funds from the miners' treasury to defray the costs incurred in the early stages of organizing workmen in the mass-production industries. Of all the major steel companies, for instance, only United States Steel forestalled recourse to violent tactics; and that was in the form of a secret compact—one more instance of top-level strategy—the Traylor-Lewis understanding, which in 1937 granted, as already indicated, the Steelworkers Organizing Committee bargaining rights in any plant where the majority of employees so voted.

Lewis brought with him from the coal miners' union a team experienced in this type of militant organizing—men like Philip Murray, Van. A. Bittner, and Allen S. Haywood. Thus, even though a large segment of local workers in the centers of heavy industry may have been discontented and desirous of union organization, it was old, seasoned leaders from the miners, to whom were added veterans like Sidney Hillman, David Dubinsky, and Emil Rieve from the needle trades and textiles, who took over and directed the campaigns. Thus, the very militaristic origin of trade unionism propelled unions into a centralized form of government.

Logic of Negotiation

Then, after the union is already recognized and doing business with corporations, the very logic of negotiations strengthens the tendency toward centralization. As demands by the membership for wage increases and economic gains are repeated at each contract negotiation, they lose some of their value and potency. The far-sighted leader has to conceive of new demands which he can justify.

For instance, Philip Murray launched the demand for pensions in 1949 and led his men into a strike to secure noncontributory pensions. It was an open secret that the rank and file entertained little enthusiasm for the strike, and Murray had personally to visit steel communities to maintain their morale. The men walked out in loyalty to him, but, as typical Americans, they would rather have had a larger pay envelope immediately than enjoy a pension in the dim future. Similarly, in 1955, Walter P. Reuther projected a plan for guaranteed annual wages or what in reality became supplementary unemployment benefits.

Here, incidentally, is a desirable function of leadership—to be able to shift strategy with changing conditions and, above all, to look ahead and provide for future contingencies. *Vox populi* may be *vox Dei,* but it is often fixed on immediate, earthy desires. The leader must think of the morrow.

Finally, the actual requirements of negotiations when the adversaries meet around the table call for centralized decision making. Under the conditions of present-day America, a strike is questionable because unions have achieved status and influence. Wages are already at a high level. A strike spells hardship and debt to the workers; also lost business to the employer and to all those in the community dependent indirectly upon the enterprise. Therefore, the union leader engaged in negotiating must, as the zero hour approaches, decide whether to put a strike into effect or to make compromises—as offers and counteroffers are being placed on the table. Indeed, at this final stage, negotiators are usually reduced in number to a few on each side to expedite matters without too many debates by the crowd. It is not feasible under these circumstances to go back to the ranks for a plebiscite. Commitments must be made, and with a fairly good degree of assurance that they are enforceable.

Again, after the settlement has been made and the agreement signed, the union official must be sure that the members will live up to it in the various plants of the corporation. There is always the danger of "dragging feet" or even of walkouts. Hence, the leader must have a bureaucracy ready to go out into the field and obtain ratification of the agreement; and, if ranks break away and engage in strikes, he must be certain of a strong enough following to feel confident that before long the men will be brought to their senses and return to their workbenches. The commitment made to management must be carried out if he is to enjoy confidence at the next negotiation.

Authoritarian Nature

These factors, among others, make the government of unions characteristically authoritarian. The president is the "boss." The constitution provides for an executive council, but a majority of those on it are usually his men. Conventions are held and the delegates are elected by local unions, but he usually appoints the international representatives and organizers, who are the ones that get out the votes for the administration, whenever necessary. Essentially, it is a leadership function which the president discharges, and therefore he must be sure he has a loyal group that will go along with him.

It is also in the interest of the corporation that the union leadership be centralized and authoritarian. The keeping of commitments at the work level is a matter of life and death to management. It must price its commodity and be able to make deliveries. If the successive steps in reaching compromises had to go back to the union hall for debate and ratification, one would run the inevitable risk inherent in political hustlings—the delays and interruptions that arise from political oppositions and factions.

Indeed, the intrinsic logic both of union administration and of corporate economics makes the practice of grass-roots democracy within unions almost impossible. Once the management of a corporation and union officials begin to appreciate each other's needs in this respect, there arises some understanding of the range of bargaining limits in a practical world, even though the astute union official will always try to stretch the limit to the utmost, whereas the prudent company executive will try to stay well within the limits of adding to his costs.

Thus, we find that, although union officials and corporate managements start from opposite sides of the pole—one elected, the other appointed—they end up pretty much at the same point: both are highly centralized, authoritarian governors of power systems. One vital difference does remain; management need not face political campaigns for reelection. Union presidents start out as elected officials; reelection is required under the constitution. Nevertheless, they are reelected again and again until death or voluntary retirement. And often the trade-union president, like the corporation president, may have a decisive voice in his succession.

In what we might call personality structures, too, union and corporate presidents have a striking resemblance. They are both strong men, enjoy power, and do not suffer dissidents gladly. Thus John L. Lewis—an extreme example of the autocrat—had his erstwhile and lifelong comrades, William Green and Philip Murray, expelled from the United Mine Workers when their paths parted on his withdrawal from both the AFL and CIO. He did not retire to his own tent to sulk, though, but issued fulminations against all and sundry (including President Roosevelt) who would not go along with him.

In this one respect, indeed, the union president still resembles the former owner-president more than the modern professional administrator. It is *his* union, he bled and fought for it, just as the rugged individualist of a generation ago brooked no interference in his business which he had fought and bled for. John L. Lewis, George Meany, Walter P. Reuther, and David Dubinsky, though differing in so many ways, have in common the quality of making themselves felt whenever they enter any conference, be it in an executive suite or hotel negotiating room, in the White House or Madison Square Garden.

The moral is clear: such men accentuate the centralizing drift that is inherent in the institutions they lead.

Indifferent Members

It is doubtful whether union members are much concerned about the course democracy has taken in their unions or feel seriously deprived because they do not participate actively in the government of their organizations.

For one thing, unlike earlier generations, current members do not have the fervor or excitement of founders. The pioneers were workers at the bench who, smarting under harsh conditions and an oppressive atmosphere, faced personal risks when they rallied to the call for organization as a way of obtaining a voice in their industrial destiny. They were discharged and blacklisted or, if kept, faced constant discrimination. In one way or another, they were punished for their audacity in attempting to form unions. Strikes were long and bitter; physical violence and imprisonment were not unknown consequences. Thus, out of risks and self-sacrifice, a spirit of dedication arose.

At least until World War II, large numbers of workers participated in the struggle—breaking through the historical resistance of heavy industry to trade unionism.

With the advent of the war, however, several million members were added to union ranks largely through decisions of the War Labor Board granting unions "maintenance of membership" as a way of avoiding strikes under the necessity of uninterrupted war production. Usually the checkoff was also part of the agreement. Millions of workers were enrolled, not only new to unionism, but even—particularly in the case of many recruits from the South—new to modern industry. And since the war, the four million new members in industry know even less of the sacrifices their predecessors underwent so that they could now enjoy the best working conditions and the highest wages in the world.

As corporation after corporation, under the constant pressure of governmental and union power, yielded recognition and bargaining rights and negotiated contracts from year to year, the rank and file became more and more apathetic. This is not to say that today's workers do not know what they want. On the contrary, they look on unions as a vehicle primarily for getting them higher wages, along with more and better fringe benefits and sundry improvements in working conditions. Having made no real sacrifice to bring their unions into existence, they regard the dues which they pay as tantamount to buying an insurance policy guaranteeing them more and more of the good things of life. Remember that most of these members have never had to suffer the adversities of depression and prolonged unemployment; they know nothing but sustained prosperity and constantly rising wages. These new workers have also, on the whole, been spared the privations of prolonged strikes which their forefathers conducted—and generally lost because employers could keep open and hire new workers in a surplus labor market.

Today, strikes are both effective and less costly in human suffering. There is no surplus labor for employers to recruit, and workers usually have wives or younger members of the family contributing to the total family income. Under these conditions, unions have been able to break through to new levels in industries like autombiles, steel, rubber, and electrical manufacturing, which have been profitable and hence in a position to pay high wages. Thus, General Motors, Ford, and United States Steel have been pacemakers in setting high standards of compensation and fringe benefits—*after* tough bargaining with the United Auto Workers and the United Steelworkers. In other words, trade unions have been of material benefit to workers.

Pressure for Gain

Yet workers are dissatisfied. Since wage increases and other benefits have been passed on in prices, they feel that they are always chasing a rising cost of living–higher rent, higher grocery bills, higher clothing costs. All of which highlights the constant pressure exerted upon trade-union officials in serving their members as salesmen, in forever seeking more and more benefits from year to year, from contract to contract.

These new union members are bent on continuing to enjoy the good things of life and having their aspirations for a rising standard fulfilled. They respond to the constant stimulus of advertising and sales promotion. They are good customers for cars, television sets, homes, furniture, travel, and vacations. They would also like to see their children enjoy the benefits of higher education. They do not hesitate to take advantage of credit facilities, even though it means going into debt. Thus, all the inner logic of the modern American trade unions is to propel trade-union leaders to ask for more material gains every time they enter into collective bargaining.

Herein lies the fallacy of attributing inflationary pressures primarily to labor leaders and to trade unions as organizations. To the extent that the wage push is a factor in the complex economics of inflation, the pressure—and it really is pressure with a full head of steam—is from union members as individual workers. The very role of union leaders as politicians makes response to these pressures inevitable. Like all politicians, even though they may build good and sturdy machines, they have to keep their ears to the ground. No politician, no matter how powerful his machine, can long survive unless he articulates the basic sentiments and desires of his electorate.

It should not be overlooked, however, that trade-union leaders are wedded to the Keynesian doctrine that the prosperity of the country is determined by the propensity to consume. No matter how conservative, they hold to the doctrine that high purchasing power is the key to prosperity. Accordingly, they take the position that the constant demand for higher wages and better working conditions not only is justified for workers but is good for the whole country.

Democracy Reconsidered

I trust that what I have depicted as developments in unions will not disillusion the reader about democracy or in any way give the impression that I am cynical about its actual and potential worth. The lesson to learn is that pure democracy is not always appropriate to all social and economic institutions. We ourselves, after the founding of the nation, had to rely on political parties to make our Constitution work in a practical, rivalrous, and competitive world. Thus, unions having to meet the exigencies first of fighting and then of negotiating and making commitments, had no alternative but to devise a form of government that would centralize strategy, tactics, and decision making.

Nor should it be overlooked that, in a very real sense, the concept of a union as a democratic organization continues to be important. For the machinery by which those in power can be ousted is present. And arguments in dissent do take place on union convention floors.

As long as such opportunity for dissent remains, then somehow democracy continues as a vital faith. The tragedy revealed by the McClellan committee lies in the fact that in some unions—by connivance and corrupt alliances with racketeers like Dio—terrorism, violence, and murder have been introduced to stifle any opposition, and democracy has been subverted and turned into a shambles.

Perhaps it is just as well, as we scrutinize the workings of democracy in government, business, unions, or whatever the institution, to admit that in its pure sense democracy, like morality, is an aspiration rather than a living, everyday reality. Since the days of New England town government with its town meeting, we have had precious little pure democracy. Size, scale, bigness—call it what you will—added to the increasingly technical complexity of problems and their solutions has made us all leave these matters more and more to professionals and the technicians. In this regard the shape of things as they are emerging in the union world confirms the trend.

Conclusion

The year 1776 marked the emergence of three great events destined to determine the fate of the nation.

First was the Declaration of Independence, which dedicated government to the freedom and welfare of man.

Second was Watt's steam engine. It marked the beginning of modern technology and the substitution of machine power for human drudgery. It presaged ultimately automation, electronics, computers, increasing mastery of nature's power, and the realization of abundance instead of the scarcity which had always confronted society.

Third was the publication of Adam Smith's *Wealth of Nations,* which raised self-interest and private initiative, as against government-dictated activity, to the highest pinnacle of legitimacy. It became the dominant economic philosophy of our nation during the nineteenth and early twentieth centuries.

It is the forces, ideas, and allegiances around these three seminal events that have made up the strands in the weaving of our national society. For the first 150 years, technology and economics dominated the scene, under the leadership of business. A new country, with great resources, spanning a continent, together with a new people, coming in large numbers to escape tyranny and restrictions, constituted an ideal setting for self-interest and private initiative. The country developed rapidly and wealth accumulated. But success was shadowed by poverty and maladjustment; mansions and skyscrapers were surrounded by slums.

During this first century and a half, the Declaration of Independence served primarily the pride of the nation—a symbol to be invoked on holidays or times of crisis. It was inevitable that with the maturing and affluence of the nation as the twentieth century advanced, and under the shock of a great depression, the ideology of the Declaration of Independence should pass beyond the stage of symbolism to that of practical policy. So, all of a sudden, the welfare state sprung almost full grown into life with the enactment of massive social legislation to provide for the human problems of a productive, dynamic capitalism.

Business has gradually accepted—slowly, to be sure, but step by step—the measures enacting social insurance, minimum wages, collective bargaining with unions, responsibility for human relationships, and the whole idea of an inextricable interrelationship between the prosperity of business and the welfare of the whole community.

What is needed now is a maturing of the experience of the past quarter-century into a complete realization that business, labor, and government are engaged in a permanent coalition, a combined operation to fulfill the destiny of the moral as well as the material greatness promised at the beginning of the nation.

Against one hazard, the responsible business executive must be on constant guard—the danger of disillusionment and even cynicism.

The long history of mankind cautions against the expectation of any easy fulfillment of moral aspirations in the here and now. Thus revolution and war, even when crowned with victory, frequently result in the defeat of the spirit. The struggle in itself may evoke vision and sacrifice. The aftermath may well be counterrevolution, terror, and corruption. Camus traces eloquently this degradation of man in *The Rebel*; Orwell and Huxley make it vivid in fictional sociology through *1984* and *Brave New World*.

Though the West withstood and freed the world from the onslaught of Nazi tyranny, the men who won the victory on the battlefield became the "beat generation" in this country, and the "angry young men" in Britain. Our literature is streaked with self-flagellation. Our very success in creating wealth for mankind and in bringing the abolition of poverty within reach is turned into an indictment of materialism and sensualism.

Under such circumstances it is tempting to give up and retreat to self-interest. But for those who would lead, retreat is impossible. Unless the new and rapidly growing management group holds on to social and moral goals, it is doomed to lose what it now has in the way of authority and opportunity. Private enterprise in the form of the modern corporation has still to win the prize of legitimacy. The prize will continue to prove elusive without a growing faith in the community that, whatever the faltering, justice and the good life can best be realized through a decentralized industrial system manned by individuals of high purpose responsive to the ethics of our Judaea-Christian tradition.

The fulfillment of the promise of this tradition is a long and seemingly tortuous road. Saints and martyrs have suffered and even perished on it. The very people they sought to free and succor, stoned and tortured them. It is not given us to understand the saint and sinner in every man; this duality which makes man noble, or evil, or capable of both good and evil under varying time and circumstances.

We in our own recent times have created the state, the corporation, the union—all to fulfill and ennoble man. It has not always worked out that way.

Have we been guilty of overromanticizing the saintly side of man, forgetting the demonic in everyone? Have we set up a standard of perfectibility impossible of realization on this mortal earth?

Surely businessmen, accustomed as they are to all the grim realities they face every day in building and operating economic institutions, should be the last to suffer discouragement. Perhaps what they can best bring to the quest for justice and equity is the same hardheadedness that they would apply to their daily jobs in getting things done amidst uncertainty and risk. But they too must be shielded from the natural temptations to become arbitrary, capricious, and punitive—a temptation consequent upon disillusionment with their people. That is why we need some organized framework to assure a way of justice which accepts yet transcends man's fallibility and sinfulness. Hence the urgency of a framework of constitutionalism for the modern corporation.

And yet constitutionalism by itself is not enough. Justice and equity must be carried beyond the requirements of the letter. Problems arise when feelings are injured; people suffer injustices of a nature that cannot be covered by a written document or policy. Unless equity is done, constitutionalism loses its vitality. Although a business cannot be expected to function as a church or a family or a clinic, human values cannot be ignored without peril.

Indeed, the great corporation executive, as any great governor of men, is he who so conveys justice and equity in all his bearing that his people know that righteousness prevails within his realm.

Chapter 8

The depth and breadth of thinking of Eric Hoffer stands out in sharp contrast to the superficial ranting of many intellectuals currently given wide publicity from day to day over television. In his book he has stated: "Imagine an American writing about America and not mentioning kindness, not mentioning the boundless capacity for working together, not mentioning the unprecedented diffusion of social, political, as well as technological skills, not mentioning the American's ability to do the world's work with a minimum of supervision and leadership, not mentioning the breathtaking potentialities which lurk in the commonest American . . ."

Eric Hoffer, author of these words, had only a limited formal education, but his wealth of experience as a longshoreman on the West Coast and knowledge gained as an avid reader have made him an outstanding writer. He has captured the bigness of America and has placed in the forefront some of the most important parts of American life which have escaped the observation of many intellectual but inexperienced writers. The following article taken from his book *The Temper of Our Time* sets forth clearly a philosophy of America which is well worth reading.

SOME THOUGHTS ON THE PRESENT*

Eric Hoffer**

It is remarkable that after a century of incessant change the paths of change have not become smooth and easy. On the contrary, our world seems to be getting less and less suitable for people who undergo change. Never before has the passage from boyhood to manhood been so painful and so beset with explosions. The passage from backwardness to modernity which in the nineteenth century seemed a natural process is now straining a large part of the world to the breaking point. The hoped-for changes from poverty to affluence, from subjection to freedom, from work to leisure do not enhance social stability but threaten social dissolution. However noble the intentions and wholehearted the efforts of those who initiate change, the results are often the opposite of that which was reasonable to expect. Social chemistry has gone awry: no matter what ingredients are placed in the retort, the end product is more often than not an explosive.

If one were to pick the chief trait which characterizes the temper of our time it would be impatience. Tomorrow has become a dirty word. The future is now, and hope has turned into desire. The adolescent cannot see why he should wait to become a man before he has a say in the ordering of domestic and foreign affairs. The backward, also, panting to catch up tomorrow with our yesterdays, want to act as pathfinders in the van of mankind. Everywhere you look you see countries leaping. There is no time to grow. New countries want to bloom and bear fruit even as they sprout, and many have decked themselves out with artificial flowers and fruit.

Everywhere there is a greed for pridc. Pride is the only currency that will buy souls. In the backward countries an undertaking will make headway only if it generates pride. These countries find it easier to induce a readiness to fight and die than a readiness to work, easier to attempt the impossible than the possible, easier to build dams and steel mills than raise wheat, easier to start at the end and work backward than begin at the beginning. Never has giving been so urgent and the act of giving so difficult. To preserve your pride you must vilify those who help you. You accuse them of practicing the

---

*Reprinted from *The Temper of Our Time* with the permission of the editors of Harper and Row Publishers, New York.

**Formerly a longshoreman and more recently a writer and lecturer.

colonialism of giving. Rudeness has become a substitute for power, for faith, and for achievement.

Amidst the leaping, running, and shouting no one can tell whether the momentous events of our time are real and not merely the echo of words. How real are the new nations? Is the Occident really in decline? And who can tell with certitude whether the world is being Communized or Americanized?

So evanescent are world situations that we cannot suit our actions to facts. Never has the present been so perishable: things which happened yesterday are ancient history. The better part of statesmanship might be to know clearly and precisely what not to do, and leave action to the improvisation of chance. It might be wise to wait for our enemies to defeat themselves, and heed Bacon's advice to treat friends as if they might one day become our enemies, and enemies as if they might one day become our friends.

The decline of the Occident has been proclaimed on housetops for over half a century. Knowledgeable people are still telling us that Europe is finished, America rotten to the core, and that the future is in Russia, China, India, Africa, and even in Latin America. We are urged to learn the meaning of life from these bearers of the future. Yet it is becoming evident that if there is going to be anywhere a genuine growth of individual freedom and human dignity it will be from cuttings taken from the Occident. Even the Communist parties of the Occident are discovering that their historical role is not to change the Occident's way of life but to put a brake on the dehumanizing juggernaut of the Communist apparatus in Russia and China.

The fact is that the awakening of Asia and Africa has turned the Occident into a mystery. When we see to what ugly stratagems the new countries have to resort in order to make their people do the things which we consider natural and matter-of-fact we begin to realize how unprecedented the Occident is with its spontaneous enterprise and orderliness, and its elementary decencies. The mystery of our time is not the enigmatic Orient but the fantastic Occident.

The Occident is at present without fervent faith and hope. There is no overwhelming undertaking in sight that might set minds and hearts on fire. There is no singular happiness and no excessive suffering. We have already discounted every possible invention, and reduced momentous tasks to sheer routine. Though we are aware of deadly dangers ahead of us, our fears have not affected our rhythm of life. The Occident continues to function well at room temperature.

Now, there are those who maintain that lack of a strong faith must in the long run prove fatal to a society, and that the most decisive changes in history are those which involve a weakening or intensification of belief. Whether this be true or not it should be clear that a weakening of faith can be due as much to a gain in power, skill, and experience as to a loss of vigor and drive. Where there is the necessary skill and equipment to move mountains there is no need for the faith that moves mountains. Intensification of belief is not necessarily a symptom of vigor, nor does a fading of belief spell decline. The strong, unless they are infected with a pathological fear, cannot generate and sustain a strong faith. Nowhere in the Occident is there at present a faith comparable to that which is being generated in the meek, backward masses of Russia and China. The Occident has skill, efficiency, orderliness, and a phenomenal readiness to work. It would be suicidal for the Occident to rely on a concocted new faith in a contest with totalitarian countries. We can prevail only by doing more and better what we know how to do well. Those in the Occident who wring their hands and pray for a new faith are sowing the wind.

Free men are aware of the imperfection inherent in human affairs, and they are willing to fight and die for that which is not perfect. They know that basic human problems can have no final solutions, that our freedom, justice, equality, etc., are far from absolute, and that the good life is compounded of half measures, compromises, lesser evils, and gropings toward the perfect. The rejection of approximations and the insistence on absolutes are the manifestation of a nihilism that loathes freedom, tolerance, and equity.

The present Americanization of the world is an unprecedented phenomenon. The penetration of a foreign influence has almost always depended on the hospitableness of the educated and the well-to-do. Yet the world-wide diffusion of American habits, fashions, and ways is proceeding in the teeth of the shrill opposition of the intellectuals and the hostility of the better people. The only analogy which comes to mind is the early spread of Christianity, with the difference that Americanization is not being pushed by apostles and missionaries but like a chemical reagent penetrates of its own accord and instantly combines with the common people and the young. "The American way of life," says, a British observer, "has become the religion of the masses in five continents."[1]

Ironically, at a time when the world is being Americanized the American intellectual seems to be seceding from America. Here in the San Francisco Bay area, the dramatic change in the intellectual's attitude toward America has the earmarks of a historical turning

[1]David Marquand in the Manchester *Guardian Weekly,* March 17, 1960.

point. The first impression is that the American intellectual is being Europeanized, and one is tempted to see a connection between influencing and being influenced: that by influencing the world America unavoidably opens itself up to foreign influences; and in this case, as so often before, the intellectual is the carrier of the foreign influence. Actually, the intellectual's revulsion from contemporary America has little to do with the penetration of a foreign influence but is the result of a recent change in the tilt of the social landscape.

The nature of a society is largely determined by the direction in which talent and ambition flow—by the tilt of the social landscape. In America, until recently, most of the energy, ability, and ambition found its outlet in business. In *Notes of a Son and Brother* Henry James tells how, as children, he and his brother William were mortified that their father was not a businessman but a philosopher and an author. In a European country like France, where writers and artists rank high in public esteem, boys and girls probably find it humiliating to admit that their father is a mere businessman and not a writer or an artist. In France, said Oscar Wilde, "every bourgeois wants to be an artist." Now, it stands to reason that the central pursuit of a society attracts and swallows individuals who by nature are meant for other careers. In America, until recently, many potential poets and philosophers became businessmen, while in France many potential business tycoons go through life as intellectuals; and the paradox is that these misplaced individuals who do not really belong are often the ones who shape the character and style of the sphere in which they operate. It was not conventional businessmen but misplaced poets and philosophers who set in motion the vast combinations and the train of ceaseless innovation which gave American business its Promethean sweep and drive. To a philosopher who finds himself immersed in a milieu of sheer action, all action will seem of one kind and he will shift easily from one field of activity to another. He will combine factories, mines, railroads, oil wells, etc., the way a philosopher collates and generalizes ideas. In France, where the misplaced individuals are chiefly among the intellectuals, the tone and the pace of the intellectual establishment are generated not by authentic intellectuals to whom words and ideas are ends in themselves, the center of existence, but by potential men of action, potential organizers and administrators, who find themselves trapped in the mold of intellectuals. To this type of intellectual ideas have validity only as a prelude to action, and he sees commitment and history making as vital components of an intellectual existence.

Now, the important fact is that since Sputnik the prestige and material rewards of intellectual pursuits have risen sharply in this country, and the social landscape has begun to tilt away from business. Right now the career of a scientist or a professor can be more exciting than that of a businessman, and its material rewards are not to be sneezed at. A recent survey showed that only 20 percent of undergraduates intend to go into business. The chances are great, therefore, that at present many individuals with superb talents for wheeling and dealing and for building industrial empires are pawing their way up the academic ladder or are throwing their weight around in literary and artistic circles. This is a state of affairs not unlike that which prevails in France, hence the impression that the American intellectual is being Europeanized.

It goes without saying that a change in the direction of flow of social energies constitutes a turning point in the life of a society or a civilization. If the Reformation figured as a historical turning point, and marked the birth of the modern Occident, it was largely because it brought about a diversion of energies from sacerdotal to secular channels. We are told that during a twenty-year period in the sixteenth century not a student of the University of Vienna became a priest. In this country, with the opening of the West in the middle of the last century, the sons of New England divines, poets, writers, and scholars went into railroading, mining, and manufacturing, and this diversion of energies from one field to another marked the birth of modern Ameirca and also brought to an almost abrupt end the cultural flowering of New England.

There is no telling how soon and to what degree the diversion of talent and ambition from business might make itself felt in a diminution of economic venturesomeness and drive. Nor can we tell whether the inflow of energies into intellectual pursuits will result in an upsurge of cultural creativeness. But it is beyond doubt that the movers and shakers are already at work inside and outside the universities. The civil rights movement and the Vietnam war are ideal vehicles for these would-be makers of history. History making is becoming the malady of our age: the book of history seems to lie open and every two-bit intellectual wants to turn its pages.

The attitude of the intellectual community toward America is shaped not by the creative few but by the many who for one reason or another cannot transmit their dissatisfaction into a creative impulse, and cannot acquire a sense of uniqueness and growth by developing and expressing their capacities and talents. There is nothing in contemporary America that can cure or alleviate their chronic frustration. They want power, lordship, and opportunities for imposing action. Even if we should banish poverty from the land, lift up the Negro to true equality, withdraw from Vietnam, and give half of the national income as foreign aid, they will still see America as an airconditioned nightmare unfit for them to live in.

When you try to find out what it is in this country that stifles the American intellectual, you make a surprising discovery. It is not the landscape, though he is poignantly aware of its historical meagerness, and it is not the social system, particularly when it is headed by aristocrats like Roosevelt and Kennedy. What he cannot stomach is the mass of the American people—a mindless monstrosity devoid of spiritual, moral, and intellectual capacities. Like the aging Henry Adams, the contemporary American intellectual scans the daily newspapers for evidence of the depravity and perversity of American life, and arms himself with a battery of clippings to fortify his loathing and revulsion. When you listen to him or read what he writes about America you begin to suspect that what the American intellectuals know about the American people is actually what they know about each other: that they project upon America the infighting, mistrust, envy, malice, conformity, meagerness, and staleness of their cliques and sects. Imagine an American writing about America and not mentioning kindness, not mentioning the boundless capacity for working together, not mentioning the unprecedented diffusion of social, political, as well as technological skills, not mentioning the American's ability to do the world's work with a minimum of supervision and leadership, not mentioning the breathtaking potentialities which lurk in the commonest American. Who among the intellectuals would have predicted that a machine politician patronized by the Knowlands would become Chief Justice Earl Warren, that a hack politician endorsed by the Ku Klux Klan would become Justice Hugo Black, that a bankrupt haberdasher who was given his start by the corrupt Pendergast machine would become President Harry Truman, that a Southern politician would push through the civil rights legislation. The Johnsons, Trumans, Blacks, and Warrens can be met in every walk of life, and they are wholly immersed in American life.

The American intellectual rejects the idea that our ability to do things with little tutelage and leadership is a mark of social vigor. He would gauge the vigor of a society by its ability to produce great leaders. Yet it is precisely an America that in normal times can function well without outstanding leaders that so readily throws up outstanding individuals. When you talk to an American intellectual about common Americans it is as if you were talking about mysterious people living on a mysterious continent.

Yet when all is said about the intellectual's preposterous stance there remains the incontestable fact that his chronic militancy and carping have been a vital factor in the Occident's social progress. The blast of the intellectual's trumpets has not brought down or damaged our political and economic institutions. Napoleon predicted that ink would do to the modern social organization what cannon had done to the feudal system. Actually, in the Occident, ink has acted more as a detergent than an explosive. It is doubtful whether without the activities of the pen-and-ink tribe the lot of the common people would be what it is now.

The events of the past fifty years have sharpened our awareness of the discrepancy between what the intellectual professes while he battles the status quo, and what he practices when he comes to power, and we are wont to search for the features of a commissar in the face of impassioned protest. Actually the metamorphosis of militant intellectual into commissar requires a specific cultural climate and, so far, has taken place mainly outside the Occident. It is easy to underestimate the part played by Russia's and China's past in the evolvement of their present Marxist systems. A century ago Alexander Herzen predicted that Russian Communism would be Russian autocracy turned upside down. In China, where Mandarin intellectuals had the management of affairs in their keeping for centuries, the present dictatorship of an intellectocracy is more a culmination of, than a rupture with, the past.

In Western Europe and the U.S.A., where the tradition of individual freedom has deep roots in both the educated and the uneducated, the intellectuals cannot be self-righteous enough nor the masses submissive enough to duplicate the Russian and the Chinese experience. Thus in the Occident the militant intellectual is a stable type and a typical irritant; and whenever the influence of the Occident becomes strong enough the chronically disaffected intellectual appears on the scene and pits himself against the prevailing dispensation, even when it is a dispensation powered by his fellow intellectuals. We see this illustrated in the present intellectual unrest in Eastern Europe and Russia, and it is beginning to seem that dominant Communist parties have more to fear from a Western infection than the Occident has to fear from Communist subversion.

Stalin's assertion that "no ruling class has managed without its own intelligentsia" applies of course to a totalitarian regime. A society that can afford freedom can also manage without a kept intelligentsia: it is vigorous enough to endure ceaseless harassment by the most articulate and perhaps most gifted segment of the population. Such harassment is the "eternal vigilance" which we are told is the price of liberty. In a free society internal tensions are not the signs of brewing anarchy but the symptoms of vigor—the elements of self-generating dynamism. Though there is no unequivocal evidence that the intellectual is at his creative best in a wholly free society, it is indubitable that his incorporation in, or close association with, a ruling elite sooner or later results in social and cultural stagnation. The chronic frustration of the intellectual's hunger for power and lordship not only prompts him to side with the insulted and injured but may drive him to compensate for what he misses by realizing and developing his capacities and talents.

Part IV

THE ROLE OF COOPERATIVES IN A COMPETITIVE ECONOMY

Chapter 9

Four major groups in our American economy are: urban industry, labor, farmers, and government. In an industrial democracy it is essential that each group have a voice in the economy as checks and balances against the abuse of power by one or more of the other groups. And while, as stated (page 15), American cooperatives are active in many fields, farmer-owned organizations probably rank near the top of cooperative activity both as a voice of farmers in the legislative halls and in the market place, and also in service to the American people. Hence in this book, the objectives and scope of farmer-owned cooperatives are shown to exemplify the role of cooperatives in a competitive economy.

While a few cooperatives such as the California Fruit Growers Exchange were organized toward the end of the nineteenth century, most of the farmer cooperatives now in operation have come into being during the past fifty years. Through these cooperatives—some organized as marketing associations, others established for cooperative purchase of farm supplies—farmers are not only protecting their investments in farm and equipment but also insuring the continuance of our system of private enterprise. On my father's farm in Vermont, I grew up in the gradual development of farmer cooperatives. I saw the Orleans County Farmer's Exchange organized in 1916 to buy feed, fertilizer, and seed in quantity lots for the dairy farmers in the county. For several years my father was president of this organization, and he later became a director and vice-president of the Eastern States Farmers Exchange. Milk produced on our farm was sold to city buyers by officials of the New England Milk Producers Association. In his paper on the objectives of farmer cooperatives, Mr. M. J. Briggs gives us a firsthand picture of the purposes of this type of organization and of its methods of operation. In his portrayal of cooperatives in Indiana, Mr. Briggs has done an excellent job of showing the underlying principles and practices of cooperatives all over the United States.

OBJECTIVES OF FARMER COOPERATIVES*

M. J. Briggs**

In general terms, the principal and primary objective of farmer cooperatives is to preserve the existence of the family-size farm as the most vital element in the economy of this country. There are sociological, political and economic reasons for the continuity of the farm as a family-operated unit.

1. On the farms the birth rate is high compared to that of the urban areas, and since agriculture cannot absorb all the farm boys and girls, they are constantly being fed into the industry and professions of the United States. (Recently I read that three-fourths of the preachers came from farms.)

2. The farm family is the most clear-thinking, intelligent and stable element in our political economy. The farmer's record is without strikes, and his intelligent stability is most desirable in the political economy of the future.

3. Private ownership of farm property by the farm family is the best foundation for the private property system of the United States. Most of the population of this country does not know what it means to own and operate private and productive property. But the farmer and his wife, who at twenty-one years of age bought a quarter section and covered it with a mortgage of $10,000, sent three children through college and finally paid off the mortgage twenty-five years later, can tell this country exactly what it means to own private property.

4. At the present time the free enterprise system is on trial, and many businessmen raise questions about its continuance. It is claimed here that the best way to preserve the free enterprise system of this country is to tie it to the family-size farm. This is because the farmer is about the only free agent in the United States. He is the manager of his operation; he is the capitalist; he is the laborer; he is the veterinarian, the soil agronomist and the plant pathologist. Therefore, let's preserve the free enterprise system by tying to the best example in the United States.

---

*From *American Cooperation, 1949*; reproduced by permission of The American Institute of Cooperation.

**At the time this paper was written, Mr. Briggs was General Manager of the Indiana Farm Bureau Cooperative Association, Indianapolis, Indiana.

5. This country's principal interest is in low cost food, and the only way the people can be served with food at reasonable prices is through the operation of the farm as a family unit. This is because the farm family works on the farm, not for wages at time and a half; they live a life and take what they get at the end of the year.

To accomplish these purposes farmer cooperatives have been organized with certain definite objectives:

Before Cooperatives, Farmer Did Things for Himself

1. A principal purpose of the farmer cooperative is that of extending the farmer into commerce off the farm to do those things which, years ago, he performed for himself on the farm.

a. Fifty years ago, the farmer provided himself with wood for the farm stoves and lumber for the farm buildings from the wood lot on the farm. Most of these wood lots have disappeared, and from them the farmer receives the profit of the grain crops which are now being grown there. He extends himself into business and provides for himself by taking the money from the grain crops and investing in his farmer cooperatives, which own lumber mills to provide the lumber for the farm buildings.

b. In times past, the farmer stored his grain in his own farm granary and performed the storage functions of grain marketing at home. Today, he invests his money in his cooperatives and stores his grain in his local elevator and grain terminals, which he owns.

c. Years ago, the farmer procured his power from horses and mules on the farm. Through the years he has transferred his investment from horse power to tractor power. In the early days he grew his own oats and corn and hay to furnish the fuel for his horse power. Today, he takes the income from the acres previously devoted to feeding horses, to invest capital in the cooperatives which own oil wells, refineries and local distribution facilities for petroleum products.

In general, the farmer cooperative has furnished the means by which the farmer extends himself into business by the investment of his capital, performing for himself, off the farm, more efficiently, the same services he previously performed for himself on the farm.

Cooperative Puts Farmer on Competitive Business Basis

2. It is a primary goal of farmer cooperatives to place agriculture on a business basis. The farms must continue as individual and independent manufacturing operations, and to be competitive they need the cooperative to give them buying and selling power.

History shows us that early Indiana farming was essentially a mining operation. Like the laborer who digs coal from his mine, the farmer took plant food elements from the soil. For over fifty years he mined the plant food from his soil—without sufficient replacement—and sold these elements in the form of grain and livestock. At this stage the farmer was a capitalist miner.

Science came into the farm picture at about the turn of the century. The farmer began to buy raw materials such as fertilizer and feed, and to process these materials into grain and livestock products for human consumption. In other words, our farms became, every one, a small manufacturing plant. At this point the farmer was a capitalist manufacturer.

When our farmers became manufacturers they inherited all the problems inherent in this enterprise—problems of buying raw materials; those of production and processing; and those of selling the products.

These 180,000 farmer manufacturers in Indiana bought all their raw materials and sold all their products individually and separately—every one in competition with the other—until the 1920's, when it became apparent that farmers could not maintain a satisfactory income on this basis. Then it was that they began to organize the Farm Bureau and its affiliated cooperatives.

At this point let's draw a parallel.

The manufacturing industry of the United States was, in the beginning, made up of literally thousands of small independent manufacturers, all competing with each other. The competitive fight was sharp and destructive. Industrial history contains chapters about their "dog eat dog" methods and the "survival of the fittest" in business.

However, Industry found out even before 1900 that more profits could be realized by integration and cooperation than by competition. The stronger units which survived the competitive struggle, began combining or merging with other similar businesses, or eliminated direct competition through trusts and holding companies. This process has continued until the Federal Trade Commission reported last July that two-thirds the size of one of the largest steel companies in the United States was created by external expansion. In the summary of this report, published July 26, 1948, we find the following statement: "At the end of June 1948 the seventy-eight largest manufacturing corporations had sufficient net working capital to buy up the assets of some 50,000 manufacturing corporations of less than one million dollars in assets each, representing more than 90% of all manufacturing corporations in the United States."

No attempt is made to criticize or disparage this concentration of economic (and probably political) power. There is economy and efficiency in size, and, if proper statesmanship is used, the public welfare may be served. I do want to impress upon our farmers that they operate 180,000 manufacturing plants in the State of Indiana alone, and nearly 6,000,000 in the United States, all in competition with each other as buyers and sellers. The industries from whom you buy materials and to whom you sell products have, by concentration and combination, reduced their number to four or five dominating units in each field, as in petroleum, fertilizer, implements, grain and livestock.

The effect of these trends in our economy is apparent in the statistics which record agriculture's income and price relationship with that of the rest of our industries. But farmers do not want—and do not need—to merge their farms into farming corporations to cope with other groups. They have found that by merging their common interests in purchasing and marketing they can achieve the efficiency and strength that are necessary. The tool for this is the cooperative.

Farmer Investment in Cooperatives Safe

3. A well organized and managed cooperative, integrated across the board from distribution to processing and production, is a safe place for farmers to invest their capital. Farmer's investments of their capital in other people's businesses show high losses because the farm family does not *buy* stock in various enterprises of the world; it is *sold* to them. On the other hand, farmers' investments of their money in properly-operated cooperatives show extremely low losses.

Our educational, training and public relations programs should be conducted in a manner which will interest agriculture in a permanent investment in the farmer cooperatives of the country. The farmer's investment in his cooperative, which serves him off the farm, should be as permanent as is his interest in many of the tools of production, such as combines, dairy barns, farm granaries, etc.—all steps in the marketing process.

Cooperatives Stabilize Prices

4. A principal purpose of agricultural cooperatives is that of stabilizing prices at fair and equitable levels. In 1920, the margin on a ton of fertilizer was $12. At the present time it is less than half

that. In 1924, the margin on a gallon of gasoline, with distribution from local bulk plants to the farms, was 6⅞¢. Today, when costs are higher, it is around 3.7¢. In the early days proprietary feeds were distributed to dealers on a mark-up of $20 per ton in some cases. Today, with the competition of the efficient feed mills of the co-operatives, the margin has been reduced to one-fourth of that amount.

More Research Needed

5. It is the task of farmer cooperatives to do applicable research on services for the farmers, and to conduct some pilot plants to ascertain the costs which the family-size farm now pays in distribution and marketing. Between 1940 and 1944, the Government spent two billion dollars in research; one billion of which went to private laboratories. About all the one billion went to sixty-eight corporations. This story of research is one of the greatest technological potentials in history, but it is not going to be available to small business or to cooperatives. Out of it are coming new products and combinations of products, techniques, etc., to both serve and lure the public. Our cooperatives are slow and weak on research and more attention must be given in that direction in the future.

International Markets Should Be Sought

6. Cooperatives are definitely obligated, especially under present market conditions to expand the market for the products of the American farm. Farmer cooperatives must be more than just gathering agencies for private processors or private exporters. It has been clearly proven that cooperatives can meet the test in any field. Recently the Indiana Grain Co-operative sold a cargo of soybeans to an Italian firm. This shipment amounted to over 300,000 bushels, and was valued at about $1,000,000.00. The cargo was shipped from the port of Baltimore and was unloaded in Genoa, Italy. It was really a pioneering movement because it was the first time in American agricultural history that the Indiana farmers have been able to retain ownership of their product from the time it was produced on the farm until it was consumed at a foreign port. This is one way to expand our markets.

Nor must new markets be overlooked in our domestic fields. The real solution lies in new uses for farm products. High support prices, with inadequate outlets, only create burdensome supplies, and do not provide a sound solution for a prosperous agriculture. Research has added much and can contribute more toward sound agriculture.

Chemurgy gave us synthetic rubber and power alcohol during the war—both products of our own grain fields. The potentialities in this field are tremendous. It may be that a subsidy, if necessary, on power alcohol derived from grain would be of greater benefit to agriculture than restricted acreage, and a lot less expensive to the Government than the acquisition of huge grain supplies under defaulted loans.

Stability of Rural Community Strengthened

7. A chief objective of our cooperatives is to increase the income of the family farm and strengthen the stability of the rural community. The competitive system of marketing and distribution is filled with waste, duplication of investment and services, and in many cases, extremely wide margins. A well organized cooperative, integrated to a practical extent, can and does effect margins returnable to the individual patron. The margins of a great percentage of private business leave the community, while the savings of the cooperatives are returned to the patron and can be spent at home.

Cooperatives Work to Spread Corporate Control

8. Farmer cooperatives can contribute to the public respect for the corporate structure of the country.

In spite of the statistics showing widespread ownership of American corporations, it is an undeniable fact that the real basic participation in corporate affairs, and the control of American corporations, is becoming concentrated in fewer and fewer hands. The public in general is suspicious of this business system in which they have no apparent part, and which may be used to serve the private ends of the relatively few people who are in control.

Cooperatives are corporations too, but they share the control widely among all the participating farmers, and work diligently at the job of getting more participation by these farmers in the control function. Thus it is that literally hundreds of thousands of our farmers learn at first hand, through active participation, something about the functioning of corporate business, its problems and its processes. This inevitably helps all business corporations by doing a public educational job.

Independence of Farm Credit System Sought

9. Farmer cooperatives are obligated at the present time to take an interest in and give support to the Farm Credit Administration of the country in its attempt to make this agricultural credit system

more responsive to the borrower. It is a known fact that all the Federal Land Banks of the country have repaid to the Government all the capital ever advanced to them. We are all cognizant, too, of the continuous repayment by the Production Credit Associations of the United States, and of legislation which has passed the House and is pending in the Senate to permit the cooperatives of this country to begin the repayment of Government capital in the Banks for Cooperatives.

This exclusive (because there is no other general farm credit system like ours in the world) system of credit for farmers and farmer cooperatives, after the Government capital is repaid, should become more democratic in its operation and more responsive to the borrowers of the system. There should be a well-organized movement among the farm organizations and cooperatives in our country to work alongside and with the Farm Credit Administration of the United States, not only to protect the system and preserve it for our farmers and farmer cooperatives, but also to make whatever changes are necessary to get the ownership and control in a practical way in the hands of the borrowers.

Cooperatives Help Farmers Develop Self-confidence

10. It is a direct responsibility of cooperatives, and of course it is a result of their successful operation, to develop rural leadership. Farmers for the most part, have generally suffered from a complex. They have felt that the best brains were elsewhere; they have been reluctant in investing their capital; they have developed a suspicion of everything off the farm, and have never felt they could run their own business.

Our state has developed a number of local associations in which the net worth exceeds three quarters of a million dollars—one recently passed the million dollar mark. It is obvious that their well-trained and business-like annual meetings, the democratic elections of directors, the study and analysis of their operations, general discussions of the business and its management, the operation of the board of directors are developing a leadership which has confidence in itself, its business and other people's business.

Cooperatives Must Provide Opportunity for Youth

11. Farmer cooperatives have an obligation to the boys and girls who must leave the farms. Part of them are moving into the industries and professions of the United States and are working in

conflict with the interests of the family back home. Some of them leave the farm by choice; others because agriculture cannot absorb all the boys and girls reared on our farms.

Farmer cooperatives must develop by the processing, manufacturing, financing and distributing of farm supplies, and in the wholesaling and retailing of farm products, to the place where they can absorb the best boys and girls who leave our farms. The boys and girls of the agricultural colleges must in the future be fed into the system of farmer cooperatives where, off the farm, they can be performing business functions in the interests of the rest of the family back home.

If "life, human value and interest" are not breathed into our cooperative corporations we tend rapidly to become "just another business" headed toward the "monopoly in the order of the day."

Savings and sales, even facilities for service, in our cooperatives must be translated into human services and values. We must learn to project feed, fertilizer and petroleum facilities, and we must visualize their service in terms of human improvement on American farms.

Cooperatives must recognize individual farmers as patrons, as "part of the show," not solely as stockholders. Our purpose is to dignify our stockholder as a human being. It is our task to free farmers from slavery in industrial tyrants.

Let me impress upon you that cooperatives, in their corporate structure and procedures, dignify the individual; they recognize "persons and people." In cooperatives, human values are not junior to monetary or property values; instead, "humanity ranks first and people are supreme."

For example:

1. *In a cooperative every stockholder has one vote regardless of shares held.* (In a for-profit corporation he votes his shares, and in a proprietary corporation with 100,000 stockholders, one person with 51% of the shares is the boss.)

2. *Cooperatives look to people, not property alone.* In the cooperatives in Indiana, stock, either common or preferred, can bear 6% interest, and no more. (In the profit corporation, interest on stock is unlimited.)

3. *Cooperatives recognize people, not money alone.* In the cooperatives, savings are paid to patrons, not stockholders. (In the ordinary corporation, profits go to stockholders only. One person, *not a patron,* can receive all the profits.)

Cooperatives account to the people who create savings by participation. This common justice which runs through the principles and operations of our cooperatives has a distinct human appeal which must be emphasized more and more by our leadership. In fact, the two principal assets which intangibly appear on our combined balance sheets are (1) the development of people for leadership, and (2) our contribution to the dignity and independence of the American farmer.

Summary

These, then in my opinion, are the objectives of farmer cooperatives:

To strengthen the family-size farm by conducting the off-the-farm business of agriculture in a business-like and efficient way, so that the standard of living of our farm families can be maintained and improved.

To carry on those functions in purchasing and marketing for farmers, in such a way that they will have the benefit of the savings that can be made by large scale operation, while still retaining the individual family farm as the production unit.

To provide a safe and profitable investment for farmers.

To prevent exploitation of farmers in the distribution of farm supplies and the marketing of farm products, through competitive pressure.

To pioneer in new methods of marketing and better supplies.

To expand the market for farm-produced products, so that farmers can continue their historic role of full production in the interest of an ever-increasing standard of living.

To strengthen the rural community by channeling back to farmers the savings made in purchasing and marketing, rather than to have this wealth drained away to the urban centers through abnormal profit-taking.

To build respect for our whole system of free private corporate enterprise by actually letting more people participate in its function.

To develop rural leadership that will be both devoted to the continual improvement of farming and the rural community, and with the ability to organize projects that will accomplish this objective.

To see to it that our business system never loses sight of the fact that the people are the most important part of our economy, and that no interest, profits or property shall be allowed to detract from their dignity or their well-being.

Chapter 10

Some business leaders still think that farmer cooperatives are socialistic and depend primarily upon government support to compete in the business world. In fact, this concept is not true. Farmer cooperatives, which market around 25 percent of the products from American farms and purchase a somewhat higher proportion of the supplies used by American farmers, are a definite part of our free enterprise system and can survive only by operating efficiently. When I was in my senior year at Cornell University, H. E. Babcock, as Professor of Marketing, taught a course in cooperative marketing. Mr. Babcock had his feet on the ground and believed in teaching the realities of the world rather than unattainable philosophies of varying types of socialism or of monopoly. I well remember a trip with Professor Babcock from Ithaca to Syracuse to hear Aaron Sapiro discuss his philosophy of iron-clad contracts in promoting a cooperative for New York potato farmers. Both of us agreed that this monopoly approach was, in large part, wishful thinking and utterly impractical. Most of the Sapiro-formed cooperatives disappeared in a short time. The following year Mr. Babcock became manager of the Grange League Federation Exchange, a cooperative engaged in the purchase of farm supplies. From near bankruptcy, this organization became, under Mr. Babcock's leadership, the pacesetter in the United States by its efficiency of operation. His article is worthwhile reading for anyone interested in farmers cooperatives.

SCOPE OF THE COOPERATIVE MOVEMENT*

H. E. Babcock**

I have the choice of two courses of action:

I can present to you a statistical report of the amount of business transacted annually by farmer-owned, farmer-controlled cooperatives. Were I making this presentation before the advent of the New Deal, I should undoubtedly follow such a plan. I would be able in such a Presentation to roll up totals of millions, tens of millions, and I might even by dint of some exaggeration work into my figures a solitary billion or two. Since 1932, however, the cipher has lost its significance. The average citizen has become utterly calloused as to whether three ciphers or six or a dozen are included in a figure. In short, statistics of the ordinary garden variety, in the light of the New Deal's billions, have lost their power to impress. What few figures I do use therefore, I shall state wherever possible in terms of percentages. You see, I am counting on your having kept alive your sense of proportion, even though your comprehension of mass is temporarily paralyzed.

The other course of action, the one which I am going to follow, lies along the line of leaving with you some impressions of the present and possible future significance of the agricultural cooperative movement in the United States, impressions which I hope will be both accurate and unforgetable.

If I have my way and am as convincing in this talk as I hope to be, all of you, whether you are connected with the cooperative movement or entirely outside of it, will be stimulated by its independent spirit. This independent spirit is thoroughly demonstrated by the program of this Institute. Read this book through from cover to cover. You will find that the field of subjects considered covers highly technical accounting practices, methods of processing and merchandising farm products, all phases of farm finance, and provides for the most thoughtful consideration of this country's monetary policies yet undertaken by any group of citizens in the United States.

---

*From *American Cooperation*, 1953; reproduced by permission of the American Institute of Cooperation.

**At the time this paper was written, Mr. Babcock was General Manager of the Grange League Federation, Ithaca, New York, and Chairman of the American Institute of Cooperation.

You will note that, by and large, even the most difficult subjects scheduled in the program are handled by men drawn from the ranks of farmer-owned, farmer-controlled cooperatives. You will note an absence of government super-planners and regimenters. Nor is the absence of these gentlemen the only indication of the independence of farmer-owned, farmer-controlled cooperatives. Bankers, politicians, and the country's business leaders have not been needed to handle the program.

On the other hand, as chairman of this Institute, it has been my very great pleasure and privilege to welcome all such interests—governmental in so far as its representatives will lend an ear, bankers, business executives, and politicians—to this Institute. I invite you to continue to sit down with farmers engaged in the cooperative movement and discuss such important problems as our country's monetary policy.

What I am trying to bring out is this: The cooperative movement among farmers in the United States has progressed to a point where farmers know that, independent of all other interests, they can make a success of the operation of cooperative corporations in the field of business. Whether they proceed from this point with the friendly cooperation of the financial and business leaders of the country as well as with the support of a tolerant and far-seeing government is for such interests to decide. We invite such cooperation.

You can put it down that the cooperative movement throughout the United States represents an intelligent determination upon the part of farmers to secure economic and spiritual independence by their own efforts without too much dependence upon any other group.

Cooperative Movement Self-contained

Continuing, it seems to me that the next most important characteristic of the farmer cooperative movement throughout the whole United States is that it is a *self contained* movement. To a greater and greater degree each year, it is training and bringing forth its own leaders and its own business executives. The movement has existed long enough so that many of the business executives of cooperatives have connected with them men in the prime of life who are the most experienced men in their fields in the United States.

At the risk of appearing in bad taste but just to drive the point home, I am the employee of a cooperative purchasing corporation servicing about 100,000 farm families. In my capacity as general manager of this corporation, I have supervised the buying and processing of more tons of feed stuffs than any man in the United States with the possible, but not probable, exception of two or three others. John Brandt, president of Land O'Lakes, has probably merchandised more butter than any other man in this country. Earl Benjamin, manager of the Pacific Egg Producers Cooperative, certainly has merchandised more and better eggs than any other single individual. What Mr. Brandt and Mr. Benjamin have had in the way of experience is not outstanding. Mr. Teague, president of the California Fruit Growers Exchange has had even more experience with the marketing of citrus fruits.

The point I am making is this: In order to man adequately their cooperative enterprises throughout the United States, farmers no longer have to go outside their cooperatives to get executives who are well trained and experienced; and here I am not referring to men like the ones I have mentioned, but to the hundreds of junior executives employed by cooperative corporations and the thousands of college trained men and women who each year leave school to enter the field of cooperative service.

I have tried to give you an idea that the cooperative movement is marked by a spirit of self help. I also want you to appreciate that it is a self reliant movement, capable of generating its own man power.

Bulwark Against Radicalism

The third point is one to which bankers and business leaders should listen quite carefully. It is that the farmer cooperative movement is a substantial bulwark for the type of competitive capitalistic society which many of us hold so dear. Such a society is inevitably based on a spirit of independence and the ability of a people to take care of themselves.

I say it unequivocally and with all the emphasis of which I am capable, that the farmers of the United States who are members of *bona fide* cooperatives, almost to a man, are for a continuation of the constitutional principles and the type of society which has made this country great.

You leaders outside the cooperative movement who mistakingly think of cooperation as an expression of Socialism or Communism and who mistakingly fight it should wake up. Should you deny the farmer his right and opportunity to seek a fair measure of economic independence in society as it is, then you create a citizen who is potentially an ally, and a most effective one, of those who would change our form of government. Thank God, the American farmer in the cooperative movement has not yet even thought of such a thing.

By this time I imagine you have arrived at the conclusion that I really have not any figures which will give you an idea of the amount of business transacted by farmer cooperatives in the United States. I have. They interest me less than the fact that throughout the United States the cooperative movement among farmers is an expression of an independent spirit, an ability to take care of themselves, and a willingness to fit agriculture to the conditions imposed on it by a competitive, capitalistic society.

A Farm That Is 100 Per Cent Cooperative

The states in which farmers transact the largest amount of business through cooperatives are, in order: California, Illinois, Minnesota, New York, and Iowa. In these and other states many farmers are in a position to do almost one hundred per cent of their business through cooperative corporations which they own and control.

Perhaps another personal illustration will better impress this fact upon your minds. I own and live on what used to be a whole farm located in the Inlet Valley, four miles from Ithaca. The other night about a third of this farm washed down into Cayuga Lake, but I still live on and farm what remains.

As a farmer, I buy all such farm supplies as feed, seed, fertilizer, and spray materials through a local cooperative farm supply store. As a matter of fact, 75 to 80 per cent of all similar farm supplies used by farmers in this community are purchased through this store. The financial statement of this particular cooperative business enterprise is one of the strongest financial statements of any business house in the city of Ithaca. I produce on my farm principally eggs, milk, and beef. I ship my eggs by truck to a cooperative egg auction in Brooklyn. This auction sells my eggs for as much as it can get for them, deducts the expenses of selling, and returns the proceeds to me. I know that it is efficiently run and on the job to protect my interests because one of my neighbors, a man whom we all very much respect in this community, is on the board of directors and is currently conversant with what goes on. Incidentally, because he is a larger producer, he sells more eggs through this auction than I do.

The milk which I produce I deliver directly to a dealer's plant, but I am paid for it with the check of a cooperative milk marketing association, the Dairymen's League Cooperative Association, Inc., which acts as my agent in selling my milk to this particular dealer. This means, because this particular association is financially very strong, that I always get paid for my milk and get paid on time. It also means that my rights in weighing the milk, testing it for butter fat, and determining its bacteria count, are constantly protected.

When I have a load of steers ready for market, I simply load them in a car or truck and bill them to a livestock marketing cooperative in either Buffalo or Jersey City. When the manager of either one of these cooperatives receives my cattle, he becomes my personal representative in the market to protect my property and to sell it to the best possible advantage.

Possibility of 100 Per Cent Cooperation

Thus you will see, as a practical farmer, I do one hundred per cent of my farm business, both buying and selling, through cooperatives which I own and control along with other farmers. I am not an exception. There are thousands of other farmers in New York State, which I happen to know most intimately, who do likewise.

Let the illustration suffice, however, to drive the fact home that it is practical and many times advantageous for a farmer in the United States to transact one hundred per cent of his farm business through farmer-owned, farmer-controlled cooperatives.

With all the emphasis at my command, may I state that in my opinion it is never going to be either desirable or practical for all farmers of the United States to do this. What I have brought out in my own case, however, does, I am sure, indicate the possible scope of the movement so vividly that you will not forget its future possibilities.

Among the commodities handled by farmer-owned, farmer-controlled cooperatives in the United States, dairy products come first in volume, grain next, then fruits and vegetables, followed by live stock, cotton and cotton products, and poultry and poultry products. In dollar volume the cooperative purchasing of farm supplies also ranks well toward the top among cooperative enterprises.

Giant Consolidations Stimulate Cooperation

Try as I may, I can see but one relationship between the volume of cooperative business transacted in any one line and the general business conditions under which that line is handled. It may be important for you to remember, particularly when under-writing or purchasing securities. It is this: You can put it down as an axiom, that whenever any great aggregation of capital seeks by consolidation, organization, and the sheer power of money to dominate the handling of any particular farm product that such action immediately originates and stimulates cooperative action upon the part of farmers.

I will be glad to have you make your own independent check-up of this statement.

If I am right, you may therefore form your own idea of the present and potential scope of the cooperative movement in the United States by reading the Wall Street Journal and noting what is taking place in consolidating control of products which farmers produce and must purchase into the hands of a few great corporations. Also, you may get an idea of the probable success of such monopolies.

If I headed a great trust dealing in farm products or handling farm necessities during the next 25 years, I should expect to see farmer-owned, farmer-controlled cooperatives entering my field; and if I did not want such competition, I would set out to render the farmer the best possible service without sole regard for return on invested capital, enormous salaries, or bonuses. I confidently believe that such will be the course—in fact, must be the course—of the comparatively few corporations which have their particular farm fields to themselves.

Volume of Business Large

The best estimate that I have been able to get of the number of farmers who are now connected, for some service or other, with farmer-owned, farmer-controlled cooperatives is 25 to 30 per cent. The claim is made that the gross volume of business handled by cooperatives of the United States has totaled two billion dollars in a year. Before I personally can accept any such figure, I should need to know definitely what year and therefore what dollar was being talked about. I doubt whether any such total has been even approached since the gains of gold in the dollar more than doubled in value. Should the price of gold be raised so as to re-establish a dollar of normal debt-paying and exchange value, I would expect that the total volume of business transacted by farmer-owned, farmer-controlled cooperatives in the United States conceivably might well exceed two billion dollars annually. As a practical business man, however, dollar volume figures seem to me too misleading, to pay much attention to, as a measure of business activity.

Tonnage figures constitute a much safer measure, but I run into difficulties with them also. Since we started drowning pigs and plowing under cotton in an endeavor to become wealthy through a program of scarcity, it is too hard to keep track of 100 pounds of pork or a bale of cotton.

In conclusion, therefore, I tell you frankly that I do not know, nor can I find anyone who does know, how much of the annual farm business of the United States is transacted annually through farmer-owned, farmer-controlled cooperatives. On a single farm, as I have illustrated, the scope of this business can range from nothing to one hundred per cent. Throughout the United States, it would appear that at least 25 per cent of the farmers are using cooperatives in one capacity or another. Finally the potentiality of the movement is unlimited. It is an expression of an independent spirit and a higher degree of self reliance than is evidenced by any other group of our citizens; it is a self contained movement; and it is a movement which fits one hundred per cent into the American tradition.

If the movement as a whole goes wrong, it will not be the fault of farmers, but the result of mishandling by the government, misrepresentation by demagogues, and misunderstanding upon the part of the American business man.

Part V

THE ROLE OF GOVERNMENT IN A COMPETITIVE ECONOMY

Chapter 11

Dr. Edwin G. Nourse has long been among the top leaders of our country in the field of economics. His leadership was recognized in 1924 when he was made President of the American Farm Economic Association and in 1942 when he became President of the American Economic Association. Dr. Nourse probably reached the peak of his professional career when he was appointed the first Chairman of the Council of Economic Advisers in the Truman administration and continued in this position for several years. In the following article on "Economic Enterprise and National Planning," Dr. Nourse discusses the place of government in providing a favorable environment for private enterprise. Unlike some of those who followed him as Chairman, Dr. Nourse believed that the principal purpose of this Council was to provide the President with economic facts which could serve as guidelines for policitcal action but that Council members should be kept free from political action which the President might take as the recommendations of the Council.

I have had deep respect for Dr. Nourse from the time when, as a graduate student at Cornell University, I first heard him speak, to the more recent time when he was a guest speaker at the University of Illinois' Agricultural Industries Forum. The following article is an excellent presentation of Dr. Nourse's philosophy; it shows the changes which have taken place in our economy, and how the government can aid in the growth and expansion of private enterprise.

ECONOMIC ENTERPRISE AND NATIONAL PLANNING*

Edwin G. Nourse**

We have talked of economic forces in terms of three "propensities" of economic man and the mechanisms through which these forces may most productively be directed. Nothing was said of "the spirit of enterprise," which sometimes is thought of as the master force of economic life in free countries. Nor was much said about the agencies of government as economic mechanisms which, in civilized times, have always played at least a conditioning and sometimes a very active role. The real value and the desirable limitations of this government role have been brought under recurrent if not constant review. They were major issues in connection with the New Deal and will be major problems of the new Administration if it is confronted with a depression threat or as it undertakes, under whatever conditions, to carry out the declared policy of the Employment Act.

This act makes a vigorous reaffirmation of the principle of "free competitive enterprise" and, at the same time, a positive declaration of enlarged Federal responsibility in the economic sphere. Hence this chapter will undertake a brief restatement of the problem of economic forces and mechanisms in terms of the concept of economic enterprise. This discussion will deal with "enterprise" not merely as a global activating or regulating force in economic life but will differentiate its two hemispheres, one of which can properly be called private business enterprise and the other, no less properly, public enterprise.

The "Spirit of Enterprise"

Business enterprise has generally been identified with proprietorship or the managerial function. As such it connotes not only the diligence of the productive worker but, still more, the ambition, the planning ability, and the daring of the man who feels competent to

*Reproduced from the book *Economics in the Public Service* (New York: Harcourt, Brace, and Company, 1959) by permission of Dr. Nourse.

**Formerly Director of the Institute of Econoimcs of the Brookings Institution and Chairman of the Council of Economic Advisers for the President, Washington, D. C.

organize a working group and to direct its labor and the marketing of its product. This of course means that he is magnifying his chances of gain but also is taking on himself additional risks. The pattern of small independent proprietorship survives in vigorous form in the family farm and the small store and shop of the merchant and mechanic. But modern commercial, industrial, and financial development has caused the individual proprietor to be superseded over wide areas by the corporate organization, attaining at times a size of billions of dollars of assets and hundreds of thousands of employees. This development has been accompanied by important emancipations and frustrations of the spirit of enterprise as it motivates the actions and determines the rewards of a large part of our population.

The advent of modern industrialism and the coming of the corporation opened the door of opportunity to the creative and ambitious individual. The principle of limited liability enabled him to break the bonds of his own capital and credit limitations and to become the administrator of other people's money. Modern technology opened the door for more productive use both of other people's money and of other people's labor. These developments, taken together, multiplied the scope and power of the profit motive in the hands of the aggressive promoter as never before.

Thus the first epoch of modern industrialism witnessed great growth in personal power and personal wealth for an able and daring group. There was a sort of elephantiasis of individual business enterprise that gave us the "tycoon," the "captain of industry," the industrial Napoleon. These upstarts were able to gratify a love of money and/or power to a degree undreamed of before by anyone not "born to the purple."

Along with the public benefits of this private enterprise there were popular resentments against the pre-emption of natural resources, monopolistic tactics in the market, and the "exploitation" of labor. We are still far from having come to general agreement as to how we can suitably protect and reward capital savers and capital managers respectively and yet ensure the optimum progress in technology and proper recognition of the needs and rights of workers and consumers.

By the time the Industrial Revolution rounded out its first century of progress, we had concluded that business enterprise could be too free. As private capitalism developed the industrial, commercial, and financial corporation as its major mechanism, the public, jealous of its rights, proposed many a curb as it felt that its interests were being prejudiced. It tightened the loopholes in laws that had been quite adequate to control small proprietorship. From the Interstate Commerce Commission Act of 1887 and the Sherman Antitrust Act of 1890 through "trust-busting Teddy" and scholarly Wilson to the present time, there has been a reinterpretation of capitalist-manager enterprise and re-examination of the institutions and practices through which we hope to keep its dynamism and avoid its abuses. The verdict has not been that the large corporation must be destroyed, taken over by the state, or put under rigid control. General standards have been laid down for quality of product or service and for business practices, but wide latitude has been left for innovation and for growth.

But what is equally important is that, besides sharp challenge from the outside there has also been self-examination from the inside. Company managers have been using the tools of analysis to see just how corporations, big and little, actually function in organizing the use of resources, natural or human, and what is the impact of their policies and practices on the economy as a whole. Even before the modern corporation comes to maximum size for operative efficiency, it is brought by public prodding or the searching of its own experience to a realization that the very nature of its being calls for high standards of performance and a large measure of public service, not maximum short-run acquisition by either its owners or its managers. The large corporation has become a semipublic institution, not merely a personal venture. For such an institution to be permanently successful, it must formulate and follow enlightened policies not only in the technological and managerial sense but also as to its administration of the stream of wealth that flows through its hands, that is, price policies, wage policies, investment policies, and dividend policies.

In the old theory of capitalistic enterprise, it was held that the entrepreneur should use his bargaining power fully to push prices as high as possible and costs of labor, materials, and equipment as low as possible so that his capital would grow at the maximum rate. The practice of this theory accelerated capital formation in the hands of entrepreneurs, to be plowed back into existing companies or used to launch new ones. It resulted also in the amassing of great private fortunes. The newer theory of managerial enterprise is focused much less on acquisitions of great personal wealth in the hands of strategically placed capitalists. It is concerned rather with developing a system of private economic administration in which professional corporate managers see to it that the process of wealth creation and distribution shall go on steadily because the system is directed both with scientific skill and with a high sense of responsibility for the efficient continuation of the process of production and sale.

The spirit of enterprise of these professional administrators is gratified by a sense of technical achievement, by social prestige, and by places in the top bracket of professional salaries. The mechanics of corporate management permit them pretty much to write their own salary ticket, and they are not inclined to be modest as to the value of their services in top administrative posts. But the amount of the total product which is drawn into their hands under current practices is small indeed compared with the amounts acquired by the proprietary or promotional entrepreneurs of the nineteenth century. Both their salaries and the profits that they succeed in making for the company are subject to high levies as a source of tax revenue.

Under both the older proprietary theory and the newer professional-salaried theory of capitalist enterprise, the country enjoyed rapid economic progress from the Civil War to World War I or indeed until the decade of the thirties. This in spite of interruptions from time to time by frequent mild and occasional severe periods of depression and unemployment. Capitalist business leaders had full confidence in their own ability to achieve brilliant success not merely for themselves but for the economy and, by and large, workers and consumers were ready to "go along" in spite of minor socialist or other utopian grumblings. But when, after the collapse of 1929, we failed to get the quick recovery that we had enjoyed after all previous depressions, three new notes were struck in American thinking.

(1) Businessmen rushed to Washington to invoke the aid of government, apparently ready to admit that the forces with which they were then contending were too great for even the largest and most capable private management.

(2) Reinforcing this pressure was a demand on the part of labor and the public that some way be found for getting the economy back into vigorous operation through public enterprise if private capitalist and managerial leadership had faltered or had been outgrown. One theory was that private enterprise is adequate only to the pioneer or adolescent country, that we had now attained economic "maturity" and that, from this time forward, responsibility must shift in larger measure to the central government for the maintenance of prosperity and progress, with private management held accountable only for operative efficiency.

(3) At this time also there was explicit expression and wide popular acceptance of the doctrine that it was no longer necessary for us to have recurrent periods of slack production and low consumption. The people and the times demanded that we so modify our institutions and practices as to permit or indeed assure the continuous employ-

ment of the whole working population and capital equipment. This demand was eventually expressed in tempered form in the Employment Act of 1946. If we are to accomplish the purpose of the act, we shall need to give both opportunity and incentive to all the parties to the economic process.

The Partnership of Private Business Enterprise

In the early days of the Industrial Revolution, the disappearance of many small proprietorships and the increase in the number of hired workers led to the charge— with much justice—that their enterprise was being extinguished or superseded by "wage slavery." History, however, has amply demonstrated that the spirit of enterprise does not die that easily among the national or racial strains that have gone into the melting pot of industrial America. We think of freedom of economic choice, private property rights, and the profit motive as the major economic forces that animated the small proprietor and that have carried over into corporate business, large and small. As many erstwhile small proprietors (and yeoman farmers) found themselves recast in the role of wage workers, they found ways of reasserting these tenets of free enterprise.

Looking at the matter comparatively, it is easy to see similarities between the enterprise of the employer and that of the employee. Proprietary enterprise demands freedom to enter any line of production or trade which looks most promising and to pursue it by methods that produce the most profitable output. It demands the right to buy materials in the cheapest market and sell products wherever buyers are most numerous and affluent. It demands the right of ownership in intangible as well as tangible property acquired or created in the process. In this freedom to seek business opportunity and to retain the fruits of his labor and acumen, the proprietor is animated by the profit motive.

This has a fair counterpart in the motivation of the worker. As the proportion of proprietors has shrunk and the ranks of factory, store, and office workers have grown, the individuals have not been content merely to preserve their freedom of choice in shifting from one kind of employment to another or of improving their position in the labor group as they advanced in training or education. Beyond this, they have preserved, retained, or revived the spirit of economic enterprise in their ranks in three distinctive ways: (1) through effectuating a claim to as large a share as possible of such increased productivity as commercial and industrial progress brings about; (2) by asserting their right of "belonging" to the economic process in the productive and directional sense rather than being mere cogs in the industrial machine or accepting the theory that "labor is a commodity"; (3) more recently, by acquiring something of a capitalist role of their own and thus resuming a proprietary position and the functions of economic enterprise in the more conventional sense.

To say that "they," the labor group, have done all this means, of course, that leadership individuals amongst them have, in varying degrees, done so. From local union officers or even active members, up to the presidents of the great union federations, these leaders of the group express a spirit of business enterprise from the employee side, even as the corporate hierarchy of big and litte managers express it from the employer side. The spirit of business enterprise on the proprietary side has manifested itself in the building of corporations, in effecting mergers, and in developing intercorporate relationships of subsidiaries, affiliates, and less permanent contract relations. A similar spirit of enterprise among workers led to the organization of unions, the development of bargaining methods, the elaboration of wage structures, working rules, and seniority rights. These have been the mechanisms through which the worker's spirit of enterprise has continued to find expression in an economic society in which the avenue of proprietorship was closed to him.

As to bargaining for wages (and better working conditions), the unions first nibbled at such gains as they could get with their limited power. Now they have moved on to greater strength and larger claims and have pressed the principle of "ability to pay" to the point where, if fully successful, they would become in fact the "residual claimant" to profits as such. In the matter of management, they have at times established working rules which in effect invoke product restriction as a distributive principle. On the other hand, they have at times made themselves a factor toward better productivity (as in the garment trades) and have made claims that if they were allowed to participate on a freer basis in the laying out and conduct of productive operations they could increase production importantly. This would be in part because of their intimate knowledge of operative conditions and in part because of a latent productivity that would be released by this incentive—to the advantage of both parties. Such recognition of the worker's spirit of enterprise is to a degree recognized in practice through opportunities for promotion to foremanship or even executive position and to a limited but increasing extent through financial rewards to "employee suggestions." But, in general, management looks on this ferment of employee enterprise as "an invasion of the prerogatives of management."

It should be recognized, however, that labor is actually participating in management every time it collectively bargains a wage contract. It asserts its power against the authority of management and on behalf of its own spirit of enterprise. At times it forces the employer to introduce more efficient management to recoup the cost of a wage advance. At times its raising of labor cost constrains him to recoup by adjusting his prices or by curtailing the capital formation that resides in his profit margin. When unions bargain for security provisions, working rules, or an annual wage, their participation in business management is even more marked. The question is, will they show capacity to use this power in such ways as to contribute to economic progress? Or will they use it so blindly or stupidly as to impair the employer's ability to give jobs?

The third way in which we noted that workers gain an avenue for the expression of their business enterprise is by acquiring enough capital within their own treasury so that the labor organization as such becomes a business enterprise in the more conventional sense. Familiar illustrations are the entrance of unions into the banking business, the ownership of office buildings, or occasionally of productive plants. Union accumulations were first referred to as their "war chest" to finance strikes. But as the exchequer grows and strikes are avoided, the union finds itself with a generous reserve or endowment fund which needs to be invested. As pension funds under union control (such as the United Mine Workers') grow to large proportions, so do the possibilities that the union may acquire a capital stake as well as a labor stake in the business in which it is employed or in some other. Only a few months ago the newspapers reported the incident of employees of a butcher-shop chain using their accumulated pension fund to acquire ownership of the corporation.

Finally, organized labor today is demanding not only a voice in private management but also a voice in public policy-making. The worker's spirit of economic enterprise, of "belonging" not only to the company but to the economy and of being entitled to an active voice in its direction, comes to its largest expression in the demand for labor representation in state or Federal administrative agencies and on national policy-making boards or commissions. This claim has now received considerable recognition in both peace and war agencies. The former president of a national craft union sits today in the President's Cabinet.

In fact, it is often said that we have now developed a system of laboristic capitalism, in which government as well as management must respond to the demands of organized labor. It has not been alone in response to labor dictation but also to broad public sentiment that government has been so active in recent decades in establishing health and safety requirements, limitations in women's and children's labor, the eight-hour day, and the minimum wage. Management, labor, and government all have made their contribution to the growth of our present still-inchoate system of social security, and new frontiers of discussion and action have been opened up in terms of "the annual wage" and government-guaranteed "full employment." Management has by no means seen its way clear to bring the annual wage into its private practices. Nor did the 79th Congress see its way clear to write a commitment of full employment into Federal law. These are the growth frontiers which we must still explore in trying to find ways in which, under modern technological conditions and financial institutions, the enterprise of the whole people—that is, their desire to apply their labor with high efficiency to the satisfaction of their wants—can be realized.

This involves not merely an understanding and peaceful partnership between capital and labor, employer and employee, giant corporation and massive union. It involves also the relation between the co-ordinated partners of private enterprise and the government as a parallel or complementary agency through which national resources, labor, and capital may be efficiently employed in rendering services and in facilitating the production of goods for our people. While the expression "public enterprise" has not come into any such general usage as has "private enterprise," it is in fact a logically co-ordinate aspect of free economic enterprise.

Economic Enterprise of the Citizen

When we have gloried that America is the land of the free enterpriser and the home of the businessman brave enough to take capital risks, we have not claimed that government had no part in the economic process. *Laissez faire* meant that the proprietor, the worker, the saver, and the consumer should be let alone to make their business choices within a structure—of security and often of aid—provided by the state. Government was looked to protect the economic man against conquest from without and violence from within, to provide a sound and adequate currency, an equitable legal structure, and various consumer facilities such as post offices and public roads, harbors and lighthouses, statistical information, and commercial standards.

By and large, it has been our national and state policy to allow the private enterprise of property owners and workers to organize itself freely for the actual production of practically all goods and most services. Such regulation of private business practices as has been undertaken was designed to prevent fraud or undue restraint of others' enterprise, not to stifle individual initiative or choice.

Though, generally speaking, we have given the individual and the privately organized group the first chance to perform a given economic service and to reap its gains, this doctrine has not been followed to ideological extremes. When it has become clear that private resources were insufficient or private venturesomeness too feeble or the terms of private trade incompatible with social need, we have quite freely invoked community organization, state activity, or Federal aid or outright operation. Sometimes—as in the carrying of the mail—the people have prejudged the case and launched a public agency without giving much opportunity for private business to show what it could do. Sometimes, on the other hand, the public has put up with poor service because of a feeling that the field should, as a matter of principle, be left to private exploitation.

> In a surprisingly large number of economic functions we have organized along parallel lines of private and public activity. We have accelerated or checked the expansion of postal, highway, education, health, power, forest, and amusement services as local and temporary circumstances seemed to require. It is nonsense to say that we have had any consistent or rational policy or economic or social theory in these matters. We have been opportunists trying to get something done, and to *preserve freedom of action of the citizen as well as the business enterpriser* in the process of getting it done.[1]

Two familiar cases are quite adequate to illustrate the point. From Colonial times forward, we have had a lively realization that providing every child a good opportunity to develop his abilities and talents for productive work and to prepare himself for citizenship was essential to the soundness and the progress of the country. From "the little red schoolhouse" to the superb "consolidated schools" today, we have gone on to make public education free up to high school commencement day. And state colleges and universities make advanced general, technical, and professional training available on a low-cost subsidized basis up to the top limit of formal education. But have private schools, parochial schools, academies, seminaries, institutes, and endowed colleges been liquidated or denied the right to be born

[1]Edwin G. Nourse, "Public Administration and Economic Stabilization," *Public Administration Review,* Spring 1947, Vol. vii, No. 2, p. 85.

and live? Everyone knows better. Though many a youngster has even learned to fox trot or rhumba in a public school or college, the private enterprise of Arthur Murray—and many a lesser dancing master—is doing all right. A boy can learn a trade or a girl can take a secretarial course in a public high school. But thousands of trade schools and "business colleges" flourish from Portland, Maine to Portland, Oregon. The stream of free competitive enterprise flows strongly and harmoniously through both public and private channels.

My second illustration comes closer home to the businessman. He may not think of education as a very important field for business exploitation, and may be well satisfied that government is taking major responsibility for giving basic training to the labor force that the employer draws upon. But how about transportation? Government always has carried responsibility for a system of military roads, depots, and transport suitable to the time. But, beyond any potential military need, we have always expected government to supplement private enterprise in seeing to it that there was a local and national system of highways, railways, waterways, and now airways that gave private producers and traders quick and adequate means of moving materials, personnel, and product.

If, to cite a single case, we had not shown the public enterprise, as the automobile age burst upon us, to push the whole country over from dirt and gravel to concrete, growth of the automobile industry—and the vast industrial structure that depends upon it—would have been stunted. County road commissioners had to give way to State Highway Commissions. A Federal agency had to co-ordinate a national system of primary highways and, at strategic places, super channels or freeways. Uncle Sam put many millions into overhead cost and aid to states. States and even counties spent as they had never spent before and bonded themselves, often to the legal limit. That's "deficit spending" in any man's language.

In spite of local mistakes, wastes, or even abuses in the rush of this big economic development, I think we all agree in retrospect that it was good business all around, Government did not "invade" the transportation business. It played a necessary "facilitating" role but did not get into the operative field. The roads were built by private contractors, and their orders made profitable business for cement and steel mills, machinery manufacturers, and many others. As the roads were made available, bus and truck companies arose and flourished, the farmer's marketing problems and costs were eased, and the whole manufacturing and distributing system benefited.

As the twentieth century has unfolded, problems of the proper or desirable role of government and particularly the Federal government, in the economic areas have increased in number and become more controversial in character. In the early years of the century the issue of government action of "control" centered largely around questions of the conservation of natural resources. To this issue, which still plagues us, have been added the complications of our participation in wars of worldwide scope and our precipitation into a depression of great depth and greater persistence than we had previously experienced. And while these developments were taking place, we were passing from a largely automatic money-credit system with a gold standard and an almost free banking business over to a central bank organization and "managed money." Finally came active espousal of a national policy of sustained "full employment," though it remains to be seen whether this concept is to be interpreted fantastically or realistically.

All five of these challenges to more aggressive governmental action have become mutually involved in complex ways. The strain of war involves the question of adequacy of resources and policies for their conservation or development, particularly the provision of plant capacity. Both war and depression tempt, if they do not actually require, more active participation by government in financing, in risk-taking, or even in the actual provision of facilities. Full employment as a social goal tends to run beyond the risk-taking propensities of private enterprises.

Public concern about conservation led to extensive withdrawal—particularly by Theodore Roosevelt—of forest lands from private ownership to an active program of fire prevention and reforestation on government lands or on private lands in cooperation with the government. Both the reclamation of arid lands and the desire to accelerate the development of hydroelectric power and to prevent its monopolization led to a program of dam-building which was both ambitious and costly according to previous standards of Federal public works. These developments inevitably were involved with transportation problems and revived the perennial public interest in "cheap" water transportation.

The depression of the thirties provided an effective link between (1) those who wanted to see all types of resource development aggressively pushed, (2) those who wanted to have government leadership or direction of soil conservation, forest preservation, water transportation, public power, and the protection of wildlife "integrated" into a single government program, and (3) those who felt that the recurrence of deep depression demanded that the Federal government take a new or at least more decisive role of public entrepreneurship. Thus the Tennessee Valley Authority was born as a comprehensive government plan of integrated leadership in dealing with the whole congeries of problems of co-ordinated economic production as part of a bold action program for leading the country out of depression.

This is not the place to analyze the sweeping ramifications and implications of the TVA development or of subsequent proposals of like but larger scope for the Columbia River valley and the Missouri River valley. By some enthusiasts this kind of development was intellectually projected to include the smaller as well as the greater river valleys down to the Kennebec and the Penobscot. Since all our land drains into some river system, the logical end of this road would be an integrated or planned administration of the economic resources of the whole country under a series of Federal Valley Authorities which would be superimposed upon or even supersede municipal, state, and even Federal authorities as we have known them.

Whatever the future may hold as to any such recasting of the politico-economic structure and practices of the United States, the TVA serves admirably for the purposes of this book to illustrate the issues as to the scope of public enterprise and its relation to private enterprise and the several types of "action programs" that the government has been pressed into by the demand of the people under stress of war or depression during recent years. The conservation and development of natural resources is linked with the problem of public works. The magnitude and timing of public works is in turn linked with the problem of business cycles and the possibility that government activities could become a significant or even decisive factor in promoting the recovery of general business. That raises the problem of how public spending is to be financed. The question of how much money we undertake to channel from private pockets and corporate treasuries into the public coffers and out again to create facilities and services of general usefulness links in turn to the question of fiscal policy, public debt, and the reinterpretation of private property rights. Our ideas of the most desirable interplay of public and private enterprise have been very much in flux for the last twenty years.

Free Enterprise and Economic Planning

Undoubtedly the frustration of millions of people, able, willing, and seeking to work during the early thirties heightened popular dissatisfaction with our "mixed system" of predominantly private business enterprise and complementary public enterprise as it was working out. There was deep resentment about "the planlessness" of a situation that had allowed the country to come to such a state of demoralization. There was a demand that some top leadership come forward with a comprehensive plan for getting things going again—and so they would stay going. Thinking along these lines had in fact been going on abroad as well as at home for almost two decades before the depression of the thirties broke upon us. It had developed under the name "economic planning" or, more ambitiously, economic and social planning.

The general idea had two phases. One was simply the better application of constantly improving methods of statistics, accounting, and economic analysis to any and every business operation. In the field of private business, planning in this sense had always been practiced at least in some rudimentary or amateur way. The growth of industrialism caused it to take on systematic and formal development in the "scientific management" movement. This movement sought to link engineering and economics in the "rationalization" of industry. In its full aspect, the planning idea emphasized coordination of detailed plans and working programs with general business or economic policies adopted for the individual company or the industry.

On the public side, economic planning involved assistance and some guidance by the government to private industry in its efforts of co-ordination, and particularly, coordination of recognized government functions (monetary, fiscal, labor, social, etc.) in such a way as to develop a consistent national program for sustained and balanced economic growth. While this came to be designated as "central planning," its exponents did not advocate either a more centralized form of government or the elimination of private enterprise. They were strongly opposed to any form of authoritarianism. What they had in mind was to use the democratic forms of the American government to give direction to the unco-ordinated trends and policies which were impinging on the economy. They hoped in this way to facilitate changes toward greater stability, fuller use of all resources, and equitable distribution of the product. In other words, the planners quite generally sought more active leadership, and even some more control, in economic affairs on the part of government than had been considered necessary in the past but in line with basic American democratic traditions.

Those who were anxious to see broader patterns of industrial management developed in the private sphere, more systematic handling of public affairs, and a better articulation between the private and the public sphere were at considerable pains to distinguish American "planfulness" in business affairs from the Russian Five-Year Plan or other developments toward authoritarianism in Europe. Herbert Hoover, as Secretary of Commerce, had devoted his engineering talents toward promoting "simplification in industry" and, as President, had tried to captain a voluntary recovery movement of private business when depression got under way early in his Administration.

In June 1931, President Hoover adroitly entitled an address at Indianapolis "A Twenty-Year Plan for America." He repudiated the idea that "we should use force instead of co-operation in plans and direct every man as to what he may or may not do." He aligned himself with "our American system, which holds that the major purpose of a state is to protect the people and to give them equality of opportunity, that the basis of happiness is in the development of the individual, that the sum of progress can only be gauged by the progress of the individual, that we should steadily build up co-operation among the people themselves to these ends." As to specifics, he said:

> I am able to propose an American plan to you:
>
> We plan to take care of 20,000,000 increase in population in the next twenty years. We plan to build for them 4,000,000 new and better homes, thousands of new and still more beautiful city buildings, thousands of factories; to increase the capacity of our railways, to add thousands of miles of highways and waterways; to install 25,000,000 electrical horsepower to grow 20 percent more farm products.
>
> We plan to provide new parks, schools, colleges and churches for these 20,000,000 people. We plan more leisure for men and women, and better opportunities for its enjoyment.
>
> We not only plan to provide for all the new generation, but we shall, by scientific research and invention, lift the standard of living and security of life of the whole people.
>
> We plan to secure a greater diffusion of wealth, a decrease in poverty, and a great reduction in crime.
>
> And this plan will be carried out if we just keep on giving the American people a chance.

President Hoover, however, did not interpret "giving the American people a chance" as meaning that the Federal Government must limit itself to the functions it had exercised prior to March 4, 1929 or to the institutions it then had. Three important extensions of Federal responsibility for economic revival or stabilization secured his support as we shall note more fully in the next chapter. But Hoover never went out for any general planning or economic policy-making agency.

Not so some of the "progressive" members of the Republican party. Early in 1931, Senator Robert M. LaFollette, Jr., introduced a bill (S. 6215, 71 Cong. 3 sess.) to establish a "National Economic Council." "The bill," he said, "breaks away from the stereotyped idea of restricted production, in the direction of enhanced consumption ... the question of national economic planning in the United States of America has left the realm of theoretical discussion and become an issue of practical politics."[2] The LaFollette bill proposed a National Economic Council with specific powers for fact-finding and recommendation. The Council was to be composed of nine members, appointed by the President and confirmed by the Senate. They should be men of deep understanding of national economic problems and include at least one expert in each of the following fields: finance, transportation, labor relations, agriculture, scientific management. The term of office was four years, the salary $15,000 (equivalent to that of Cabinet members), and each member was to give full time to his office. The Council was to make an annual report, on or before the first Monday of December, to the President or the Congress, together with recommendations for legislation or other action, and special reports as they saw fit.

In February 1932, a similar bill was introduced in the House by Mr. H. S. Person of Michigan. While neither of these bills passed even in the chamber in which it was introduced, they brought forth lengthy and unusually well-organized hearings and a great volume of discussion.

Both management and labor were, in this depression period, intrigued by the idea of planning for recovery and for subsequent stabilization of the economy. The Chamber of Commerce set up a Committee on Continuity of Business and Employment. Its report, recommending "a rational program of production and distribution, to be initiated by business itself," was adopted by a large majority of the Chamber's membership in a referendum vote (1931). It stated that, "Planning by individual concerns and even by whole industries, —while it offers very definite promise as a means of eliminating waste, curtailing excess production, anticipating seasonal fluctuations and maintaining a scheduled rate of production throughout the year,—may not suffice to remedy such a severe lack of adjustment between production and consumption as we are experiencing." The committee doubted that a Planning Board, with "power to assemble

[2]The idea of economic councils was stimulated by the writings of Lewis L. Lorwin whose booklet on Advisory Economic Councils was published by the Brookings Institution in 1931.

the facts then direct the people and resources into the various activities where they would be most useful . . . would, in view of the extreme complexity of our industrial organization . . . be a satisfactory way out of our difficulties."

On the other hand, advisory "planning on a national scale seems to be urgently needed." The chamber therefore recommended a National Economic Council of three to five members "of the very highest ability and integrity (with) experience and background which will enable them to understand sympathetically the circumstances of all the essential elements of our industrial life, but they must think and act for the country as a whole, and be without obligation to any particular constituency." Appointments were to be made by an appointing board chosen by the Chamber of Commerce to represent the various interest groups—agriculture, manufacturing, banking, railroads, public utilities, distributive trades, the law, engineering, and professional economists, the United States Department of Commerce, and the chamber itself. The council was to co-operate closely with existing trade associations and encourage them to establish strong central committees or economic (trade) councils.

The general purpose of this proposal was "to retain the benefits of private initiative and at the same time to supply, if possible, some degree of control or influence that will help to maintain a better balance and thus reduce the severity of business fluctuations. . . . In the methods by which industry brings science and engineering to its aid with physical problems, we have a clue to an appropriate procedure for dealing with economic problems: to use and control the great research establishments as an effective tool for guiding engineering advance, to charge scientists with the problems, to support them liberally, and to act with courage to make their findings effective." The chamber report specifically explained that it used the term National Economic Council rather than Planning Board "because of the implication of detailed plans with autocratic powers of control which the latter carries and which we oppose."

From the business side, there was also forthcoming at this time the widely publicized "Swope Plan." Gerard Swope, president of the General Electric Company, presented this suggestion in a paper before the National Electrical Manufacturers Association in December 1931 under the title: "Stabilization of Industry." Mr. Swope argues that "Industry exists basically for serving the needs of the people. Consumption is by the mass of the population, not by the few. These, the wage earners, must be sufficiently assured of the future to feel that they are safe in spending their money."

In order to "correlate into a comprehensive whole the present undirected efforts of forward-looking business enterprise toward stabilization, Mr. Swope recommended that "all industrial and commercial companies with fifty or more employees may form a Trade Association under the supervision of a Federal body," either the Federal Trade Commission, the Department of Commerce, or a special supervisory agency. There was to be a General Board of Administration of each trade association, with three representatives of the employer, three of the employees, and three of the public. The associations were to collect and distribute information on volume of business transacted, inventories of merchandise on hand, simplification and standardization of products, stabilization of prices, and like matters. This plan did not win the full support either of management or of labor, and the powers proposed include several that have been consistently denied to trade associations under our antitrust laws.

Labor, on its part, also gave support to the planning idea. The American Federation of Labor urged the calling of a National Economic Conference by the President of the United States. The AF of L pointed out (Vancouver Convention, 1931):

> We have everywhere throughout industry very successful attempts at planning by industrial undertakings, by industries, by unions, by communities, by states, and by geographic sections. But this is not adequate—there must be comprehensive planning by all groups which affect each other.... The principles of balance in industry are the key to sustained progress .... Balance is not a result that can be obtained by arbitrary decision; it comes through working with laws in the light of knowledge and facts. . . . The interchange of information through reports, documents and conferences is basic to developing balance.... Unless organized labor is in the councils, national planning and balanced progress are impossible .... To accomplish teamwork by the whole industry and teamwork between all industries there should be comprehensive planning by an advisory body, representative of all production and consumer groups. Such a National Economic Council should plan the machinery for achieving economic equilibrium, and undertake to secure the co-operation of voluntary associations and government agencies in a co-ordinated undertaking.[3]

[3]Matthew Woll, vice president of the American Federation of Labor, called upon the National Civic Federation to summon a great American Congress of Industry representing all forms and characters of industrial organizations in the country "to outline a recovery and stabilization plan." As to a general approach, he said: "There is a growing conviction that unless industry finds and applies a remedy, the Federal Government will attempt to find and apply a remedy. But it is the conviction of organized labor in America that political government lacks

Such was the general background of American thinking about the government's role in economic affairs as brought about partly by the growing size and complexity of the economy but, in perhaps larger part, by the severity of the depression following 1929 and the persistence of special problems such as those of agriculture after World War I. The very word "planning" was anathema to many people,[4] whereas others saw it as the key word to near-term recovery and long-term progress. Quite independent of this explicit and general "planning" philosophy, the Federal Government had been setting up agencies in several areas of the economy which expressed policies as to how the operations of the economy might be stabilized or at least how particular destabilizing forces might be dealt with.

---

of guidance. Permanence of machinery is vital to industry's salvation from an onslaught of state political control, which cannot be avoided in the absence of self control."

[4]"The word 'planning' has been widely and loosely used. It has meant different things to different people. To crusaders it has been a Holy Grail leading to the sunlit hills of a better day. To conservatives it has been a red flag of regimentation heralding the dawn of collectivism and the twilight of the old order of free private enterprise and the democratic way of life. But to the humble practitioners of the art, viewing the matter with the cold eye of engineering rationality and a matter-of-fact indifference either to crusades, Red hunts, the class struggle, or the omnipotent state, it has been merely a process of co-ordination, a technique of adapting means to ends, a method of bridging the gap between fact-finding and policy-making. Planning is the opposite of improvising. In simple terms it is organized foresight plus corrective hindsight.... In peacetime the aim of American planning is to promote progressively rising material and cultural levels of living for all the American people through reasonably full use of the productive resources of the nation. In time of war the common aim is victory." George B. Galloway and Associates, *Planning for America,* pp. 5, 8.

Chapter 12

In the early 1930's the so-called public utilities usually provided electricity only to those farms close enough to villages or cities to be serviceable at a low cost. In 1935 only 11 percent of the farms in the United States were electrified. At present, over 98 percent of all farms have been electrified, over half of which are receiving service by systems financed by the Rural Electrification Administration (REA). REA, created in 1935, made loans for all phases of rural electrification including generation, transmission and distribution. This system was the culmination of a dream nourished over two decades by George Norris, formerly a U. S. Senator from Nebraska. Since 1935 the REA has made loans to more than 1,000 electric distribution systems and provides service to 5,000,000 families, about 20,000,000 people. Each of these loans was sponsored by a local cooperative or similar organization of the users of electricity. Currently there are 930 local cooperatives which are active borrowers. Each of these loans—of government funds, made available at a low interest rate—is amortized over a period of years on a self-liquidating basis out of current income for the users of electricity. When a loan is repaid, the users of electricity in each local cooperative are the owners of the distribution system and the government steps out of the picture. The story of REA is an excellent example of how government can operate to provide a needed service and help to strengthen our system of private enterprise. The methods used in this highly successful venture may well serve as a pattern for similar projects in the developing countries throughout the world.

THE REA PATTERN:

ORGANIZATION AND OPERATIONS*

1. The industrial revolution of the 19th century, which had transformed life in cities the world over, scarcely touched life on the farms of the United States of America. As a result, the American farmer at the dawn of the present century was earning his living in a way that had changed but little since the earliest days when the first colonies were established along the Atlantic seaboard. The tools he used were simple and ancient: the wheel, the lever, the block and tackle, the plow. For the most tasks, he could draw only on his strength or that of horses and other animals. His children studied by the dim light of a kerosene lamp; his wife was a slave to the wood stove and washboard.

2. For people in the cities and towns, life was different. Electricity for power and lights was available to them, and was among the attractions which pulled people away from the farms and into the cities. Some towns and cities were served by municipally owned electric power plants. Typically, however, the American city was served—and still is served—by an electric power company. These companies were organized as stock corporations to build generating plants and distribution systems to serve urban areas where concentration of consumers assured profits. In almost all cases, operation of the power company is based on a charter granted by the city. The distribution of electric power is almost in its very nature a monopoly. In recognition of the industry's monopoly status and of its nature as an indispensable public utility, electric companies are subject to varying degrees of regulation by public commission in almost all of the Nation's 50 States. Controls differ from State to State, but they usually cover rates the company may charge for service, standards of service, territory to be served, and sometimes jurisdiction over financing and capital investments.

3. In the United States, the Federal Government does not provide retail electric service over distribution systems either to urban or to rural people. The role of the U. S. Government in the electric power industry is fourfold:

---

* REA Bulletin 1-8. Rural Electrification Administration, U. S. Department of Agriculture, April, 1963. Written by officials of the REA.

(a) The Federal Power Commission exercises licensing control over the utilization of hydroelectric sites on navigable rivers of the country, and maintains certain controls over the interstate transmission and sale at wholesale of electric energy generated by the electric companies.

(b) The Bureau of Reclamation, the Army Corps of Engineers, and the Tennessee Valley Authority build and operate some of the Nation's hydroelectric generating plants. The TVA also builds steam plants.

(c) The Bureau of Reclamation, TVA, the Bonneville Power Administration, and similar agencies build and operate transmission lines to market the power wholesale.

(d) The Rural Electrification Administration makes loans for rural electrification, including generation, transmission, and distribution.

This, then, is some of the background against which to look at the development of rural electrification.

4. The notion that electricity generated at a central station could be distributed to every farm in the United States took hold of men's minds slowly. Electric service was theoretically within the reach of rural families with the discovery that alternating current voltage can be "stepped up" for transmission and then "stepped-down" for utilization, so that power can be delivered economically at distances from where it is generated.

5. But technological theory was not sufficient to electrify the rural areas. Financing on a large scale had to be provided. In the United States, farmers live on the land they cultivate. Farmhouses therefore are widely scattered across the countryside. In some of the ranch areas of the Western States, the houses are many miles apart. In such thinly populated rural areas, the electric companies could see little prospect for profit. Rates were high. Farmers usually were required to pay the construction costs of individual line extensions to provide service. Most of them could not afford this and remained without electricity.

6. Some farmers were wealthy enough to pay the high cost of electric service; others installed their own individual generating units. These units were generally very small and did little more than provide minimum lighting. For many farm chores the tractor and the stationary gasoline engine had replaced animal power and human labor. But in most respects there was little evidence of the progress which characterized the cities.

7. As early as 1923, some efforts were made to determine the

potential uses of electricity on the farms. Representative farm organizations, Government agencies, power suppliers, equipment manufacturers, and others formed a Committee on the Relation of Electricity to Agriculture (CREA). This group, financed largely by the electricity companies, set up a rural electrification demonstration at Red Wing, Minn., which showed how electricity could improve farm living.

8. This and similar experiences enabled the participating farm families to become acquainted with and to make liberal use of electric lights, appliances, and equipment to do farm chores and provide household comforts. Over a period of time, the very careful cost and production records showed that while electric usage increased sharply, agriculture production also increased and the overall operating expenses of the farmers dropped. Electricity was saving human labor that could be applied to other activities. The whole level of life on the experimental farms was happier, healthier, and more productive.

9. There were other experiments in rural electrification. In a few places, usually on the outskirts of towns with municipally owned systems, very small farmer-owned cooperatives were formed to distribute electric power. There were increasing demands for rural electrification, but little was actually accomplished. The farm family was secondary in the utility companies' planning. They were preoccupied with service in the cities, except for a few farms and other rural consumers along the urban fringes and main highways. Rural electrification was neglected because it appeared unprofitable. In 1929, only 9.5 percent of the farms in the United States received central station electric service; by 1935 the figure had crept to 10.9 percent. The economic depression of the early 1930's further limited the electric companies' progress into farming areas.

10. In 1935, President Franklin D. Roosevelt created the Rural Electrification Administration as an emergency relief program. In its initial form, the new agency found itself unable to accomplish much rural electrification. The Executive order which set up REA anticipated that grants of money and other forms of outright subsidy would be used to relieve some of the unemployment which existed at that time. It was found, however, that construction of electric lines called for various kinds of skilled labor not likely to be found, without extensive training, on the relief rolls nor in the rural areas where lines were to be built. Another obstacle was the difficulty in finding some way to use the available Government funds effectively. Existing power companies seemed to be the only organizations with trained personnel who could build and operate the rural systems; but many representa-

tives of the electric industry professed to see no need for rural electrification on the scale proposed by the Government. A report by major executives of 15 of the largest power companies, dated July 24, 1935, stated in part that in the light of earlier extensive research work "there are very few farms requiring electricity for major farm operations that are not now served."

11. REA therefore sought other ways to accomplish rural electrification. The first step to future success of the program was a decision to rely on a program of Government loans on a favorable credit terms. The second step was the development of consumer-owned, nonprofit cooperatives as borrowers.

12. A year later, in May 1936, the Congress of the United States passed the Rural Electrification Act, which established REA as a lending agency of the Federal Government with the responsibility of developing a program for rural electrification. The act authorizes and empowers REA to make self-liquidating loans to companies, cooperatives, municipalities, and public power districts to finance the construction and operation of generating plants, transmission and distribution lines, and related facilities for the purpose of furnishing electricity to unserved persons in rural areas.

13. These loans are made for a maximum period of 35 years, and bear interest at 2 percent per annum. They are 100 percent loans, secured generally by first mortgages on the electric systems. REA advances funds on the loans it makes only as fast as the money is needed. Interest is paid only on the money actually advanced to the borrower. REA customarily grants a deferment on repayment of principal until the borrower can put its plant into service and have revenues coming in. The REA loan is repaid by the borrower over the 35-year period out of revenues from the amounts paid by individual consumers each month for electricity used.

14. REA also makes loans to these borrowers for relending by them to consumers on their lines who need financing to purchase and install electric wiring, plumbing, and electrical equipment and appliances.

15. In addition to making loans, REA furnishes technical assistance to its borrowers in engineering, management, accounting, public relations, power use, and legal matters. REA does not construct, own, or operate any electric facilities.

16. The success of REA and the rural electrification program in the United States and Puerto Rico is outstanding. By January 1, 1963, not quite 28 years after REA was established, 98 percent of the farms were electrified. More than half were receiving service from

systems financed by REA. A very high proportion of the remainder received service much sooner than they would have, thanks to the competitive stimulus provided by REA.

17. The REA-financed systems provide electric service not only to farms but to nonfarm rural households, schools, churches, motels, garages, resorts, commercial establishments, and industrial plants of all kinds located in the countryside, often far from cities. REA has made loans to more than 1,000 electric distribution systems, and these provide service to 5,000,000 consumers—about 20,000,000 people.

18. Total loans in this program amount to a little over $4,800,000,000. Of this amount, a little over $4,000,000,000 already has been advanced to borrowers for their use. Approximately 100 borrowers have repaid their Government loans in full. Only two small systems were financial failures, resulting in losses to the Government of $43,500. Borrowers have now repaid more than $1,000,000,000 in principal on their loans, plus about $600,000,000 in interest payments. Only two borrowers are currently in arrears on their scheduled payments. This record of REA repayment is remarkable by any standard in financial circles.

19. Consumers of REA borrowers have doubled their consumption of electric energy about every 10 years, as they find additional uses for it. Farm and residential consumers now average 400 kilowatt-hours per month. Demand for ever-increasing amounts of power has made it necessary for a greater proportion of REA financing to be directed into cooperatively owned generating plants and transmission systems in recent years.

20. A principal accomplishment of the rural electrification program has been the steady lowering of both the wholesale and the retail price of electric power. This has occurred against a background of generally rising prices in the American economy. The electric energy supplied by rural electric systems is one of the few things—if not the only thing—that costs farmers less today than it did before World War II. Currently, the wholesale cost of power purchased by REA borrowers averages about two-thirds of a cent per kilowatt-hour. The average retail price to the consumer on borrowers' lines is a little under 2 1/2 cents per kw.-h.

21. Most REA borrowers are rural electric cooperatives. There are about 930 of these nonprofit organizations which are active borrowers—that is, currently paying off their loans. Each is an independent, locally owned business enterprise, incorporated under laws of the State in which it operates. All consumers served by a cooperative are members, share ownership of the system and have a

voice in its operation. Each member has one vote in the election of the board of directors and in any other decisions brought up at the annual meeting of the organization. Bylaws adopted by the members set forth the rights and responsibilities of members, procedures for electing directors, how the nonprofit character of the business is maintained, and other guarantees for a democratically run association.

22. Members of these rural electric cooperatives pay a membership fee of $5 to $10 which is usually returnable in case the member leaves the area. These cooperatives do not issue stock. Ownership equity of members accumulates from amounts in excess of the cost of service which they pay on their monthly billings.

23. The rate for electric energy is set high enough to cover the cost of providing service, plus an amount to repay the REA loan on schedule, plus a small margin to assure sufficient operating capital and reserves. Service is on a nonprofit basis; the bylaws in most cooperatives specify what shall be done with margins which remain after the payment of all expenses. Some organizations return the margins in the form of rate reductions, others as cash patronage refunds. Most of the rural electric cooperatives have written into their bylaws a provision for "capital credits." This is also known among cooperatives as a "deferred patronage refund."

24. Capital credits or deferred patronage refunds work as follows. If a cooperative had a net margin of $10,000 remaining after billing and collecting $100,000 from consumers for service used, the refund rate would be 10 percent. A member who paid $90 during the year for electricity billed to him would then have $9 credited to his account out of the cooperative's $10,000 net margin.

25. Capital credits bear no interest. It is a way by which investment by the member-consumers gradually replaced the Government's investment, as the REA loans are paid off on schedule. When the board of directors determines that the net worth of the cooperative is high enough to assure financial stability and sufficient operating cash, repayment of these capital credits is undertaken.

26. Use of member-owned cooperatives to provide nonprofit service in thinly populated and poor areas has been one of the principal factors in the phenomenal success of rural electrification in the United States. Other important features were: the concept of area coverage, the reduction of construction costs for rural lines, the provision of consumer credit for wiring, plumbing, and appliances, the intensive education and promotion of consumers' use of power, and

the availability of REA's technical assistance along with the Government financing.

27. In order to understand the significance of area coverage, it is necessary to keep in mind that the traditional line extension policy of the electric companies was to construct lines to new rural customers or into new areas only when there was assurance that the addition would produce a profit. The electric company generally required that the consumer pay the construction costs of an extension line built to provide service, but the line so paid for by the customer remained the property of the company. This frequently amounted to several hundreds or even several thousands of dollars, and there were few farmers who could afford the price.

28. As lines were built into the richer, heavily populated rural territory, and along the highways between towns, many pockets of poor farmers and isolated households were cut off from the possibility of service. When rural electric cooperatives began building lines with REA financing during the late 1930's and subsequent years, many power companies accelerated construction in the choice service areas. Some of this hurried extension of lines actually prevented the building of cooperative systems on an areawide coverage basis.

29. In developing full coverage, REA borrowers: (1) build a backbone electric distribution system adequate for providing service to everyone in the area who might want service; (2) determine feasibility by whether or not revenues are sufficient to meet all costs and repay the REA loan—computed on the entire system of the borrower rather than on a particular line extension; and (3) in general do not require individual consumers to pay construction costs of individual line extensions.

30. When REA engineers first faced the problem of rapidly expanding rural electrification in 1935, they found that the cost of constructing electric lines had to be reduced. They found, also, that the requirements for electric lines in rural areas were quite different from what had been developed for use in the cities. Engineers working on REA-financed projects had to consider the long distances between consumers (about three to the mile), natural hazards of lightning, windstorms, and heavy icing conditions, and the interference of trees and fast-growing shrubs along the rights-of-way.

31. REA engineers developed system designs and specifications to meet the needs of the rural areas. Light-weight, high-strength conductors permitted the use of lighter poles and much greater spacing between poles. Production-line techniques speeded system construction and reduced costs. These and other innovations brought

down the cost of line construction. Development and use of standard inspection for preventative maintenance of the system, improved specifications in purchasing materials and equipment, periodical inventory and warehousing methods, and better techniques for clearing trees and brush from rights-of-way all help to reduce operating costs of the rural systems and thus keep the price of electricity low for all consumers.

32. It was recognized quite early that the electric industry is an industry of decreasing unit costs. Once the system is built and the consumer is connected for service, a certain minimum amount must be charged to offset the fixed costs. But after that, additional amounts of energy can be furnished at progressively reduced rates. The result of this situation is twofold: (1) Within certain limits, the more electricity the cooperative sells the lower the price per kilowatt-hour and the stronger the financial position of the cooperative becomes; and (2) it is to the advantage of the electric cooperative and of the individual consumer, therefore, to encourage and promote the use of greater amounts of electric energy for doing more farm and home chores. There are more than 400 different uses of electricity on American farms. Electric power is in most instances the cheapest source of power available.

33. A single kilowatt-hour of electricity, billed to the consumer at perhaps 2½ cents, will do any of the following:

Light a 100-watt bulb for reading or working for 10 hours;
Pump 500 gallons of water from a well;
Grind 400 pounds of feed—enough to feed 3 pigs for a month;
Protect food by running a freezer for 12 hours;
Milk a cow twice daily for 15 days;
Hatch 5 chicks in an incubator;
Run a TV set for 4 hours;
Operate a washing machine for 3 hours.

Farmers soon learned that a 1-horsepower motor can do as much work in an hour as a man can do in a day. Usually the more repetitious the task and the more drudgery connected with it, the more easily an electric motor can be harnessed to take over.

34. When the rural electric cooperatives were building their first lines, some directors doubted that the average consumer could use as much as 40 kilowatt-hours per month. They soon found that new consumers started with a moderate use of electricity, generally for a few lights, an iron, a radio, a refrigerator. The list grows rapidly, however, when the rural family finds what a bargain electricity can be. REA urges its borrowers to hire home economists and agri-

cultural engineers who can show consumers how to use their electric service more effectively.

35. Everyone gained from the tremendous increase in the use of electric power. For farmers it meant greater production and improved quality of his products for market. For his family it meant better health and safety, new comforts, and free time for other activities. For the rural community it meant more jobs; higher income to be spent locally. For the electric appliance and equipment industry it meant a whole new multi-million dollar market. For the rural electric systems it meant unexpected margins that speeded up repayment of the REA loans.

36. REA had originally expected that the electric companies would construct and operate the rural systems, because the companies had the trained manpower, the skilled employees to do the job. When it became apparent that rural electrification would have to be done by local cooperatives organized by farmers and other people who had no experience with electricity or engineering, and very little in other industries or businesses, REA realized that training and technical assistance must go along with the construction loans.

37. The pattern of REA assistance to the borrower—mainly rural electric cooperatives—developed slowly and with some hesitancy. There was, at first, some apprehension that Government guidance in the formation of cooperatives might lead to governmental interference and control. Circumstances nevertheless compelled the fundamental policy step of providing help at virtually every stage of loan application, system construction and operation. In some instances, REA found it necessary to help the prospective cooperative organize and incorporate, where there was lack of experience with cooperatives or where local legal obstacles had to be overcome.

38. Technical assistance to borrowers was necessary to safeguard the security of the REA loans. Guidance was provided in three ways: through field personnel to work with applicants and borrowers; through staff specialists in Washington, D. C.; and through publications.

39. REA did not establish field offices, but its electrical engineers, accountants, loan specialists, and management consultants are stationed at various points throughout the country convenient to borrowers' headquarters. These field representatives travel an itinerary which takes them periodically to each borrower or applicant. The employees are carefully selected to assure exceptional professional skills and sympathetic understanding of the rural electrification concept.

40. The REA offices in Washington, D. C., provide assistance as

needed by borrowers in such specialized fields as retail rates, negotiations for purchase of power at wholesale, safety programs, power use promotion, public relations, legal consultation, and a wide range of other materials.

41. Over the years, REA's experience with its borrowers in rural electrification has produced an invaluable array of printed reports and bulletins available free of charge to borrowers and other people interested in rural electrification. These range all the way from one-page statements of policy to detailed construction contracts, specifications, and drawings. There are established procedures and practices in printed bulletins on practically every aspect of rural electrification. All are listed in an index which is revised periodically.

42. Despite all of the help and guidance available, REA borrowers are independent and separate entities. REA's long-standing basic policy reads as follows:

> In carrying out the loan programs and in protecting loan security, REA's activities in its relations with borrowers are limited to the requirements of each particular case and are based on the following considerations: "That each borrower is an entirely independent corporate body, locally owned and controlled, subject to applicable State laws and responsible for the management of its own affairs, including proper and successful construction and operation of its system and the repayment of the REA loan.
>
> "That the relationship between REA and an REA borrower is basically that of lender and borrower.
>
> "That the underlying objective shall be to move as far and as fast as is feasible toward a situation in which every borrower possesses the internal strength and soundness to guarantee its permanent success as an independent local enterprise.
>
> "That REA activities shall be carried on in such a way as to promote the ability of borrowers to handle their own affairs effectively.
>
> "That, as the borrowers gain in experience and maturity, thus becoming better able to meet their obligations to the Government and to rural people, REA's activities for the protection of loan security shall progressively diminish."

43. A great deal of time and energy during the early years of REA went into experimentation—trial and error methods in a field where there were few precedents and very little experience. Today rural electrification of a new area can be accomplished faster and easier because there are policies, patterns, procedures, and experience to serve as guides. Experience suggests a sequence of steps to be taken in developing a rural electrification project for an integrated area.

44. First comes a determination—by local people, the governmental lending agency, or others—that there is a definable geographic area which shows sufficient need for electricity to form the basis for a project. Then there must be a determination of what kind of an organization is most likely to do the job: a stock-owned commercial power company, a consumer-owned cooperative, or some sort of publicly owned body such as a public power district. If the choice is a cooperative, local community leaders take the initiative and begin to develop a responsible electric service organization for the rural area. The REA field representative begins a preliminary survey to determine feasibility of a rural electrification project.

45. As with most new ventures, the hard work of organizing falls to an energetic few. In many instances, the county agent, who is already experienced in working with farmers on problems of production and marketing, meets with six or eight farmers who have indicated a marked interest in securing electric service. It may happen that several of these organizers are well known in the rural neighborhood for their work on the school board, in church groups, in farm organizations or a cooperative. The task of such an informal group of volunteers is to persuade their neighbors to start an electrification project with REA financing.

46. The promotional campaign can best be launched from a public meeting. Such a gathering may be held in a suitable public building or church or meeting hall of some farm or community organization. Full publicity through all available media is essential for a good turnout of people who are potential consumers on the lines of the proposed rural electric system. The volunteer organizational committee uses posters in store windows and along the country roads, announcements on the public service programs of local radio stations, articles in the local newspapers. They also appeal to ministers and other community leaders to spread through word of mouth, information concerning the meeting.

47. Prior to the organization meeting, the volunteer committee arranges for an REA field representative to be present to explain the agency's program of loan financing and technical assistance. The organizers also select some respected community leader who is sympathetic to the idea of cooperative rural electrification to be chairman of the meeting.

48. The purposes of the first public meeting are to stir up interest in securing rural electrification, to present information on how it can be done, and to select a steering or planning committee. This committee then undertakes a survey to establish feasibility for an REA

loan, conducts a sign-up campaign to determine who will take service, and arranges future public meetings so that progress reports on the project may be made to local people who are interested.

49. There will be many questions at these meetings. Farmers want to know what the cost of power is going to be, how soon the lights can be turned on, who will own the system, and who will be responsible for repayment of the Government loan. Answers should be factual and encouraging, avoiding over-optimism and promises that cannot be fulfilled. No one can predict rates or the prospective completion dates at this early stage, but examples of neighboring systems can be cited to indicate limits. Prospective members are told that the cooperative corporation which they will own jointly carries the responsibility to repay the loan, and they are assured that their individual farms will not be mortgaged as security for the REA loan.

50. Some prospective consumers sign up for service and pay the $5 or $10 membership fee at the organizing meetings. Others have to be solicited in door-to-door visits by volunteer teams working with the planning committee. The sign-up teams learn that, despite years of talk about rural electrification, some rural people are not sure they really want power. They have lived so long without electricity that they doubt it is worth the expense. Some are afraid of something as unfamiliar as electricity. Or they are worried about getting involved in a large debt.

51. While the publicity and sign-up campaign is progressing, the planning committee and the REA field representative undertake the initial survey of the area. This includes a study of: the people in the area—their income, standards of living, and power needs; the economy of the district—with its potentialities for improved agricultural yields and rural industry; its water resources, transportation, communications, and power sources. The organizers look into possible sources of electric power that the cooperative will need for distribution to its consumers.

52. One of the big jobs in the preloan stage of a rural electrification project is the formation and incorporation of the cooperative as a nonprofit business enterprise. In the United States during the early days of the program, this required new legislation in many of the States. REA provided legal advice and counsel for applicants who found themselves baffled by the highly technical legal requirements for establishing a rural electric cooperative and operating a distribution system. REA provided model bylaws which many organizations used in drafting their own.

53. The rural electric cooperatives had to select a board of direc-

tors and officers and be incorporated as a legal entity qualified to do business, before REA would make a loan. To assure the new organization that financing would be available when all requirements had been met, REA established a procedure for "allocating" funds. This was an earmarking or tagging of funds short of making the actual loan.

54. Another of the big jobs that had to be undertaken prior to a loan was the engineering study. Here, too, REA offered the assistance of its staff engineers to assure satisfactory maps, system design, standard specifications, and contracts.

55. Other technical assistance includes: estimating the size of the power load to be anticipated at given points at given times, determining rates to be charged, forecasting estimated revenues and expenses, and deciding the amount of financing that would be needed. Not until all of this was done could feasibility be determined and a formal application for an REA loan be submitted.

56. Under certain conditions, borrowers may use REA loan money to pay interest during the construction period before the system goes into operation, to provide working capital for initial operations, and to reimburse the borrower's own general funds which have gone into REA-approved plant.

57. As soon as the borrower has complied with all requirements, REA makes the loan and notifies the borrower that the money is available to undertake construction. A new cooperative getting its first loan will have to hire a manager. This is a responsibility of the board of directors, but REA helps new borrowers locate applicants, if requested to do so, and retains a seldom-exercised veto power in the selection of a manager.

58. Before construction of the system can begin, the cooperative has the task of obtaining easements from property owners across whose land the lines will be built. It has been general practice in the United States for power companies to pay for right-of-way easements. REA decided not to approve the use of loan funds for purchasing rights-of-way from members, feeling that payment would be inconsistent with the idea of nonprofit, member-owner cooperatives. REA borrowers have had to solicit millions of these easements, explaining to individual property owners in each case that the pole line would not unduly interfere with farming nor constitute a hazard, and that it was a requirement for electric service.

59. REA required that borrowers award construction contracts on the basis of sealed bids in order to secure the lowest prices. Many rural systems now have enough experience to build their lines with their own construction crews. This is impractical for new cooperatives.

60. To insure economical construction and a well-built system, all construction must conform to REA standards and specifications. REA field engineers inspect the lines to assure that materials, design, and construction meet required standards.

61. Over the years, the rural electric systems have built their lines section by section on an area coverage basis that brings electric service within the reach of every farm, every household, every potential consumer. This did not finish the job, of course. A great many families in poorer sections of the country did not feel they could afford electricity. Before REA, it cost an average of $70 for minimum wiring of a house and barn. This was beyond the reach of so many potential consumers that REA staff members met with representatives of the contracting industry and worked out a group wiring plan which cut home wiring costs to around $55. A number of manufacturers cooperated with REA in offering for sale a lighting package which contained fixtures for an average-size farmhouse at about half the prevailing price. Similar mass purchase plans were applied to electric running water systems and basic appliances.

62. These plans helped the farmers and helped the new cooperatives. At the same time they opened up a vast new market for the manufacture and sale of electric wiring, appliances, and equipment. It was obvious that rural consumers unfamiliar with their new electric service would need some help in learning how to use it most effectively. In response to requests from the cooperatives, REA organized a traveling demonstration—a sort of road show where farm families could gather under the carnival tents and see electrical equipment in operation.

63. Equipment manufacturers and appliance dealers cooperated by furnishing samples for the power use demonstrations—to show how electricity could be put to work cheaply and easily for cooking, refrigeration, pumping water, grinding, hoisting, and a variety of other farm chores and household uses.

64. A large number of rural electric systems added power use advisers to their staffs as an extra service to members and also to help boost revenues from increasing consumption of electric power. These employees usually have experience as home economists or agricultural engineers. They arrange demonstrations for groups of members in different neighborhoods, talk with individual consumers about their plans for house and farm wiring and purchase of appliances, and help members arrange financing. In rural communities where consumer credit for such purchases is not readily available, the cooperative may borrow money from REA under section 5 of the

Rural Electrification Act and relend it to individual members on favorable terms.

65. All of these efforts have helped build rural power consumption to levels far beyond early estimates. When the cooperatives were first organized, many directors wondered how farmers were going to use all the electricity that the lines were built to carry. Such apprehensions were short-lived. The two-wire, 60-ampere service has long ago been replaced on most farms. The rural electric systems have had to come back to REA and borrow additional funds to rebuild their lines to provide the much greater capacity that is now demanded. Consumers have had to rewire their homes to take care of farm and household loads far heavier than anticipated.

66. Transmission and distribution voltages have had to be increased, and now considerable attention is being given to the use of higher voltage in the wiring of consumers' premises. Consideration is being given to the power supplier extending ownership beyond the meter—to include the entrance wiring and fuse box.

67. The former practice of restricting power for water heaters and other loads which caused peaking of system demand is recognized as a mistake. Rural systems are concentrating their efforts on adequate facilities and ample power supply to meet whatever power demand arises.

68. Mistakes in the REA program have been easily offset by the overwhelming growth and success of rural electrification. Here was something that started out as a small effort to relieve unemployment during a period of acute economic depression. Much of the early effort was amateurish and experimental. It was freely predicted that the farmers could not pay for electric service, and that the REA borrowers would not be able to repay their Government loans. Both predictions were set aside by the facts. The REA pattern proved flexible enough to be used in all kinds of rural territory, under all kinds of conditions. It has been used with modification in Puerto Rico with great success.

69. Rural electrification in Puerto Rico has been responsible for a dramatic rise in the standard of living of dwellers in the rural areas of the Commonwealth. Here the organization which provides electric service is not a cooperative but an agency of the Government. The Puerto Rico Water Resources Authority is one of REA's most interesting borrowers.

70. The Authority's program for rural electrification must be considered an integral part of the island's famous Operation Bootstrap which has attracted world-wide attention. Essential to the program of

education, sanitation, agricultural improvements, and industrial development is an ample supply of low-cost power. The Government's program uses REA financing to help achieve goals which include checking the exodus of rural dwellers to the city, with the consequent formation of slums, unemployment, and other social problems.

71. A good many years ago, the Government asked three utility companies operating on the Caribbean island to extend their lines to small towns and the adjoining rural territory. They were then serving the urban areas and a few well-to-do rural homes bordering the electric lines between the generating plants and the cities. The companies rejected the proposal on the grounds that the extensions would not operate at a profit.

72. By 1952 the details of a plan were worked out by the Water Resources Authority to assure complete area coverage, so that all people could have electric power no matter how remote they lived from the cities. The program is quite simple.

73. For those who can afford to guarantee a minimum consumption of power to justify the necessary capital investment or for those willing to contribute a part of the investment to make service economically feasible, the Authority makes electricity available without delay. REA financing is used to construct the distribution lines.

74. For low-income rural families who cannot afford to pay a high enough guaranteed minimum bill, service is made available through a special plan which involves REA loan funds plus annual contributions from the Commonwealth government. These payments cover the difference between revenues derived and the cost of service. Since 1952, REA has loaned the Authority $58,450,000 for the construction of transmission and distribution lines and for construction of a 44,000 kilowatt steam plant.

75. Experience has proved that in a matter of 5 to 10 years, when average consumption of electricity reaches 75 kilowatt-hours per month, the increased usage of low-income families is sufficient to put the rural electrification projects on a payout basis. The Authority is now bringing power to about 16,000 additional rural households each year. Puerto Ricans consider this expenditure a wise investment, in order to raise the standards of living and to make available one of the basic conveniences of 20th century living to all the people on the island.

76. Once electric service is made available to a rural consumer, the consumption growth follows an almost standard pattern. Lights, the table radio, and the electric iron are followed by an electric re-

frigerator and the TV. The Water Resources Authority offers consumers two programs which help build the electric load rapidly.

77. The first of these is the rural home wiring program, which aids rural consumers in securing good interior wiring at a low price and on easy payment terms. Families are permitted to pay the cost of the installation through small monthly installments included in the billing for electric service. The average cost is about $25. The Authority selects an electrical contractor by bid to make the installations, and then inspects the completed jobs.

78. The other form of direct consumer assistance is the basic rural appliance program. The Authority found that many rural families were prevented from buying appliances and equipment due to low income, the great distance from stores which sell electrical equipment, and credit limitations in rural areas. Working with appliance dealers in Puerto Rico, the Authority awards a contract by competitive bid to supply electric irons, table radios, and two-plate electric cooking units. All appliances carry a service guarantee. The supplier delivers the appliance to the purchaser and then is paid in cash by the Authority. The purchaser reimburses the Authority in easy installments which include a small charge for interest and for handling the account. The payments are included in the monthly bill for electric service.

79. To promote rural electrification and to educate the rural people of Puerto Rico on how to make effective use of their electric service, the Authority has a mobile rural electric exposition which travels from village to village. Demonstrations of appliances and talks on the benefits of electricity are presented in a carnival atmosphere. In Puerto Rico, as in rural areas of the United States, rural electrification has required Government assistance.

80. One lesson learned from efforts made over more than a quarter century of REA experience is that the program must, on the one hand, be standardized enough to keep down costs and assure high quality performance, but, on the other hand, be flexible enough to fit the needs and the capabilities of the people getting service. There are great differences from one geographical area to another in climate, in the type and level of the economy, in the living habits and customs of the population, and in technical development.

81. The success achieved by the Rural Electrification Administration offers a pattern which may be useful to nations where widespread rural electrification has not developed. Of particular significance is the role occupied by consumer-owned cooperatives. REA, as an agency of the Government, can provide financing and technical

assistance for rural electrification, but continuing development and growth of this program must depend in the long run upon the initiative, ownership, and control exercised by the local people who benefit from the program.

82. The REA-cooperative approach has brought many benefits into the lives of rural people. It has: increased production and quality of farm products and at a lower cost; introduced new or stimulated existing businesses or industries; produced better living conditions and increased income; promoted better health and sanitation; and stimulated education and self-respect. Participation in cooperatives has developed community leaders and increased interest in local and national affairs.

83. In a very real sense, the REA pattern is an avenue free men everywhere can use to realize their goals.

Part VI

THE ROLE OF PRIVATE ENTERPRISE IN SOLVING PUBLIC PROBLEMS

Chapter 13

Beginning August 11, 1965, riots broke out in the 46 square miles of the Watts area in Los Angeles. As a result of these riots, 34 Negroes lost their lives and 200 buildings were destroyed, with a total value of $40 million. Following this, businessmen of the Los Angeles Chamber of Commerce organized the Management Council for Employment, Training, and Research with H. C. McClellan named as chairman. The purpose of this Council was to assemble the essential facts underlying these riots and take positive measures to bring about improvements in the areas where the riots had taken place.

Studies showed three fundamental causes for the riots, namely; (1) unemployment, that for Negroes in the Watts area being two to three times that for Los Angeles County as a whole; (2) inadequate schooling which despite the fact that there was a shortage of semi-skilled and skilled workers in the county, many unemployed did not qualify for those jobs; and (3) resentment of police authority resulting from rebellion of the jobless demonstrated in many different ways.

The Management Council's major work has been in breaking down barriers of communication between Negro leaders and businessmen, and in getting jobs for unemployed after a period of retraining. By the end of 1966, two years following the riot, a total of 17,903 unemployed in the Watts area had been given jobs as a result of the activities of this Council. By the end of 1967, the number of unemployed given jobs in this area had increased to 23,500. As pointed out, these figures include a few duplications.

This paper by McClellan and associates is a progress report of a very practical way of meeting the problem of riots and unemployment in Los Angeles County. From the beginning the activities of the Management Council have been founded as a private enterprise program, and it may well serve as a model procedure for other cities in the United States.

THE MANAGEMENT COUNCIL FOR MERIT EMPLOYMENT, TRAINING, AND RESEARCH, LOS ANGELES*

H. C. McClellan and Associates**

The Watts Riots of 1965

A drunk-driver arrest sparked the Watts riots of 1965. Obviously, the circumstances which made the disturbance possible were complex, varied and diverse. It is not easy even now either to identify or fully understand all of the factors responsible for this trouble. It appears logical that the inner frustrations which had smoldered and burned for many years in the minds of Negroes across the country and the strong sense of denial, both real and imagined, finally exploded into rage and violence unprecedented for this community.

Background

Immediately following the riots which occurred here in Los Angeles beginning on August 11, 1965, the Los Angeles Chamber of Commerce appointed a Rehabilitation Committee of seven members. . . . H. C. McClellan was named Chairman.

The committee was charged with the responsibility of doing what it could toward rehabilitation of the stricken area. No specifics were given.

The committee met immediately and reached several conclusions. When the riots ended great controversy was taking place in Los Angeles over probable causes and possible remedies for the situation. Complaints were registered against the Police Department, the schools were criticized, the Welfare Departments were maligned, charges of every kind were voiced, including some against the Negroes themselves for their conduct. . . . The committee decided that it should

---

*An abstract of some of the principal facts presented in Part I of "The Management Council for Merit Employment, Training, and Research, Los Angeles: Our First Three Years, 1966, 1967, 1968." Part II which is not included here, sets forth suggested procedures for organizations affiliated with or similar to the Management Council. A copy of the complete report can be obtained upon request to the Management Council, Chamber of Commerce Building, 404 South Birel Street, Los Angeles, California 90054.

**Chairman of the Board, Old Colony Paint and Chemical Company, and President of the Management Council of Los Angeles.

stay out of the controversies in order to be effective to the maximum without appearance of bias or partisanship ... The committee decided that before determining a course of action it should assemble the essential facts. We got some chilling ones. The findings were as follows:

1. Approximately 650,000 Negroes reside in Los Angeles County, 450,000 of this number living in the curfew area.
2. The riots which lasted six days cost 34 lives. "There were 3,438 adults arrested ... The number of juveniles arrested was 514 ... Of the adults arrested 1,232 had never been arrested before; 1,164 had a 'minor' criminal record (arrest only or convictions with sentences of 90 days or less) ... Of the juveniles arrested 257 had never been arrested before; 212 had a 'minor' criminal record."
3. The riots covered an area of slightly more than 46 square miles and resulted in the destruction of 200 buildings with an economic loss of approximately $40,000,000.
4. In 1964 the Negro communities in seven Eastern cities were stricken by riots and in each case the fundamental causes were the same; not enough jobs to go around, inadequate schooling, and resentment of police authority.
5. In 1964 the Urban League made a national study concerning Negro conditions in 68 major cities in this country. Included were ten economic factors such as housing, job opportunity, etc. Of the 68 cities studied, Los Angeles emerged as the one offering the best score.
6. It was clear that unemployment in the Negro community was two to three times that in the white community; from all indications, there were some 25,000 unemployed Negroes in the central section of Los Angeles County and probably an equal number of unemployed Mexican-Americans.
7. There was an actual shortage of semi-skilled and skilled workers in Los Angeles County.
8. Welfare costs in Los Angeles County were running in excess of $400,000,000 annually (perhaps one-fourth of this being expended in the curfew area).
9. Transportation to and from the Watts area was poor. Los Angeles covers an area of approximately 450 square miles. Industry is not concentrated in any one area. It is dispersed. A worker residing in Watts may be called upon to travel a considerable number of miles from his home to his place of employment. This circumstance, however, while especially diffi-

cult for the disadvantaged did not apply to him alone. There was no fully adequate rapid transit system in Los Angeles. Most citizens tended to rely upon private means of transportation rather than upon any public transit system.

Philosophy of the Job Program

The war on poverty has many facets. The problem is immense. This fact is clearly recognized by the Management Council for Merit Employment, Training and Research.

Fundamentally, there are two parts to the poverty program, each of which is important, although each is different from the other. Part I has to do with welfare. We believe that any nation should see to it that the poverty-stricken should be cared for by society to the extent that none go hungry, unclothed or without shelter. Charity should be participated in by all who can afford it and welfare should be the concern of all of the people. Provision for the needy should be generous. In the ordinary sense, however, welfare programs, like simple charity, tend merely to accommodate the poor, making their unfortunate circumstances more bearable by making the recipients of charity more comfortable.

Desirable as welfare programs are, however, and generous as they must be, more than mere charity is needed if poverty is to be significantly reduced. Thus the second part of the poverty program should concern itself with the *means of escape; the means by which those in need can permanently remove themselves from the disadvantaged category.*

It is to the "escape" part of the poverty program that the Management Council addresses itself. *While we certainly consider that we are a part of the war on poverty, ours is not a welfare plan nor is it charity.*

The Management Council was organized to help the disadvantaged help themselves. They welcome this approach. Our experience has convinced us that almost without exception, the disadvantaged, who are in this area made up principally of Negroes and Mexican-Americans, *would far rather hold a respectable job and earn a living, than to subsist on welfare payments of any kind.* We have also learned that, given opportunity, incentive and a reasonable amount of encouragement, the disadvantaged will respond and perform productively and with good results.

For those who need pre-job training (there are many in this category), training is now available in numerous areas of our community. There are five Skill Centers and eight adult vocational schools in the disadvantaged areas of Los Angeles.

Once the disadvantaged unemployed learn the reasonable amount of pre-job training results in their getting a job opportunity, training is readily accepted. Three years ago, some reluctance was displayed to accept training in the Skill Centers; there is now a long waiting list, simply because most of those graduating have been and are being placed in meaningful jobs.

Our Management Council in Los Angeles is now working in direct relationship with 1200 employer firms.

In addition to our direct relationship with employers in our immediate area, we have working relationships with what we have called "AFFILIATES" and with other Management Councils.

An affiliate is simply an employer organization operating under a different name. Most of our affiliates—they now number 18—are Chambers of Commerce. A Chamber of Commerce, having established a relationship with our Management Council, conducts its own independent program, utilizing its own membership and its own staff organization.

The other Management Councils which have been organized with our cooperation extend up and down the State. They are located in San Diego, Orange County, Pasadena, Monrovia, Fresno, Monterey and San Francisco. Others are in the stages of development . . .

Financing

Financing of the Management Council has been achieved as follows:

Initially, the aerospace industry at the request of H. C. McClellan, subscribed $23,000 as the foundation for broader based underwriting. Thereafter funding of our operating budget has been obtained entirely from private foundations.

In 1966 a grant was made by the Ford Foundation in the amount of $50,000 as partial underwriting for 1966 and 1967.

Also in 1966 the Haynes Foundation of Los Angeles contributed a total of $65,000 as partial underwriting of our budget for the years 1966-1967.

Subsequently the Haynes Foundation granted the Management Council an additional $35,000 for the year 1968 and has committed $25,000 for the year 1969.

Another foundation, which does not wish to be identified in this report, has provided $200,000 toward our operating budget for the years 1967 and 1968 and has committed an additional $100,000 for the year 1969.

The total of these grants has made it possible for the Management Council to operate without deficit and to be financed through the year 1969.

In addition to the above mentioned grants which have been for the purpose of the Management Council's operations, additional sums have been provided for specific projects sponsored by the Council. Among these are the following:

$5,000 has been subscribed by private industry to underwrite the cost of planting 1,000 trees in the Watts area.

Efforts to Meet the Problem of Unemployment

Recognizing that job opportunity was certainly a fundamental need and believing that unless opportunities were provided for any man to have an equal chance to earn a decent living and support his family, there was little hope of correcting the social problems involved, our Rehabilitation Committee concluded that our efforts should be restricted to one simple purpose—placing the qualified unemployed jobseekers from the curfew area in appropriate contact with willing employers who needed workers. There was one other reason why this decision was made. Any competent executive knows that when a difficult problem is confronted which he would solve it is wise to reduce that problem into manageable dimensions before the task is undertaken. Job opportunity seemed a big enough problem.

We thereupon adopted the following objectives for our organization:

> The objectives of the Rehabilitation Committee are relatively limited when considering the problem as a whole. In order to be effective to the maximum in our work we believe that it is essential that our function be limited to one simple purpose–providing job opportunities for the disadvantaged.
>
> The fundamental objective of the Rehabilitation Committee is, therefore, to place qualified job applicants from the disadvantaged areas of our community into appropriate contact with willing employers needing workers.
>
> Toward this end it is our purpose to arrange, if possible, such pre-job training as may be necessary to enable the job applicants from these areas to meet minimum job entry requirements.
>
> The Rehabilitation Committee will serve as the catalyst in bringing together employers and the disadvantaged unem-

ployed. We will also serve as a coordinator to insure that the many agencies and organizations which are earnestly trying to be helpful work in full cooperation rather than at cross purposes with each other.

A major function of the Rehabilitation Committee will be to encourage employers to reach into the disadvantaged areas for the purpose of recruiting qualified disadvantaged unemployed to fill open jobs.

Our plan, we thought, was businesslike and practical.

First, we persuaded a group of prominent Negro businessmen from the curfew area to form a "counterpart" committee of fifty. We needed dialog with the Negro community. (Our Rehabilitation Committee was expanded to a membership of thirty-five).

The Negro committee, at our suggestion, selected an executive committee for purposes of conference with our Committee. Over a period of several weeks nine meetings were held which were attended by members of the executive committee from each side. Some of these meetings lasted into late night hours. Beyond doubt the benefits which resulted from the forthright discussions which took place were substantial. But the going was not easy . . .

It took several weeks of lengthy, drawn out, ofttimes bitter discussion before we finally convinced the Negro panel that we were limiting our function as the means of accomplishing the maximum within our capabilities. It seemed to us that the breakthrough came late one night following a rather high tension meeting at one of the hotels. The discussions had been lengthy, vigorous and at times bitter. Finally, after a somewhat forthright statement from Chairman McClellan in which he made an appeal for objective understanding, one of the Negroes stood up and said: "Mr. McClellan, we are beginning to trust you." Mr. McClellan rose somewhat indignantly and said: "Well, gentlemen, I have news for you—it is justified." This seemed to break the ice and it turned out to be the best joke we had had together since the conversations began weeks before.

From that point forward we addressed ourselves to the problem of job opportunity and how to achieve it.

Why Communication Was Difficult

It puzzled us at first that we could not seem to establish friendly, objective, down-to-earth discussions with the Negro Executive Committee. We believe now, after our experience of these past three years, that our problem is the same one that plagues many well wishing organizations trying to work with minority groups. We believe, incidentally, that what we discovered here is something that the American people to this day do not fully understand. It is the degree of resentment, frustration and bitterness and even hatred that permeates the Negro society.

From our viewpoint, few among us are fully aware of what all Negroes suffer as a consequence of the prejudice which still persists in our society as a whole. Little by little we learned, as we spent hour after hour with our Negro counterparts, what was in their minds and the depth of feeling which resided there.

They did not talk about it much and they never fully stated the degree of their resentment, but it was there—always there—and we sensed it in time.

Every Negro in the nation, regardless of what his name is, awakens in the morning conscious of the fact that he is black. He knows what he must face all day every day in little ways and sometimes in big ones. He feels degraded, insulted, denied or humiliated. It is on his mind until he falls asleep at night.

While these human displays of prejudice may differ in various parts of the country, some parts being much worse than they are here in California, even here they get the message: They are looked down upon and every Negro man and woman hates it.

Thus it was as we sat down to talk with residents of the Watts community; we found the going rough. They welcomed the opportunity for dialog, but they wanted it to be, in part at least, on their terms; they were in the mood for complaints and as time went on we found their attitude understandable.

While it would not be appropriate to over-state progress made during the first meetings there certainly was some. In all fairness it must be stated that the Negroes finally joined with us in an honest effort to approach the problem of job opportunity objectively and reasonably.

Negro Resolution

During our discussions with the Negro businessmen's committee we urged that a resolution be adopted by the full membership of the Negro businessmen's committee rejecting the concept of rioting as a means of achieving their goals. We had prepared a suggested resolution, but urged the Negroes to put it in their own words—only, we asked, please don't leave anything out.

This proposal resulted in long discussion and some resistance, but when it was explained that such a resolution would be helpful to us in persuading employers to cooperate, a resolution was adopted. The language follows:

> Actions contrary to the concepts of law and order such as took place here recently can never be justified in a civilized society.
>
> There were, nevertheless, underlying causes for these incidents which must be identified and understood as a first step toward permanent cure. Governor Brown has appointed a commission made up of leading citizens for precisely this purpose. In addition, many other investigation bodies are at work.
>
> We earnestly hope that these investigations will be thorough, penetrating and unbiased. We sincerely believe they will be.
>
> When all the facts are in hand and the full truth is known, appropriate and adequate steps must be taken to immediately correct whatever is wrong in this community. Our city of Los Angeles, particularly the Negro community, deserves no less than this.
>
> In the meantime, we join wholeheartedly in the coordinated effort by business, industry and government to rebuild, repair, restore and create new jobs and improve conditions in our city.

The above resolution was adopted unanimously by the entire 50-member committee. Immediately thereafter the Chairman of our Committee escorted the Chairman of the Negro businessmen's committee to our leading newspapers where good publicity was awarded the action. In one instance, an excellent editorial commending the Negroes for their forthright statement was carried.

Our Committee made it clear to the Negroes that our program would be strictly private enterprise, without government finance, yet conducted in full cooperation with all agencies, public or private, designed to provide job opportunities for the qualified minorities. We declared time and time again that we would only recommend that employers hire *qualified* applicants. That employers would not be asked to lower their standards to accommodate the deficient. This we said would only create "second-class" employees who would be the first laid off in an economic slump.

We told the Negro committee that we would not participate in marches, boycotts, picketing or the like to achieve these ends. We declared that, in our opinion, the persuasive efforts would work far faster and deserve the first chance; therefore we opposed the militant method as being less effective.

If we failed to produce, we said, we would step aside. But if the Negroes insisted on militant action we as a committee would depart the program and address ourselves to other matters. After long discussion, the Negro committee unanimously agreed to work with us in developing persuasive, non-militant means of attaining our common objectives. *To the date of this report they have kept that commitment fully.*

Coordination with the California Employment Service

At this point, as a result of discussions which had already taken place between top local officers of the Department and members of our Committee, it was agreed that there should be close coordination between the California Employment Office and our Committee. We discovered, incidentally, that up to this time there had not been as effective employment service delivered to industry from the disadvantaged areas as has been needed.

In the first place there was no employment office in the Watts area. Secondly, for whatever reason, the Negroes had developed an unfriendly attitude toward the California Employment Service generally and were reluctant to use it. Thus employers themselves, failing to achieve solid recruitment through that means, made only limited use of such offices as were open and operating at that time.

Mr. Arthur Morgan, Los Angeles Area Manager for the Service, joined with our Committee enthusiastically in the development of a workable, compatible plan in the hope of attracting not only Negro job candidates but willing employers as well. New procedures were developed. Attention was given to employers' specific needs and an attitude was created in the Department's Service Office which would tend to encourage increasing employer participation. A State Employment Office was opened on 103rd Street in Watts.

Initial Employer Contacts

Having worked out a seemingly workable arrangement with the California Employment Service to recruit, screen and refer Negro job candidates we turned our attention to the employers themselves ...

The attendance was outstanding. Most of those invited came to find out what was going on and, we discovered, to help if they could. This initial employers' meeting proved to be highly successful. It set a pattern which has been followed throughout the many, many similar employers' meetings which have taken place since that day.

The meeting lasted only one hour and fifteen minutes. During that time, however, the situation in the crisis areas of our city was depicted with clarity and purpose. The facts as reported earlier in this document were revealed, including the penalties which had been suffered by our community as a consequence of the riot and certainly indicating the possibility that another riot could occur at any moment unless appropriate steps were taken by the community as a whole.

It was not suggested that industry or our employers could or should by themselves solve the problem. It was not recommended that industry engage in a welfare or charity program. It was suggested only that the fundamental issues involved here did indicate that industry itself should bear some responsibility out of pure selfish interest, if nothing more.

It was pointed out that unemployment in the distressed area was perhaps three times that of the County area; those assembled were reminded that welfare costs out of taxpayer funds exceeded $400,000,000 annually in our County. *It was declared that a shortage obtained even then of both skilled and semi-skilled workers throughout industry in the metropolitan Los Angeles area.* It was declared that investigation had revealed that half of the unemployed in the curfew area were well equipped to meet minimum job entry standards for jobs then open . . .

Those assembled were urged *not to lower employment standards* nor to hire the unqualified candidates. They were, however, urged vigorously to *have a look at the large number of candidates then available who were actively seeking jobs and whose applications were now on file at the new California Employment Service in the heart of Watts in their search for qualified workers.*

Our Committee explained the new relationship with the California Employment Service which had been developed. A representative of that agency was present to make his own statement of purpose and plan and to demonstrate willingness to cooperate to the maximum by seeking out qualified candidates and screening them carefully in order to serve the employers as best they could. The response was unanimous, enthusiastic and affirmative. We requested that the "word" be passed on to the personnel departments . . .

The Los Angeles Black Congress

Out of the tragic assassination of Dr. Martin Luther King emerged a concept in the Los Angeles Negro community called "operational unity." Developed within the framework of the Los Angeles Black Congress, a coalition of over forty organizations in the Black community, "operational unity" maintains that all black people and organizations can and should work together regardless of any individual differences in philosophy and program. The development of the unity concept and the other work of the Black Congress are credited with playing a major role in keeping Los Angeles calm in the wake of the assassination of Dr. King.

The chairman of the Los Angeles Black Congress is Walter Bremond whose academic training in social work and experience in the civil rights movement made him a logical choice to head the coalition group. With a coordinated plan of action, the Black Congress is working in every problem area in the Black community including education, police community relations, political participation and economic development. The Congress has established task forces to work in each major area of concern.

On July 21, 1968. the President of the Management Council hosted a dinner meeting with Congress Chairman, Walter Bremond, and the entire executive committee with twelve of the Black Congress ...

The meeting centered on a discussion of developing more effective means of achieving the needed dialogue between the Black community and the key forces in the White community that were interested in solving the basic problems confronting the community. The President of the Management Council described the work of the Urban Coalition to the group and cited this coalition of key leaders in business, labor, government, education and community groups as one logical organization with which the Black Congress should deal directly. The Council President also stated that because of the need to have effective representation in the Urban Coalition from the Black community, he had nominated Walter Bremond as a member of the Board of Directors of the Coalition. He urged the Congress to maintain this key link with the Urban Coalition.

Throughout the meeting it was evident that the Los Angeles Black Congress had taken a giant step forward toward achieving the kind of unity of purpose and program that had long been talked about in the Negro community.

Conclusions

Obviously, with the flow of 100,000 to 150,000 new citizens annually coming into Los Angeles County alone—at least 12,000 of them Negroes—we simply cannot, overnight, eliminate unemployment problems for the Negroes in our area.

Historically, we have had a somewhat higher unemployment rate in this area than in other parts of the country, as indicated in the figures which will follow. Furthermore, the difficulties responsible for higher unemployment in the minority groups have not themselves been fully resolved nor will they be quickly resolved. Deficiencies, because of unfortunate past experience, doubt and suspicion, prevail; adjustments in attitude are constantly needed which will take patience and cooperation from all of us. Equally important, industry "involvement" must be developed to the maximum; motivation and recruitment of the disadvantaged must be improved. Finally, there still remains some degree of discrimination through prejudice in industry itself which, though diminishing, still has to be dealt with.

It cannot be denied, however, that due to the outstanding and enthusiastic cooperation thus far provided by industry in the Southern California area substantial progress has been made.

The following is a capitulation of the principal achievements in placing formerly unemployed or unemployable from the disadvantaged areas of our community on to regular jobs in industry.

The Management Council in Los Angeles is working directly with 1200 employer organizations throughout this area. *Not one of these has indicated unwillingness to co-operate in the recruitment and hiring of formerly unemployed disadvantaged minorities.*

A survey was made by the Management Council of 250 of these corporations, through a letter written to the president or chief executive officer. A request was made for a written report indicating the number each company had hired during the first twelve months following the riots of 1965. *201 companies responded. The net employment report was 17,903.*

A comprehensive survey conducted by the University of Southern California tracing the success stories of the individuals hired under the program indicated a high percentage were successful on the job, the pay was good, employers were content, and were disposed to continue the recruitment and placement of formerly disadvantaged minorities.

Eight Management Councils outside the city of Los Angeles have been organized and put in motion covering areas from San Diego to the San Francisco Bay Area. While these several Management Councils are operating with varying degrees of success, some of them are doing work comparable to that achieved in Los Angeles. All are trying.

In addition to initiating the organization of other Management Councils, eighteen affiliates have been established composed of employer organizations, such as chambers of commerce and groups like the Industrial Council of the City of Commerce in the Los Angeles area. These organizations, working independently, with their own employer groups, are carrying out work similar to that of the Management Council and in many instances using precisely the same techniques. The effect is substantial and favorable.

It is a generally accepted fact that following the riots during the summer of 1965, many thousands were unemployed in the South Central City area alone. The unemployment rate in that area was judged to be two and one-half to three times the prevailing unemployment rate for the County of Los Angeles. Furthermore, at that time it was discovered that half of those seeking jobs were qualified to fill job opportunities then open if a candidate could only be matched up with employers willing to use his services. *Today the situation is different.*

More than 90% of the job candidates in the South Central City area today require pre-job training to meet minimum job entry standards. The qualified have been hired and are working.

Based upon a comprehensive study made by the U. S. Department of Labor, the results of which were published on February 20, 1968 the unemployment picture is different from what it was three years ago. According to that study (U. S. Department of Labor Release No. 8584), these are the statistics.

This report deals with the current unemployment rate for Negroes in major urban areas as compared to the over-all unemployment rate in the same areas. The comparison follows:

In Chicago the unemployment rate, urban area, for whites was given as 2.4%. The unemployment rate for Negroes is given as 8.3%.

In Detroit the unemployment rate for whites was given as 3.2%—for the Negroes 10.9%.

In Newark, New Jersey, the unemployment rate shown for the whites was 3.5% and for the Negro 9.8%.

In the Los Angeles-Long Beach area white unemployment was given as 5.3% while the Negro unemployment was given as 8.0% which represents a major change in the situation as it appeared to be three years ago.

This change was achieved notwithstanding the fact that approximately 1,000 Negroes move into Los Angeles County from other states each month.

Not only has there been considerable progress in dealing with the unemployment situation in the South Central Negro area, but also the Mexican-American East Los Angeles area as well as in the San Fernando Valley area where both Negroes and Mexican-Americans reside.

Almost of equal importance, there has been a significant change in the opportunities for training and education in the metropolitan Los Angeles area. We now have five Skill Centers which are underwritten by the Manpower Development and Training Act—through

Federal subsidy. *Each of these Skill Centers is operating at budget capacity.* There are approximately 2,000 enrolled at the present time. We have just checked the official record on the placement in industry of those graduating from these Skill Centers.

The official report for the 1st. quarter, 1968, is a record 91.3% of those graduating remaining in the work force who were placed promptly on regular jobs in industry.

Because of the success of this program, thousands more have expressed willingness to take the training as soon as they can be enrolled. (Initially—Negroes were reluctant to enroll claiming past experience bad—no jobs. Our first Skill Center was even picketed.)

Quite apart from the industry effort to recruit, motivate, train and employ formerly unemployable disadvantaged minorities, there has been a development by industry in cooperation with the Government that will make a substantial contribution in the months ahead. . . .

Chapter 14

Early in 1966, the University of Southern California was retained by the Los Angeles Management Council to make a survey of those hired under the Council's program and to learn what happened to them following employment. Professor Reynolds, who directed the study, did his graduate work in public administration at the University of Chicago, taught at the Illinois Institue of Technology, worked with the Office of Salary Stabilization during the Korean conflict, and was with Ford Motor Company for over ten years before joining the U.S.C. faculty. His study showed that the turnover among the Negroes interviewed averaged less than among employees generally in manufacturing firms in Los Angeles. Employers reported that their new, Council-program employees were much like their other employees on most measures of job performance. The results of this study should encourage businessmen generally to make fuller use of the human resources represented by the Negro community. This accomplishment, tied in with greater understanding and improved income, would appear to be one of the most practical ways of resolving, at least in part, the racial problem which is with us.

EXPERIENCE OF LOS ANGELES EMPLOYERS WITH MINORITY GROUP EMPLOYEES*

William H. Reynolds

The study was sponsored by the Management Council for Merit Employment, Training & Research, a non-profit public service corporation which was formed in March of 1966. The Council is an outgrowth of the Los Angeles Chamber of Commerce Rehabilitation Committee appointed shortly after the riots of August 1965.

The President of the Council is Mr. H. C. (Chad) McClellan, and the Executive Director is Mr. Murray A. Lewis. The Council is supported primarily by funding from the John Randolph Haynes and Dora Haynes Foundation, the Ford Foundation, and firms in the aerospace industry.

Immediately after the riots 100 major Los Angeles firms were solicited directly by the Council to encourage them to employ Negroes from the "curfew" area. This was followed by an enlistment of another 167 companies. A short time later the full resources of various trade associations were brought into the program. These additional resources of various trade associations were brought into the program. These additional resources were channeled not only to the curfew area but to the East Los Angeles area as well. (Population in this area is predominantly Mexican-American.) There are at present 2600 cooperating employers in the Management Council program.

In the formal study itself, three groups were selected for interviewing:

1. Personnel directors or employment managers of firms which responded to the initial appeal of the Management Council and hired Negro employees through the Employment Service Section of the Watts Service Center.
2. First line supervisors in the same firms.
3. Negroes who were placed in jobs through the Watts Service Center following the initial appeal of the Management Council.

All three samples were drawn on a random basis from the files of the Watts Service Center.

---

*Reynolds, William H., "Experience of Los Angeles Employers with Minority Group Employees," *Report to Management,* No. 16, Graduate School of Business Administration, University of Southern California, March, 1967, 56 pp.

Three factors may have operated to bias to some extent the responses of the employer samples in a positive direction: first, a possible reluctance to express negative attitudes toward minorities; second, the possibility that the firms that responded to the Management Council are in fact more favorably disposed toward minority groups; and third, the possibility that the Negroes initially placed were more readily "employable."

Nevertheless, the findings presented *can* be taken as more-or-less accurately reflecting the experience of firms which actively sought out Negro employees after the riots in August 1965.

The Employee Study

A random sample was drawn of 100 Negroes placed in jobs from the Watts Service Center by the California State Employment Service from September 1965 to April 1966. Certain information on the respondents was drawn from the files of the Center and other information obtained in personal interviews. These personal interviews were conducted by Negro staff members of the Employment Service Section of the Watts Service Center. It proved impossible to locate four of the members of the sample. (Interviewing was conducted in October and November of 1966, six to fourteen months after the employees were placed.)

The Employer Study

A sample of 74 firms which had employed Negroes through the Watts Service Center from September 1965 to April 1966 was drawn from the files of the Center. Mail and telephone were used to contact these firms and make appointments for personal interviews with their personnel directors and with one member of first line supervision with Negroes in his work force. It was not possible to arrange interviews with all of these firms, and the data below are based on interviews with 59 personnel directors and 58 supervisors. All of these interviews were conducted by students in the USC School of Business Administration.

Major Conclusions

The Employees

1. The Negro employees interviewed were a relatively good sample of the Negro population of South Central Los Angeles. The data obtained on age, education, length of residence in Los

Angeles, etc., are reasonably consistent with internal California State Employment Service analyses. It should be emphasized, however, that the sample was not representative in at least two ways. First, all of the respondents were at least sufficiently motivated to find work to register with the State Employment Service (although some registered only after employers began active recruiting). Second, the respondents were immediately employable, or at least were considered so by the firms which hired them. Nevertheless, all of those interviewed were people who were looking for jobs and were helped to find them.

2. Once on the job, the Negro employees seem to have done well. Two-thirds were still with the firms that had originally hired them, and, among these employees, about half had been promoted and almost all had received pay increases. (In many cases, no doubt, the pay increases were due to company policies providing for automatic increases after so many months on the job.) Their median wage was $2.75 an hour and almost all said that their present job was better than other jobs they had had in the past.
3. One-third of the Negroes placed were no longer with the firm that had originally hired them. (This was six to fourteen months after they were hired.) About half of those who had left their jobs were working some place else and in many instances described their present job as better. About 15 per cent were unemployed again at the time of interview. In effect, positive results were obtained in the case of approximately 80-85 per cent of the Negroes placed.
4. Not one of the employees who had left the jobs in which they had been placed said that they left because of discrimination. (Recall that they were being interviewed by other Negroes.) Their replies were frank. One respondent said: "There was no future with the company. It wasn't discrimination though. There wasn't any future for anybody." Another said simply that he was caught sleeping on the job. Perhaps the most significant difference between the employees who had stayed with the companies that had hired them and the employees who had left (either voluntarily or not) was that the former group were placed in higher paying jobs. Most of the employees who had left had been in jobs paying less than $2.00 an hour.
5. The Negroes in the sample did not seem especially concerned about job discrimination. Only about ten per cent mentioned discrimination when asked if the company hiring them had

given them an opportunity based on their ability and performance. Similarly, when asked specifically what they saw as the major factor holding back Negro employment, only 20 per cent said discrimination. Almost monotonously, the respondents said lack of education, lack of training, lack of experience, lack of skill, lack of qualifications.

This is important. It points up the fact that the Negro community itself—or a major segment of it—believes that education and training is an answer to Negro unemployment and underemployment.

The Personnel Directors and First Line Supervisors

1. No less than 26 different organizations, agencies, and groups were named by the personnel directors when they were asked what private or public agencies they had worked with in hiring minority group employees.
2. All the firms interviewed have listed job openings with the California State employment Service Centers, most have worked with other organizations trying to place minority group employees, most have advertised in minority group newspapers, most have sent recruiters into minority group neighborhoods, and almost all have tried to use their present minority group employees to recruit other minority group employees.
3. On the other hand, the study produced some evidence which would indicate a continuing need for employers to evaluate employment standards and tests as they relate specifically to actual jobs. For example, is a high school certificate required for certain jobs? Do the tests that are administered tend to bar some minority group applicants from being given the opportunity to get into a job? In fact, do the standards and tests tend to limit the supply of manpower that would prove to be productive if more realistic measures were used? Few tests are culture-free, and personnel directors tend to agree that Negroes and Mexican-Americans do not do as well on the tests used as other applicants. Some companies, including several of the largest in California, are developing standards which relate more specifically and realistically to the requirements of the job.
4. Most firms said they try to treat minority group employees exactly like other employees. More recognition should be given to the problems arising from the cultural environment of the Negro community.
5. With respect to performance on the job, personnel directors

and first line supervisors agreed that Negroes and Mexican-Americans were much like other employees. First line supervisor ratings of minority group members were somewhat higher than personnel director ratings on a list of job performance factors.

Only about one out of five personnel directors and only about one out of ten members of first line supervision felt that Negroes required more training than other employees.

6. Turnover among Negroes and Mexican was reported to be about the same as among other employees. The number of minority group employees who received pay increases or promotions was also reported as about the same as in the case of other employees. Overwhelmingly, poor education and the lack of basic qualifications were cited as the principal factors holding back minority group employment. About ten per cent of the personnel directors and first line supervisors also mentioned "poor attitude" as a problem among Negroes and about 15 per cent mentioned "language" as a problem among Mexican-Americans.
7. Over-all, the experience of companies that have hired Negroes and Mexican-Americans has been significantly favorable. About one-third said that their experience has caused them to plan to hire more minority group employees in the future than they had in the past and about two-thirds said they planned to hire about the same number as in the past. *None said they planned to hire fewer.*

Comments and Recommendations

The author assumes sole responsibility for the comments and recommendations made below. They do not necessarily represent the views of either the Management Council or the Graduate School of Business Administration of the University of Southern California. In part, they are based on the data gathered in the formal interviews with employees, personnel directors, and first line supervisors. They also reflect the impressions formed in the course of the informal interviews with officials and employees of groups actively concerned with the problem of minority group employment. They also—inevitably—probably reflect to some degree the biases of the author.

1. To the 96 Negroes and 59 firms interviewed, discrimination *per se* at this time appears less important than other factors impeding the employment of minority groups in Los Angeles. Negroes themselves appear to attach more importance to lack

of education, lack of training, and lack of basic qualifications. Businessmen agree that the shortage of qualified applicants is the principal reason they do not hire more Negroes.

2. This suggests that remedial action may take either or both of two different forms: First, it would be advisable for more employers to review their job standards to determine if they are in fact realistic, and do not amount to *de facto* discrimination against minority groups. Second, further efforts should be made to up-grade the Negro working force to meet the employment standards they are certain to encounter in looking for jobs.

   a. With respect to the first of these two proposals, it is certainly not suggested that employers should arbitrarily revise employment standards downward. On the other hand, it is probable that some employers are looking for "career" people to fill entry level jobs, for people with "potential". Realistically, many "floor maintenance specialists" will stay "floor maintenance specialists," and a high school education and the ability to pass a written test are irrelevant for many jobs of this kind.

      If we are to approach a solution to the problem of unemployment among the disadvantaged, more consideration should be given to job applicants with police records. The kind of job, the nature of the offense, whether the record consists only of arrests or also of convictions, how long ago the offense occurred, and similar factors should be carefully considered.

   b. A second recommendation is that minority group members should be provided with the education and training to permit them to participate effectively in our economic system. Many kinds of training have been proposed. Basic education (reading, writing, and arithmetic) and pre-vocational training seem mostly likely to be productive in bringing the hard-core person to a level of employability. "Coupled programs" in which on-the-job training is provided by employers and more basic training is provided institutionally seem to offer promise. Remuneration while being trained seems to be a powerful motivation for people to seek training.

      Attitudinal orientation which would constructively deal with the sense of hopelessness and other psychological barriers among the disadvantaged is also indicated. The recognition that job opportunities exist can provide a strong stimulus to higher levels of motivation and confidence.

3. Assuming that employment standards and employees qualifications can be brought into line, the problem will still remain of bringing together the prospective employer and the prospective employee. The Management Council, the California State Employment Service, the Urban League, and dozens of other organizations, agencies, and groups have been active in trying to solve this problem. Two recommendations are indicated: First, more coordination is required. Second, the employer himself must take an active role in seeking out minority group employees.
   a. It is hoped that ways can be found to solve current problems of funding, duplication of work, red tape, and lack of communication among concerned agencies. The Management Council is functioning as a coordinating influence on the employer side. Various agencies and organizations have valid functions to perform; what is necessary is the kind of coordination that would make for more efficient utilization of the resources of these various groups.
   b. Some minority group individuals simply do not believe that they stand a chance of being hired by a major firm and do not even appear at the hiring gate. *Employers need to find ways to reach the minority community more effectively.* Also, in "treating minority group employees on the job exactly like other employees," some employers may be failing to recognize the special problems faced by such employees. Finally, minority groups should not be looked upon as a source of cheap labor. Over half of the employees in our sample who had been placed in jobs and who had left them had earned less than $2.00 an hour. Jobs at this level are often part-time or intermittent and do not provide adequate incentive for the employee to continue work.
4. To conclude with a point made repeatedly throughout this study, the employers who have hired minority group employees report almost uniformly good experience. Turnover rates, attendance and tardiness, the quality and quantity of work produced, raises and promotions, and other measures of job performance show that minority group employees do not differ from other employees. Expected resistance from first line supervision and fellow workers has not materialized. *Other Los Angeles employers should be encouraged by the results of the study not only to provide entry level opportunities to minority group members, but, once they are employed, to make full utilization of their skills and talents.*

Chapter 15

Critics point out, and frequently rightly so, that government's attempts to resolve problems are sometimes bungled or outright failures because of poor management. These critics believe that private enterprise can do the job better at a lower cost. Among those who hold this viewpoint is George Champion, who points out specific private-enterprise projects which have already proven themselves. One of these was undertaken in East Harlem by the U. S. Gypsum Company, to refurbish—dilapidated tenements it bought, because the company saw this project as the first step in a plan to gain a share of an important market for its products, and at the same time improve the lot of the people living in a depressed area. Mr. Champion points to other projects, among them some on air and water pollution control. The objectives of improving housing in the slum areas of our cities and tackling the problem of air and water pollution through private enterprise are most commendable. Since demand is desire coupled with purchasing power, the costs for housing renovation in the East Harlem area make me wonder if the present residents of these tenements can afford to pay for the improvements. But from an overall viewpoint, I am very much in sympathy with Mr. Champion's approach.

CREATIVE COMPETITION*

George Champion**

In recent months a slum clearance program undertaken in New York City's teeming East Harlem by the U. S. Gypsum Company has attracted considerable attention. The company has completely refurbished one of the half-dozen dilapidated tenements it bought, redoing the interior, installing new bathrooms and kitchens, and painting the outside light gray with bright yellow trim.

Within six months of the time the job had started, the original tenants, who had been living amid almost total deterioration, were able to enjoy housing which was as good as that provided in a nearby public housing development. The residents, many of whom had lived in the building for a number of years, had their lives changed without having to rip out their neighborhood roots and become faceless inhabitants of a large, impersonal apartment complex. The remaining buildings owned by U. S. Gypsum are now in the process of rehabilitation.

While what U. S. Gypsum did was good for the tenants, the company was not acting completely out of charitable instincts. The first building, which had cost U. S. Gypsum $30,000 to buy and $219,000 to rehabilitate, now produced $33,700 in gross annual rentals. The rehabilitated structure itself has been privately appraised at $300,000. These figures show that the project was a practical one, even though U. S. Gypsum is not interested in going into the real estate business and plans to sell the properties it rehabilitates to a nonprofit fund.

There are also many side benefits that U. S. Gypsum has gained from its $1.25 million investment in East Harlem. On the job, the company utilized its new radiant heating system embedded in gypsum ceiling panel, an asphalt-gypsum compound that aids in leveling floors, and a line of long-lasting epoxical paints. In addition, it has tested a new gypsum wallboard which is a prefabricated partition system with space to allow for utility pipes and wiring.

The company sees the East Harlem project as the first step in a plan to gain a share of an important market for its products. The

*Reprinted from the *Harvard Business Review,* May-June, 1967, pp. 61 to 67.

**Chairman of the Board, Chase Manhattan Bank, New York City.

overall market for rehabilitation has been estimated at some $4 billion annually, with New York City alone containing some 50,000 to 60,000 structures that lend themselves to treatment. U. S. Gypsum has already developed plans for rehabilitating rundown housing in sections of Cleveland, Chicago, and the West Coast.

All this is impressive and intriguing, but the most striking aspect of the U. S. Gypsum slum clearance project is not so much the work itself as the amount of attention it has generated. The company has received untold column-inches of publicity on its project. More than 100 cities have inquired about how the new approach works. Several hundred letters have been received from contractors, housing authorities and other interested parties clamoring for more information.

Why should a building project which, on the face of what has been done, is not especially spectacular cause such a public stir? One reason is that, unfortunately, it *is* news today when a private business organization strikes out on its own in a full-scale attack on a major problem deep in the heart of an area of our economy—the social field—which the government has regarded for several decades as its exclusive preserve.

However, the important aspect of the U. S. Gypsum project and others essentially like it is not their news value. It is that we are witnessing in them the first phase of development of an exciting and challenging new concept of the relationship between the public and private sectors of our economy.

Ambitious New Role

One way of describing this concept would be to use the term "sociocommercial enterprise." For what we are considering here is an entirely new view of the true "business" of business and its role in the so-called "public" sector of the economy. In essence, sociocommercial enterprise is based on the theory that if we are going to be successful in solving such crucial problems as water and air pollution, race relations, unemployment, and education, we must commit the vast resources of private business on a *businesslike* basis. Thus, such an approach is partially social in motivation and goals; but it is also partially commercial in that it is helping to shape an environment in which business can continue to operate profitably five or ten years from now.

What is involved here is not mass "do-goodism" on the part of business at the expense of the stockholders. Rather, it is the application of the skills, knowledge, funds, and technical resources of a company in a social problem area on a scale comparable to that on which the company attacks day-by-day commercial tasks. A blending of the awareness of social responsibility and the determination to approach the social task in a hardheaded, businesslike way is crucial to the idea. Sociocommercial enterprise, in other words, is "for keeps" —a vocation, not an avocation.

Need for Corporate Help

This new concept of the relative roles of business and government represents an encouraging reversal in the power and activity flow that has been running so strongly in the past three decades from the private sector into the public sector. Studies have shown, for example, that the federal government has recently been involved in some 24,000 activities which by most reckoning belong within the private sector.[1] The spread of government resources and power has, of course, widened under the Great Society program as the government has continued to stake out vast new areas in the social field for its own. The 89th Congress alone passed 4 new man-power training programs, 12 new urban programs, 15 new economic development programs, 17 new educational programs, and 21 new health programs.

This outpouring of social and economic legislation contributes further to a situation in which 170 different federal aid programs are on the books, financed by over 400 separate appropriations, and administered by 21 federal departments and agencies backed up by 150 Washington bureaus and over 400 regional offices empowered to receive applications and disburse funds.

Indeed, the tasks the nation must undertake in the social area imposed such a demand for funds, organization, facilities, and know-how that the machinery of government is clearly unequal to the massive burden. According to John W. Gardner, Secretary of Health, Education and Welfare:

> In almost every domestic program we are encountering crises of organization. Coordination among Federal agencies leaves much to be desired. Communication between the various levels of government–Federal, state, and local–is casual and ineffective. State and local government is in most areas seriously inadequate.[2]

There is and will continue to be a widening disparity between the cost of the programs and what the government—even with its

---

[1] *The Wall Street Journal,* April 27, 1965, p. 1.
[2] *The New York Times,* November 23, 1966, p. 38.

seemingly unlimited ability to obtain funds from the taxpayers—is able to pay for. Senator Abraham Ribicoff of Connecticut, for one, believes that the cost of rebuilding our decaying cities could run as high as a trillion dollars. He said:

> With the war in Vietnam, the space program and other projects, the Federal Government doesn't have a trillion dollars available. We're going to have to get help, massive help, from private enterprise.[3]

Belief in Private Business

There is another element adding to the pressure for a significant private advance into the social sector. When it comes to a choice between having a job done by private enterprise or by the government, the conviction of most Americans is that the job should be done by private enterprise. Polls have shown repeatedly that whenever the people see a viable alternative to government action, they are likely to support it. They favor government intervention only when there seems to be no other way. Consider evidence like the following:

> The results of a survey, conducted by Louis Harris & Associates and published in *Newsweek*, showed that by large majorities the people want business to assume active leadership in broad social areas. The poll showed that of those questioned, many wanted business to help eliminate depressions (92%); to help rebuild cities (87%); to help find cures for diseases (72%); to aid college education (83%); to contribute its resources to the war against poverty (80%); to play a role in eliminating race prejudice (83%); and to become involved in controlling pollution (90%).[4]
>
> In a 1962 California poll, conducted by Belden Associates for the Purdue Research Foundation, 62% of those questioned believed it would be better if private business did more of what government now does. Only 21% believed the opposite.[5]

Such opposition to "letting government do it" represents much more than a quaint quirk in our national personality. It arises from the bedrock philosophy of individual freedom and self-reliance on which our democratic way of life is built. Also, there are undeniable economic truths involved. When government takes over an activity

---

[3]*The National Observer,* December 5, 1966, p. 1.
[4]*Newsweek*, May 2, 1966, p. 84.
[5]Richard Cornuelle, *Reclaiming the American Dream* (New York, Random House, 1965), p. 10.

that should be handled by private organizations, resources such as labor and materials are siphoned off from the private sector. This reduces the productivity of the private sector and decreases its contribution to government operations. The loss is accentuated when the government takes over a revenue-producing private activity, because the government operation, rather than supporting itself, usually feeds on taxes. Funds for government projects can be derived only from an expanding base of revenues, which in turn means a growing private economy.

Competing with Government

Yet, while sociocommercial enterprise would seem to be a logical response to these forces for change—and the one most in keeping with freedom of competition—another concept has been gathering a head of steam over the past several months. This is the idea of forming economic units which would be vehicles for business-government "partnerships" in attacking social problems. Such concepts as "partnership" are, of course, the direct antithesis of the evolving philosophy of sociocommercial enterprise.

Joint ventures appear to many businessmen to be disguised attempts to put private capital at the disposal of the government in areas which the government has attempted to monopolize but could not because of financial difficulty. Accordingly, many businessmen regard these "partnership" proposals as a snare and a delusion, and are having none of them.

There is a growing conviction that business should strike out on its own in the social area, providing the government with creative *competition* there rather than becoming a party to what is labeled as "creative federalism" or some other type of business-government "partnership." As Richard Cornuelle has observed, "The Government needs competition ... not collaboration." It can also be said that competition, and not collaboration, holds the greatest promise for both business and society as a whole.

It will take a major effort to abolish poverty, unemployment, pollution of air and of water, transportation jams, and educational wastelands. But business could bring to bear the almost incalculably great force represented by the energy, initiative, ability, and facilities that have made ours the most productive society in history. This power would be thrown into the balance in the struggle to solve problems that so far either have proved unyielding or have not been attacked because of their awesome dimensions.

By adopting a policy and attitude of aggressive competition in attacking broad social problems, business could vie to supplant government in the setting up of projects that would represent beachheads of excellence throughout the country. They would be in the nature of pilot programs for attacking and dealing with social problems. They would be models for future projects. By establishing standards of quality and cost for the government to match, these projects would not only serve to get the job at hand done, but would also help to raise standards in areas where the government has already gained a foothold. To illustrate the difference between business and government standards, Carl Madonick, the real estate commissioner of New York City, recently estimated that it would cost the city 50% more than it would a private builder to erect a building. The more business becomes involved in socioeconomic enterprise, competing directly with the government in the social field, the more apparent such comparisons will be.

Exciting Markets

Traditionally, projects in the social field have not been associated with private enterprise, because they have not been considered as "balance sheet" operations. However, having raced ahead technologically, our economy is now at a point where human concerns are paramount and, in fact, may very well have become indistinguishable from economic concerns. Not only do broad social problems offer business an unparalleled opportunity to make a solid contribution to society, but the sociocommercial "market," if it may be referred to as such, could well prove to be one of the great new economic frontiers of the future.

Planned Cities

A program of the General Electric Company is highly compatible with these trends. The company plans to carry urban redevelopment beyond slum clearance and rehabilitation. It proposes to develop planned cities within reasonable commuting distance of major metropolitan areas. Like U. S. Gypsum, GE intends to test new materials and techniques in developing the projects. It also hopes to bring down the cost of good urban living—and, not incidentally, make a profit. Fred J. Borch, president of GE, has said that through the planned cities projects the company hopes to double or even triple the size of a market to which it would sell products ranging from dishwashers and refrigerators to traffic-control and transit systems.

Pollution Control

Several major companies have applied the doctrine of sociocommercial enterprise directly to one of our most serious problems—air and water pollution. Over the past 15 years, U. S. Steel and Bethlehem Steel between them have spent something in the neighborhood of $300 million on air and water pollution control. West Virginia Pulp & Paper Company has also done an outstanding job in this area. In getting a major program of stream improvement under way, the paper company first had its own experts and consulting engineers make pioneering studies to determine the best means of providing treatment for the complex wastes from paper manufacturing processes. On the basis of these studies, the company invested $4 million to install in Virginia an advanced biological process for treating industrial wastes. The company then entered into contracts to guarantee bond interest, amortization, and operating expenses for a $4.5 million plant built in Maryland by a state commission, and $1 million for enlarging an existing municipal plant in Pennsylvania.

Not only are the West Virginia Pulp & Paper plants in Maryland and Pennsylvania cleaning up industrial wastes, but they are treating domestic sewage from nearby municipalities as well. Thus these communities benefit doubly from the paper company's venture into socioeconomic enterprises.

Innovations in Education

Another area in which it is vitally important for business to offer government aggressive and creative competition is education, particularly the "new" education built around teaching and learning machines. Business must do its part in research and development in this area and provide not only the "hardware" but, in close cooperation with education, also adequate "software" to feed into the machines. Otherwise government will move into still another vacuum, and its influence will be further extended.

Already private business is providing some of the most notable advances in the field of electronic education. IBM has been especially active in this regard through its subsidiary, Science Research Associates. The company is conducting experimental projects and special studies in the adaptation of data processing "hardware" systems to teaching and learning. In the "software" area, it has created a series of computerized courses for the IBM 1500 computer in various aspects of biology, chemistry, physics, mathematics, statistics, and German.

The Xerox Corporation is another company that is turning its attention to education, both as an exercise of social responsibility and with an eye to developing a new market. Joseph C. Wilson, chairman of the company, explains, "We're starting at the other end, looking at how people learn." Xerox has a team of specialists from the behavioral sciences working in its research laboratories with human subjects. The object is to find out more about the workings of human memory, eyes, and ears in order to understand more about how individuals learn.

A project closely allied with education, yet carried on in an entirely different field, is that undertaken by the American Bankers Association. The aim is to induce the nation's 13,000 commercial banks to lend money to students who need financial help with their education and, at the same time, keep the government out of the general student loan business. The funds are provided at the relatively low rate of 6% on the unpaid balance. Under the program, commercial banks and other lenders made $173 million available to 210,000 students during the first semester of the current academic year.

The banking community has also contributed to the advance of sociocommercial enterprise in slum clearance by providing loans at low interest rates to finance renewal programs. Seven commercial banks recently agreed to lend $7 million at low rates to revive the lagging rehabilitation program on New York's West Side. The renovation of some 400 dwellings is involved. While money for this purpose has been bringing rates of as high as 12%, these banks have made it available at 6%.

Our own bank has developed a unique training program that is aimed at preventing high school dropouts among Negro and Puerto Rican youths. We hire high school juniors and seniors for part-time jobs with the explicit understanding that they will continue in school until graduation. If they work out satisfactorily—and the vast majority have—we offer them permanent jobs once they receive their diplomas and, in some cases, even finance college courses for them in the evening. Far from being just a gesture of altruism, this program is a highly practical way of attracting promising young people into the bank to fill job vacancies that currently total more than 500.

World Food Needs

As the concept of social competition on a businesslike basis is extended to the international scene, it seems likely that private business can contribute effectively to solving the problem of feeding the world's hungry. It is becoming increasingly obvious that what countries with underdeveloped economies really want is self-sufficiency in food production along with the ability to produce agricultural products within the price range of their own low-income populations.

Some enterprising companies are demonstrating that private business can met these requirements. They are introducing modified plantation schemes, directing and supervising credit, and pioneering in technical services and marketing arrangements. Companies already taking part in such sociocommercial projects include Anderson, Clayton and Company, California Packing Corporation, Campbell Soup Company, H. J. Heinz Company, Ralston Purina Company, Quaker Oats Company, Fisher Flour Mills, International Milling Company, Dole Corporation, and United Fruit Company.

Several of the more intriguing of these programs involve the processing and promoting of inexpensive but nourishing foods and animal feeds by American companies in overseas areas. For example:

> Enriched Maizena is one product developed for the low-income, mass food market. Derived from a cornmeal product, it is produced and sold by the Corn Products Company of Latin America. Enriched with proteins, vitamins, and minerals, it is an all-purpose food that can be used as a pudding or a drink. While serving useful social purposes, it also sells well.
>
> Another interesting project has been launched by Ralston Purina in Colombia. Recognizing an acute need for low-cost meat, milk, and eggs, the company decided to promote milo, a grain sorghum similar to Indian corn, as a suitable feed crop. Ralston introduced milo seed and financed local growers in Colombia by guaranteeing each a cash market for his harvest. The idea is that the increase in production in milo as a feed crop will in turn lead to the increased production of meat, milk, and eggs. Ralston Purina has also introduced improvements in local storage and transportation facilities and initiated consumer educational services.[6]

The phrase "business know-how" has become a cliché, but there is no denying that, applied to social problems, it can be as effective and rewarding as it is in the normal run of commerce and industry.

Strategic Approach

The kind and scope of projects a business tackles and the approach it takes must be determined by the nature and capabilities of the business itself. But surely some sort of social challenge offering the opportunity to apply the doctrine of sociocommercial enterprise lies within the framework of the knowledge, skills, and resources of most business organizations.

---

[6]See Ray A. Goldberg, "Agribusiness for Developing Countries," HBR September-October 1966, p. 81.

While large businesses are more likely than small businesses to have the resources and the inclination to become involved in sociocommercial enterprises, there are also opportunities for small business in the field. For instance, rehabilitating a neighborhood around a factory can be both socially and commercially beneficial to a company, no matter what its size. The residents gain, and the company gains from increased property values as well as from improved working conditions for its employees and an enhancement of its public reputation. Again, the development of new products for use in socioeconomic projects conducted on a major scale by larger organizations represents a promising market for small, specialized manufacturers. There is also the possibility that small companies with mutually supportive functions can form combinations to carry out projects in the social area.

Basic Steps

How does management get a sociocommercial enterprise under way? If we take a cursory look at what has been undertaken so far, it would seem that a logical sequence of action of a business considering such an enterprise would be along these lines.

1. *Choose an area in which the company is experienced and already successful.* U. S. Gypsum, for example, had already been extensively involved in supplying materials and developing techniques for remodeling as well as for new construction. The same can be said of most of the other companies that have initiated "paying" projects in the social field. They have literally started on their own "doorsteps."

2. *Choose an area in which there is an obvious need, and analyze the situation thoroughly.* Figure the market from a dollars-and-cents point of view rather than plunge in on a wave of crusading zeal with the primary desire of winning public plaudits. U. S. Gypsum and GE, for example, knew not only the "hows" of their enterprises but also the "whats" of costs and resources and the "whys" of practical objectives such as increased product sales and new product development.

3. *Launch studies to determine the best means of solving the problem.* Before undertaking its program to correct water pollution, West Virginia Pulp & Paper had its own experts and consulting engineers make pioneering studies to determine the best means of providing treatment for the complex wastes from paper manufacturing processes. Again, Xerox had made its participation in education a primary focus of research and development before moving

into this particular area of the sociocommercial market. IBM also is conducting extensive experimental projects and special studies.

4. *Undertake the project with the idea of making it pay, as well as accomplishing good.* There will thus be less of a chance that the project will deteriorate into one more example of aimless "do-goodism." Rather, the results will show that there is a direct relationship between the financial soundness of the proposition and the amount of good it does. The U. S. Gypsum project in Harlem, for example, not only was a financial success, but also cut rehabilitation costs by an estimated 50%—a saving which will encourage expanded rehabilitation work and bring tenants greatly improved housing at reasonable rentals.

5. *Develop new attitudes toward participation in socially oriented projects.* This is perhaps the most important step of all—and the hardest for many businesses and businessmen to take. A change in the organization's attitude must begin at the top; through deeds, policies, and plans, management must show not only that it is aware of the indispensable role of business in areas that have come to be thought of as purely "public," but that it is ready and willing to move the organization actively into these areas on a sociocommercial basis.

Personal Participation

Through internal communications and other corporate public relations activities, an environment of social awareness and action must be created within the company from top to bottom. Middle management not only should be made cognizant of the close intermingling of the fate of business and state of society but also should be encouraged to look for opportunities in the sociocommercial marketplace—opportunities that will improve the overall environment in which the company operates and that will enhance the role of the company as a social force.

Every opportunity should be taken to expose managers and other employees to the nature, needs, and meaning of major social problems and their relation not only to the future of the business but also to the preservation of the individual's own job. We must face the truth that today a company is only as good as its environment and that a man's job will last only as long as the company does.

Conversely, it should be brought home to the individual employee that his job can be expanded through company involvement in the sociocommercial market. Company employees should be encouraged to see for themselves what conditions and opportunities exist in the social field. People who become personally involved in community affairs can make a valuable social contribution; in addition, they can develop expertise which in turn may be valuable to their company in its sociocommercial enterprises.

Business has been widely criticized—especially by the young people coming out of college—for a lack of social involvement. By becoming socially *activist* through sociocommercial enterprise, using the techniques that serve it in the marketplace, business could go a long way toward improving the public's impression of it in this respect.

Conclusion

Businessmen have been complaining for too many years now about government competition in the private sector. Although many, if not most of these complaints have been amply justified, it would be a refreshing and beneficial change to hear government bureaucrats complaining that *business* is competing in *their* activities. This would also be a healthy thing for our economy and a formidable hedge against a future in which we must grapple with the social and economic "fallout" of technological advances.

Business must move from the defensive to the offensive and begin pushing the boundary line between the public and private sectors the other way. Both business and society stand to gain from the doctrine of sociocommercial enterprise. Vigorously applied, it could well become the most promising new technique of social progress.

Chapter 16

Estimates by the United Nations show that unless checked the world population for the year 2000 will be around 7.5 billion people or about double that of today. With more than half of the people now going to bed hungry, and population growth highest in the same areas in Asia, Africa and South America, the problem of world hunger is magnified to almost an incommensurable degree. And, as the experience of the past 50 years shows, the problem of finding answers to the problem of world hunger must rest largely upon the shoulders of the industrial nations operating under private enterprise because of the failure of state-controlled countries such as Russia to develop an efficient system of agriculture.

Recent experience has also conclusively shown that food exports from productive countries to hunger-stricken areas, while aiding in a temporary way, are no solution to the massive problem of hunger now existing or likely to exist in the developing nations. Rather, aside from the expanded use of birth-control measures which as yet have affected population growth to only a small degree, the principal solution to the world hunger problem would seem to be in exporting practical versions of capitalistic agriculture which can be widely used in the countries where the problem exists. The following article by Duncan Norton-Taylor covers some of the factors underlying the increasing problem of world hunger. This well-written paper includes a wealth of information pertinent to the problem of world hunger.

WORLD HUNGER*

Duncan Norton-Taylor**

The prospect of a world whose population is doubling every thirty years or so has inspired a number of nightmares. Professor J. H. Fremlin, a prestigious physicist of Birmingham University in England, has described one he had in an article in the magazine *New Scientist*. Looking ahead eight hundred years, and speculating about how all the people would be fed, he saw how "waste products could in principle be changed back into food compounds with the absorption of little more energy. Cadavers could be homogenized," and additional photosynthesis for the production of extra crops could be arranged for by the orbiting of immense mirrors that would continuously reflect the sun around the earth. But the mirrors would have created an insoluble problem of overheating, and the world, having produced a population of 12 quadrillion, would then have reached, in Fremlin's phrase of finality, a "dead end."

But there are visions, almost as unpleasant as Fremlin's, that have the more disquieting effect of being real and immediate: of the human population stabilizing itself in the manner of the animal world—through mortal conflicts between species, through degeneracy and reduction in the birth rate due to stresses of overcrowding (what one experimenter with rats calls "pathological togetherness"), and through death from hunger.

Disease may simply stalk quietly through populations debilitated by malnutrition. Such visions come into closer focus in Mrs. Indira Gandhi's India, now not only threatened again by famine, but haunted by the realization that the production of its croplands continues to fall steadily behind the requirements of its multiplying population.

The same predicament in varying degrees of seriousness has overtaken about two-thirds of the people of the world. The leaps in population are most rapid in those regions least able to support them—the so-called underdeveloped nations, sometimes politely called the "less developed," or "developing," nations. The French have a noncommittal phrase for them—the *tiers monde,* which limits the

---

*Reprinted from the June 1966 issue of *Fortune Magazine* by special permission;

**Contributor to Fortune Magazine.

grouping to those underdeveloped countries not in the Communist bloc, thus reducing to some extent the magnitude of our concern. But in this struggling area, which we cannot cast out, are most of Africa and Latin America, and an Asia that still includes, most burdensomely, India with its 500 million. This is the Third World, crying out, not always humbly, for help.

No problem presses on this generation of men more remorselessly. Few decisions or actions (outside of a nuclear decision) will be more critical in the next few years than those taken to resolve this dilemma of populations and human sustenance. All of modern humanism's skills and technologies are available to get the world out of its predicament at least in this century. The test is one of men's will to act.

The burden rests heavily upon the U. S., which for two decades has been sharing its abundance with hungry nations and now is called upon to rush emergency aid to India. But this country cannot continue on this course indefinitely, and shouldn't if it could, for such handouts merely put off crises, and even compound them. If there is any discernible solution it must be to raise the Third World to a state where it can feed itself. The point is being made over and over again today by Congressmen and the President, to each other and to the needy nations. But how is it to be brought about?

They have no simple answer—there is none. But certainly one answer must lie in what the U. S. has accomplished for itself and how it has done it. This nation has been able to grow food to a fantastic extent beyond the needs of its people. Granted its natural endowment of land, the U. S. had nevertheless multiplied the capacity of that land through the exploitation of technology and capital investment. These are the American products that both the government and American business should export in quantity to the agricultural economies of the Third World.

Capital can build irrigation canals in India, supply pumps and tube wells to tap the fresh water under the saline marshes in the Indus River basin in West Pakistan. Capital can supply tools and machinery, pesticides, fertilizers, provide training in modern methods. Most important of all, U. S. capital can create an atmosphere that is conducive to self-help. In the countless analyses of the subject, one fact stands out: that is lack of incentive in the poverty-stricken, potentially rich, farmlands of the Third World. The factors inhibiting food production are traditionalism, lethargy, and hopelessness, not, at the moment, any lack of arable land. Capital generates incentive by producing goods and creating demand, and it widens the distribution of the fruits of labor. This is the market system so familiar to Americans.

The difficulties of transplanting the process are undeniable. Socialistic prejudices, hostility, and suspicion confront U. S. capital. American businessmen are reluctant to move into such an inclement and ostensibly unrewarding environment. But in the urgency of the situation, solutions to these difficulties must be found, and some indeed, have been found and being pressed by enterprising businessmen and administrators. It is inconceivable that there should be no answer at all to the dilemma.

A Hypothesis: 48 Million Left to Starve

Let us look at the dimensions of what is sometimes sportingly called the race between people and food. The world population has doubled since 1900. Nothing is altogether inevitable, but enough female children have already been born to produce enough babies to raise the population to 7.4 billion by the year 2000. The populations of the Third World, which now number about 1.5 billion, are growing at rates of around 2.5 percent a year. The enormity of this growth comes clear when one realizes that, at the 2.5 percent a year rate, Latin America will go from 212 million in 1960 to 569 million in the year 2000.

The sudden acceleration of population growths all over the world began in the Forties, when the availability of DDT and the antibiotics transformed a problem that was only slowly evolving into the dimensions it has now attained. Death rates began dropping abruptly. Right after World War II they were as high as thirty per thousand in many of the Third World countries, and since then they have declined to around twenty. Meanwhile the birth rates in the Third World have continued to exceed forty per thousand.

Birth rates may be the more opaque side of the dilemma. While farming isn't much fun, as one corporation economist remarked, reproducing is. There is also a poignant aspect to the situation: peasants in poverty-stricken regions look to their children as a kind of social security for themselves in an uncertain old age; and the higher the infant mortality rate, the more babies they are apt to produce. But this also suggests an encouraging angle: an improvement in economic conditions tends to lower the birth rates. In highly developed Western European countries, birth rates are down to about seventeen per thousand. It would be tragic, however, to wait on such a development, for the situation also works the other way around: increasing hordes of hungry people retard economic progress.

And the hordes have been getting hungrier. Before the war according to the American Society of Agronomy, the countries of the Third World were, all together, net exporters of some 11 million metric tons a year of corn, wheat, rice, and other grains to the world's industrial nations. From 1948 to 1952 the flow reversed: the Third World countries imported an average of four million tons a year. As population growth gained momentum (and as many people migrated to urban centers), the net flow of imports increased: to 13 million tons a year between 1957 and 1959, to 25 million tons in 1964. It was not a matter of increasing trade but a matter of want. Even the 25 million tons were not enough to make up the growing food deficits.

The size of these deficits is difficult to measure with any exactitude, because opinions differ (as they differ in almost every aspect of the subject of food) as to what precisely constitutes an adequate diet. A Department of Agriculture study ("Changes in Agriculture in 26 Developing Nations") fixed on some 2,500 calories per day as adequate, which is about the average consumption in Mexico, and posed an interesting hypothesis to illustrate how short of this level was India's average food consumption in 1963. If India had distributed its supply of food as far as it would go even at only a 2,300-calorie level, 48 million out of that country's 480 million in that year would still have been left totally without food.

The study found an average per capita intake of calories below "desirable" levels in eleven of the twenty-six countries it examined: Colombia, Tanganyika (now part of Tanzania), Sudan, Tunisia, Egypt, Iran, Jordan, India, Pakistan, the Philippines, Thailand. And because of the uneven distribution of food in the other fifteen countries, many people there were suffering from malnutrition and undernutrition. Diets barely adequate in calories can be hazardously low in nutriments, such as proteins, necessary for good health.

At a seminar of experts in Estes Park, Colorado, in the summer of 1965, the prediction was made that in 1980 the deficit in the underdeveloped countries would be somewhere between 47 million and 240 million metric tons of food, depending on whether populations were to be fed subsistence diets or adequate ones. These figures included mainland China; by removing China one reduces the over-all figures somewhat (by around 25 percent) but this statistical exercise doesn't relieve the plight of the rest.

How Capital Can "Substitute for Land"

There is hope in one statement in the Agriculture Department report: most of the countries of the Third World have the potential of feeding their own people *and could have surpluses* within ten to twenty years. That hope rests on pointing economic development toward attaining self-sufficiency in food. One economist, Professor Theodore W. Schultz of the University of Chicago, takes encouragement from the way capital has transformed some of the old and congested farmlands of Europe, an experience more pertinent, perhaps, than that of the U. S., with its hugh acreages. In his book, *Transforming Traditional Agriculture*, Schultz observes that Western Europe "with a population density much greater than Asia's and with a poor endowment of farm land generally, has been increasing its agricultural production at a rate that would have been thought impossible only a couple of decades ago. Italy, Austria, and Greece, for example, with less arable land per capita than India and with farm land inferior to India's have increased agricultural production at a rate of 3.0, 3.3, and 5.7 percent per year respectively, compared to 2.1 for India."

"New land obviously is not the explanation," says Schultz. "It is the same old endowment of mostly poor land. If anything, the total area devoted to arable farming has been declining somewhat." In Israel, heavily populated by European stock, "between 1952 and 1959, production more than doubled although farm employment rose only a fourth." Israel's growth, too, was stimulated by capital investment. As in Europe, it created the factors of production "that substitute for land": modern implements, machinery, new seed strains, chemicals to fight pests and plant diseases, chemicals to enrich the earth.

India's story is a sorry contrast to this kind of progress. But at the same time India is a good case study of what capital might do to lift a poor country out of its ruck. As recently as 1952-53, India's annual output of chemical fertilizer nutrients totaled only 60,000 metric tons. Now it produces nearly 400,000 tons a year and uses more than 700,000 tons of fertilizer. It is estimated that India could increase production by 50 percent in the next five years if it improved its methods of farming and used three times this amount of fertilizer. India cannot afford to import such amounts, being lamentably short of foreign exchange. But with its own fertilizer plants, it would be freed from the need to import fertilizer and eventually the need to import food. Scarce foreign exchange could go instead into modernizing production and processing facilities. (One lack is up-to-date storage. Uncounted tons of grain are destroyed by rot and rats.) In time, India might even be able to export food and thus earn exchange for industrial development.

The injection of outside capital into the agricultural economy would also tend to draw out native capital from India's financial institutions and what is especially important, from the farmers themselves. The Agriculture Department declares that most of the twenty-six developing nations it studied "probably have a larger capacity for savings and new capital formation than their per capita incomes and past rates of capital accumulation indicate." An Indian farmer, with an investment of no more than $68 in livestock and $11 in implements and machinery, may arrive at the end of the season with a small cash surplus. But instead of using it to buy more efficient implements or fertilizers, or even to acquire more land and thus increase his next season's profit, he puts his money in jewelry, or splurges it on ceremonies of birth, marriage, or death. The hope is that deep-seated customs will change under the impact of modern capitalism.

The Critical Failure of PL 480

For a number of years, of course, the U. S. has been pouring capital into the Third World—and on a large scale. Billions of dollars worth of government aid has gone out from these shores in both currency and commodities. The unhappy part is that U. S. foreign-aid policy, for one reason or another, has so far failed in one vital respect: it has not made the indigent countries able to feed themselves.

In the last eleven years the U. S. has shipped, mostly to Third World countries, food that has cost it some $25 billion. Some of this food was shipped in emergencies and the recipient countries were not billed for it at all. Most of the tonnage was paid for in local currencies, which can enjoy only a vague kind of status in the Budget Bureau's accounts. This was the food that went out under the legislative aegis of Public Law 480.

PL 480 was originally put together in the Eisenhower Administration with the idea of disposing of some of the country's large Commodity Credit Corporation surplus; helping stave off famine abroad; encouraging the export of U. S. agricultural products, and world trade; and promoting U. S. foreign policy. The program (once called "Food for Peace" and now probably to be renamed, at President Johnson's suggestion, "Food for Freedom") has been put to many splendid uses. It saved an uncountable number of lives; it did level off U. S. surpluses—wheat, for example, is now down to what is deemed a prudent reserve. And the act did foster world trade in agricultural commodities in several instances and to the profit of American business. In 1954, Taiwan was unable to purchase anything from the U. S.; in 1965, no longer in need of aid, it bought $36 million of U. S. farm products. Japan, which has received $376 million worth of PL 480 aid since 1954, is now a spectacular world trader and the U. S.'s biggest customer for food grains. These success stories were right in line with what a lot of people kept thinking PL 480 was supposed to do in the end: put a billion and a half people in the Third World on their feet. But it never did.

The failure grew partly out of some early notions about priorities. The experts urge the Third World countries to get cracking first on industrial development, on the theory that they needed to create foreign exchange and this was the way to do it. In India, American food shipments along with some substantial improvement in India's own farm economy (which was soon to level off) gave rise to a complacency about the onrushing population and rising demands. Instead of helping India to learn how to feed itself, PL 480 had a disincentive effect on agricultural development. The Indians strove proudly to industrialize. "Nothing was dearer to their hearts than steel mills," says an Agricultural Department economist. Professors and Indians were not the only ones making the mistake. "In the mid-Fifties," the economist recalls, "American bankers and U. S. foreign-aid people examined the underdeveloped countries. They were interested in seeing them develop industry, not agriculture."

Despite the worsening food situation, the idea of giving priority to industrial development has persisted. PL 480 provides that the local currency a country pays for the purchase of American food can be borrowed back for various investments that the U. S. approves of, or given back to the countries in grants. The three countries that have received the most PL 480 aid are India, Pakistan, and the United Arab Republic, and not surprisingly, they are the biggest recipients of such loans and grants. India has put very little of such money into agriculture, Pakistan a bit more. Most of these funds went into industrial development and public works. Egypt, so far, has put almost nothing at all into agriculture, but has put $22 million into industry, $403 million into an account merely labeled "general and miscellaneous."

Let 'em Eat Sugar

U. S. policy under PL 480 was muddled by conflicts in goals and responsibilities. Legislative direction and effective control of the program lay with the House and Senate agricultural committees, whose members, coming chiefly from the South and the Midwest, had to keep in mind their farming constituencies. The Department of Agriculture has obediently carried out Congress' demands for protective restrictions. Herbert Waters, assistant administrator for material resources in the Agency for International Development, recalls how the earnest efforts of his office to promote self-help were undone by such restrictions. Shipments of U. S. wheat encouraged South Koreans to get away from their almost exclusively rice diets, as a result of which they had a rice surplus. They wanted to sell some of it to Japan. But Agriculture made it clear that so long as the South Koreans were getting PL 480 wheat they couldn't export their rice. Eventually they were permitted to do so, but only if they bought a ton of U. S. wheat for every ton of rice they exported. Such protectionism was also applied to the export of Pakistani rice to India. And since Turkey was getting PL 480 soybean oil, that country was tied down in its export of olive oil.

One promising innovation in the program was the provision for so-called "Cooley loans," named after Chairman Harold Cooley of the House Agriculture Committee. The local currency proceeds from the sale of U. S. commodities may be borrowed by U. S. firms that might want to do business in the Third World or by local people who are going to buy U. S. goods. But this borrowing is further circumscribed. A rider disallows such borrowing when the enterprises might be competitive with a domestic American enterprise. Who would have thought that a mushroom venture would come under such a ukase? But a request for such a loan in south Korea has been shelved because AID recollected how help given to mushroom growers in Taiwan had once stirred up Congressman Paul Dague's constituents in Pennsylvania's mushroom country. Dague is ranking minority member of the House Agriculture Committee.

Now, with PL 480 about to expire and the time come to devise a new program, this attitude is changing, according to Chairman Cooley. "Some members still think we shouldn't encourage people to compete with us. But the feeling is not as widespread as it was. The new concept is to help the countries help themselves."

But one exchange during the House hearings on a new bill indicated that some Congressmen may be hard to budge. Vice Chairman W. R. Poage, of Texas, expressed his exasperation over the fact that India was producing about five million bales of cotton. "That land that is producing cotton could produce food," he told Secretary of Agriculture Freeman, who was testifying before the House committee. "I see some folks are laughing about this," Poage noted, "but to me it is a deadly serious problem." Why shouldn't the U. S., he demanded, tell the Indians to put some of that cotton acreage into something they can eat? "We can say that to them. And let us say to them that we will give you cotton to take the place of what you do not grow." And, for that matter, Poage wanted to know, why should the U. S. be buying sugar from India? "They ought either to eat it themselves," he said, "or they ought to be growing something on that sugar land they need themselves."

"It is not a simple problem, as I know you thoroughly realize," replied Freeman. "If you rejected desperately needed exchange that India might get by selling sugar, which she would use to buy fertilizer, and that fertilizer in turn makes it possible for them to double their wheat and rice output—why you then would come to the conclusion that we either say, 'We concur in your producing sugar or cotton,' or we say, 'We will make the fertilizer available.' "

After this mild demurrer, the Secretary retreated, breathing at one point, "If anybody in Washington needs any advice it is me. Thank you for any you have given me."

So it remains to be seen just how Cooley's "new concept" will work out.

Message from a Dutch Uncle

President Johnson, for his part, seems determined that the Third World should now understand that the U. S. is inclined to help only those who help themselves. With an air of having reached the end of his string, he stipulated in messages to Congress early this year that the financing of the bulk of American food shipments must eventually (within the next five years) be in dollars instead of local currency. Under the current program there have been some hard-currency transactions on credit terms as long as twenty years at 2 1/2 percent. Less than 10 percent of such loans so far have been paid back.

But the most significant passages in the President's message were aimed at the Third World itself. From now on, he said, the recipients of U. S. aid must "make basic improvements in their own agriculture ... bring the great majority of their people—now living in rural areas—into the market economy ... make the farmer a better customer of urban industry and thus accelerate the pace of economic development."

The President, while sounding like a Dutch uncle, was not threatening to let the Third World starve: "Even with their maximum efforts abroad, our food aid will be needed for many years to come." Nevertheless, he gave the Third World something brand new to think about, not the least of which was its attitude toward U. S. aid, public *and* private. "Only these people and their leaders," he said, "can . . . create the climate which will attract foreign investment."

"Threats and Rumors of Expropriation"

The climate has been rough. A committee of businessmen, educators, and government and labor leaders, headed by Arthur K. Watson, chairman of I.B.M. World Trade Corp., studied the problem of "Private Enterprise in Foreign Aid." And in its report last summer it pointed out that while U. S. businessmen are used to taking risks, not many of them are accustomed to accepting "political instability, threats and rumors of expropriation, systems of pervasive discretionary regulation, prospects of rapid inflation and devaluation, and other novel features of overseas investment." And in the face of all this, the eagerness of U. S. capital to go into the underdeveloped countries is petering out.

Watson's committee found that a total of $13.3 billion of U. S. private investments had been put into underdeveloped countries up to 1964. But the *rate* at which these investments are increasing has been insignificant, compared to the needs and possibilities. And most of the increase has been in the more advanced countries, especially of Latin America; roughly 20 percent of the increased capital was from profits generated in these countries and plowed back. Petroleum and mining, not surprisingly, accounted for well over one-half the $13.3 billion; manufacturing for 2.5 billion, and "other" business activities for $3.3 billion. Very few companies have been willing to risk scratching for profits on the farms: some manufacturers of chemical fertilizers (including a few oil companies) and a few food-processing and farm-equipment firms.

The committee for its part made certain proposals aimed at the President himself. It recommended that the U. S. Government should accept the idea of international arbitration of investment disputes; it should support an investment code under international sponsorship; there should be an increase in government guarantees against overseas losses due to inconvertibility, military hazards, etc. And the income-tax laws should be amended to encourage overseas investments. The committee also recommended that AID select a number of key countries for intensive study and that an explicit program be developed for the improvement of the investment climate in those selected countries.

"We Give the Farmer a Reason to Grow"

A few companies have taken their narrow chances in the agricultural economies of the Third World. It is interesting to see how they are making out, for it does indicate what capital can do with encouragement. These ventures cannot be said to be very large, but the companies are doing moderately well or they wouldn't be planning to expand, as some of them are, cautiously.

Corn Products, for example, is introducing Latin Americans to such novelties as milk fortifiers, baby foods, custard powder, and packaged soups. Its wholly owned subsidiary in Argentina, Refinerías de Maíz, buys all its supplies locally, thus providing a cash market for the farmer. Management of the operation is in local hands.

Corn Products has also found a way to enrich edible corn starch with soybean oil, which it is marketing under the label "Maizena," and in order to increase its margin of profit on this new food the company is showing Brazilian farmers how to grow soybeans, which now have to be imported from the U. S. "We're part of the economy," said Alexander McFarlane, Corn Products' chairman. "In a modest way we give the farmer a reason to grow." What concessions does Corn Products want in a foreign investment? "No harassment. Equal opportunities with the national companies—no special favors. If we're treated equitably, we'll take our chances."

H. J. Heinz is in Venezuela with a subsidiary, Alimentos Heinz, which processes vegetables and fruits grown on small farms. Heinz introduced new strains that give better quality and yields. Junius F. Allen, in charge of Heinz's international operations, relates that the company built a factory in the farming town of San Joaquin (pop. 6,000). "We went in as the first steady industrial employer. The reactions of people to steady income were marked. They began to wear better clothes. At first they'd just peer into our cafeteria or just buy a Coke. But after a time they began to eat the hot lunch. They began to buy bicycles to get to the plant. It was the first step up, the first kind of mobility. We improved their standards in hygiene by providing clean washrooms. People respond to example. Perhaps as even greater impact was made on the agriculture of the community, for Heinz supplied a market for their produce which had not existed before. Heinz provided assistance which allowed the farmers to increase their yield and hence their incomes. The average yield of tomatoes of these farmers, for example, doubled in four years."

Sermons in Half a Dozen Dialects

In Brazil, Mexico, and Peru agricultural services are provided by Anderson, Clayton for local farmers who grow cotton seed, peanuts, and soybeans for a line of cooking and salad oils, shortening, and margarine that the company processes and markets. It finances seed, fertilizers, and insecticides, and gives advice on planting and harvesting. The plants provide plenty of local employment—6,000 jobs in

Brazil, 4,500 in Mexico, 800 in Peru—and Anderson, Clayton feels, like Heinz, that it is generating incentives by providing the means for a higher standard of living.

Not the least of the handicaps these companies have to overcome is that of communication in regions where the illiteracy rate may run as high as 50 percent. Esso Chemical, which has worldwide fertilizer operations through affiliates, has developed a system of chain teaching; they train their salesmen to train local people, who in turn train larger groups to go out into the fields and preach capitalism and modern farming—sermons that may have to be rendered in one of half a dozen different dialects. International Minerals & Chemical is carrying the message of fertilizer into every corner it can reach. The gist of its sermon: NPK (nitrogen, phosphate, and potash) is a substitute for land; i.e., it can multiply the yield of one acre as many as 500 times. The average consumption of fertilizer nutrients in the Third World countries is around five pounds per acre. Some Dutch farmers use as much as 400 pounds per acre.

Some U. S. firms have already set up fertilizer plants abroad on a limited scale. I.M.C., with Standard Oil of California, is building a $70-million plant in Visag in India with a capacity of 350,000 tons, which should be in operation in 1967. I.M.C. and Standard have accepted a minority position in the Visag enterprise; Indian interests own 53 percent. This is not the kind of situation that appeals to very many U. S. corporations; they are reluctant to grant even a minority position to Indian interests, which may not appreciate the vigorous ways American business does things. But Armour is in a deal with India's big industrial firm of Birla Gwalior Ltd. to operate a $50-million ammonia-urea complex in Goa. The two companies hold 51 percent of the equity; Indian private money has taken up the rest.

A Plan for 20 Million Peasants

These companies have been fairly bold, within the limits of their accountability to their stockholders. They have been resourceful and sometimes imaginative. But some people who have studied the problem believe that it calls for an even more creative approach.

One such person is Simon Williams, a consultant once hired by I.M.C. to do a survey of world hunger. He has a scheme he would like to test with a pilot project in Mexico, where he would set up a corporation in partnership with 1,000 small farmers under "paternal" American management. The farmers would share ownership of the corporation through stock purchased on credit and paid for out of the surplus crops Williams is sure they could produce under skillful direction. He saw such a corporation financed by some $5 million of equity capital within ten years and working capital of $2 million to $3 million. Williams admits that the decision on the part of Americans to invest must "be motivated primarily by the desire to increase food supplies and to stimulate rural economic development."

Nevertheless, he sees American investors making a "substantial profit every year, as well as recovering their investment in twenty years." In those twenty years the farmers would have acquired ownership of the corporation. Williams has confidence in their intelligence and thriftiness. "We have to find new forms of organization," he says, "that will be acceptable to both capital and the political powers. We need new institutions, new attitudes so that investment can become meaningful. The opportunity was never better than now to experiment with new forms."

But the idea looked much too experimental to one banker who studied the scheme. He thought it was a fine notion but pretty idealistic and he was not sure Williams had figured out a feasible debt-equity ratio. "No banker would touch it with a ten-foot pole," he said. I.M.C., for its part, decided it had "too many other things on its plate."

The fact is, Charles Dennison, an I.M.C. vice president, has an interesting scheme of his own for India. (I.M.C. wants it to be known that the plan is Dennison's, not the company's.) An earnest and ebullient man, Dennison proposes to set up a consortium that would include a fertilizer company, seed, insecticide, and pesticide companies, a farm-implement maker, a fisheries enterprise, and a food processor, all under one top manager. The project would be capitalized at something around $100 million. Indian private investors would be invited to subscribe for shares; most of the debt structure would be government money, in rupees, including PL 480 rupees, which could be used to purchase made-in-India components for the consortium's facilities.

The consortium would train the farmers in a selected geographical area, and would sell them the products of its various technologies. "The Indian farmer is illiterate but shrewd," says Dennison. "Education is the heart of the thing." The consortium would go into operation with 1,000 to 2,000 distributors, who should be able, he figures, to reach upwards of two million peasants.

Crucial to the whole scheme would be a generous farm-credit program, and either a free market or a government policy on farm prices that would give farmers an incentive to produce.

Dennison sees other consortiums, profiting from example, beginning similar operations in neighboring regions. The participants might well include not only U. S. and Indian partners but European companies (e.g., Montecatini, I.C.I., Dutch State Miners). This should allay Indian suspicions that their country was being invaded by an American "neo-colonialism."

With ten such projects going, India could look forward to its farmers' producing the bulk of the 185 million tons or so of grain the country will need for an adequate level of consumption in 1980. India would then be able gradually to reduce its grain imports while increasing imports of other foods, thus becoming a market, instead of an object of continuing charity, for the U. S.

Dennison has taken his scheme to Secretary Freeman, who thinks it is admirable in concept but questions whether enough attention has been given to "its nuts and bolts." Another government official feels the Indian Government would think twice before letting foreign interests cut such a wide swath into their economy. Dennison himself has told Indian officials: "Here is a scheme. Tear it down or alter it any way you want. But please recognize that it is an attempt to deal with this problem on a scale big enough and fast enough to solve it." His basic motive, he says, is to help the Indians while generating profits for everyone. No one exposed to Dennison's missionary zeal can doubt him.

The Unthinkable Alternative

There has been a modest marshaling of a variety of public and philanthropic forces on the farms of the world's underdeveloped regions. Besides AID, the United Nations' Food and Agricultural Organization and private foundations, notably the Ford and Rockefeller foundations, are supporting agricultural laboratories and training centers, helping to develop new seed strains and introducing new technologies in farm management. The foundations have sent money and personnel into the Philippines, India, Pakistan, the Middle East, Africa, and Latin America, and have contributed funds to American land-grant universities to enable them to send both advisers and equipment into the foreign field. A typical outlay of Ford Foundation funds was the $300,000 it put up to experiment in crossbreeding West Pakistan's wheat with high-yielding Mexican dwarf strains.

FAO has some 2,000 employees in its Rome headquarters analyzing data and mapping areas from African deserts to Amazon rain forests that might be turned into croplands. And some 2,600 FAO people are in the field in many roles, teaching the techniques of irrigation, helping farmers in their struggles against blight and disease.

But it is the U. S. that can do the most in the struggle because of the power of its capital, if it can be put to work, to fire up the human energy that resides in these populations. It cannot be emphasized enough that this country is unable to fill the food gap, or even supply the fertilizer needs of the Third World indefinitely from its own resources.

Any formula for transplanting capital and the capitalist revolution—Williams', or Dennison's, or anyone else's—will be slow to bear fruit among old and backward cultures. There is little prospect of a short-term profit for American investors, and no one, with the exception of Williams perhaps, is ready to vouch that there will be a sizable long-term profit either.

But American businessmen, singly and in consortiums, and with the support of their government, must face the fact that the world will be unsafe unless economic, as well as political stability, is brought to the countries of the Third World. Food riots that overwhelm all order can turn threats of expropriation or destruction of American properties into reality, so that investment of billions of dollars in oil, mining, and manufacturing may in the end depend very much on a determined movement of American capital into the agricultural economies of those nations. These are practical considerations. They do nothing to lessen the humanitarian concerns involved in this astounding race between people and food.

Chapter 17

The population explosion which may result in doubling the number of people in the world by the year 2000 is a problem of the greatest magnitude. This is particularly true since the greatest increase is expected in the developing countries where population growth is expected to exceed the rate of increase in food supplies. The underlying philosophy of this book is that in private enterprise can be found the best solution to this and the other major problems facing the world. Evidence of this is found in the way that the Caterpillar Tractor Company, under the direction of Lee L. Morgan and in cooperation with government, entered into a project in Costra Rica to clear land to produce rice. In this project, a 500-acre tract of land was divided into ten 50-acre plots to be homesteaded by native farmers. In this paper Mr. Morgan tells of one way of providing more food to meet future needs through a combination of government and free enterprise working together. This experiment in Costa Rica has already led to similar ventures in Peru and Columbia. Mr. Morgan and the Caterpillar Tractor Company are to be commended for their practical approach to a world problem.

CHANGES AND CHALLENGES*

Lee L. Morgan**

... The "changes" of the title are embodied in data on the population of the world and the outlook for the future. You know that whole epochs were required to produce a world population of one billion—in fact, it wasn't until 1815 that the figure was reached; however, world population became two billion in 1929 and three billion in 1960. A fourth billion will be added in 1975 and a fifth, sixth and possibly a seventh by 2000, a year in which one-fifth of all those born since the time of Christ will be alive. In short, the world faces an approximate doubling of its population in one-third of a century.

Unfortunately, this explosion of people will not be spread uniformly throughout the world. The United States, as well as most of the other developed nations, instead of doubling will grow less than 50% during the remainder of this century. The real population increase will occur in the less developed countries of Asia, Africa and South America, the places less able to accommodate such rapid change. These are the areas that have inadequate food production or distribution systems. Their economic structures are generally incapable of supporting a reasonable standard of living for present numbers.

Although there has been much conversation about increasing birth rates in Asia, Africa and South America as the underlying reasons for their population growth, it is clear that the major factor has been the decline in the death rate. For example, between 1940 and 1960, Mexico, Costa Rica, Venezuela, Ceylon and Malaya were among the nations that decreased their death rates by more than 50%. But regardless of cause, the net effect of all this will have been to create a gigantic change—an approximate doubling of the world population by the time you have done a pretty effective job of spoiling your grandchildren in the year 2000.

Creating an effective response to this problem is where the "challenge" part of these remarks comes in, especially for agriculturally oriented people who understand the American genius for food and fiber production; in short, a challenge to those who are capable of and want to climb a mountain mainly in order to see the view.

---

*Paper given at an All-Agriculture Banquet at the University of Illinois, April 27, 1968; reproduced by permission of the writer.

**Executive Vice-President, Caterpillar Tractor Company, Peoria, Illinois.

One of the potential responses to the world food problem is importation from other nations. In the past the United States has shipped millions of tons of food to other countries. This food relieved the hunger and suffering of millions of people. Our action from a humanitarian standpoint was admirable but we were not helping people to learn to feed themselves. Food aid, at most, will only buy time to enable these countries to get their economies moving forward. For those nations which can, it seems to me to be a most important point that those countries should become determined to produce their own food and fiber. Generally this should be the most economical way; in addition it is a means to developing a nation's natural resources. This approach suggests that it can also create an employment base in food production and distribution industries. Doing the job locally vis-a-vis importing also creates increased value for land which, in turn, contributes favorably to the taxation base of the government.

Another solution to the problem receiving much attention is birth control, especially in India; however, availability and efficacy of "the pill" and other technical means of birth control are largely ineffective until their use is understood and here, in itself, is a first class problem in communications. Even if the use of such devices is understood, they are completely irrelevant until couples are reasonably certain of having at least one son reach maturity. Here the approximate fifty fifty probability in the birth of boys and girls, coupled with infant mortality and the high death rate for children suggests that a couple may want as many as six children to assure the likelihood of having one son who will reach adulthood.

A third and more generally accepted solution to the food problem is based upon economic development. It suggests that the economies of the less developed countries need to be made to move forward more rapidly than the growth in population. It is axiomatic that no increase in standard of living for a people can occur unless this happens. We at Caterpillar believe that this condition can be best met by the combination of government and free enterprise working in their respective areas of expertise.

It was with this concept squarely in mind that Caterpillar recently gave leadership to a joint venture with other private companies and governmental agencies in undertaking a pilot land clearing project in Central America. The project was part of an experiment to see if settlement of the Costa Rica jungle and ownership of land by natives was a practical concept. Our first interest was to determine if today's mechanical land clearing methods are really low enough in cost to be practical. To that end a 500 acre tract of land was divided into ten fifty acre plots to be homesteaded by native farmers. The area selected has an annual rainfall of 150″, approximately four times the amount received by Eastern Illinois. Caterpillar machines cleared one-half of each plot and rice was planted, the remainder was left uncleared for future expansion. The first crop was harvested in the spring of 1967 and the net income for each farmer was $300. Although it may sound low, this income was above the national average and was the amount left after all expenses, including the farmer's labor, had been paid. The cost of clearing the tropical land came to about $50 per acre—a figure which we believe makes it economically feasible to clear vast areas of similar land.

This project helped trigger similar ventures in Peru and Colombia. In the Peruvian one, 500 acres of extremely heavy vegetation were cleared as a pilot plot for oil palm development. It appears this project will eventually lead to the clearing of an additional 125,000 acres.

These are small examples of the role that can be assumed by private enterprise. It happens we build the kind of machines needed for basic resource development but other companies can likewise play an important role. Manufacturers of all forms of agricultural inputs, such as chemicals and tillage and harvesting machinery, must become involved; seed companies and food processors also have a vital part to play.

Putting additional land into cultivation has an important relationship to solution of the overall food problem. This approach can make a significant contribution because according to the U. S. Department of Agriculture less than one-half of the potentially arable land in the world is now under cultivation. Most of this unused land lies in South America and Africa, either under forestation or lacking only water to be productive.

The other fundamental way of providing more food is to increase production on existing agricultural land through greater use of farm chemicals, improved tillage and conservation practices, efficient application of farm machinery and better strains of plants and livestock. This approach is especially suitable for India and it, incidentally, is where virtually all the gain in U. S. farm production has come. Total U. S. land in farms has remained about the same for the past thirty years; the number of farms is, as a matter of fact, dropping by about 100,000 per year, but productivity of the land is away up. As late as 1950, for example, the U. S. farmer was growing an average of 38 bushels of corn per acre—now the figure is almost double that and some efficient farmers are getting 150 bushels per acre. Some expect that a figure of 500 bushels by the year 2000 is quite possible—here is an indication of how much potential is in this approach to the problem.

So there are the changes in world population and the consequent challenges of feeding the increased numbers. The price for failure is fantastically high. You and I and most others in the more highly developed nations will never know hunger. There is little doubt that our ability to produce food will keep pace with our growth in population but is it reasonable to believe that people of other nations will quietly starve while their neighbors have plenty? It is most unlikely that they will remain peaceful while dying of hunger or while watching their children starve. So I submit that world peace is inexorably tied to the matter of world food production.

Agriculture has always risen to the challenges given it. During the 1930's in this country it survived the problems of the dust bowl and severe economic dislocations. Before recovering from these problems it was asked to respond to the challenge of feeding and clothing a nation at war and helping our allies achieve the same end. Based upon these demonstrated capabilities, I have every confidence that the world's agriculture will be equal to the greatest challenge it has ever faced. However, this has the prospect of being true only if people like you help. It would seem that at no time in history has it been of such vital importance that there be agriculturally trained people available to research, teach, produce, market and finance the things which will become the solution to this problem. . . .

Part VII

THE FUTURE OF PRIVATE ENTERPRISE AND CENTRALIZED CONTROL

Chapter 18

Every economic or political system ever in actual existence has at one time or other been subjected to attack by some of those who live under it. Under a system of private enterprise, a discontented individual may, on his own initiative, go about increasing his income. If he desires he can go to night school to train for a better job, he can move to another place, or he can keep in good with the boss to get a higher place on the ladder in the firm where he is working. His discontent about his income can be directed against himself and not against the system. In this way he is likely to become a more productive member of society, obtain a higher income, and resolve his discontent. Under a state-controlled system, an individual discontented with his income is more likely to direct his anger against the system than against himself. While it is possible for a younger person to attain a higher echelon in the state-controlled bureaucracy, for the ordinary man there is only a remote chance of his being permitted to change his status so as to get a higher income. A few attain the heights of income and power; the masses of people never do. Since the survival of any economic or political system depends on its ability to resolve the forces of discontent within it, private enterprise has a far greater chance of survival than does centralized state control as it has historically operated. In "Symbols for Capitalism," Professor Kenneth E. Boulding discusses the chances of survival of the two systems. His article is valuable reading, especially for those charged with the responsibility of leadership in business and government activity in the many countries of the world.

SYMBOLS FOR CAPITALISM*

Kenneth E. Boulding**

The veil which divides us from the future is opaque, but it has occasional peepholes. These peepholes are dynamic systems which can be detected in the past, and hence projected into the future, on the assumption that the systems themselves will not change. To illustrate:

> The heavenly bodies move according to dynamic systems which are fairly simple and gloriously stable, and in which the future is hardly less certain than the past (the principal uncertainties seem to be those introduced by political astronomy). Again, in a planetarium the present is a wholly arbitrary point.
>
> By contrast, human history is not so simple. Its systems are unstable and its predictions unsure. Nevertheless, all is not random. History has both rhythms and trends; societies and systems rise and fall, develop and mutate in temporal patterns which are perhaps subject to random shocks like Hitler, but which still have strong nonrandom components.

Where we go from here depends in part on where we have come from. Trends are notoriously unreliable as simple predictors—witness, for example, the debacle of the population predictions of the past generation—but they are not irrelevant. If we can detect trends of trends, or trends of trends of trends, we may discover higher-order stabilities. The solar system rests for the most part on a certain stability among second-order differentials: the planets do not continue in the direction in which they happen to be pointing at any moment, but their change of direction is fairly constant as they revolve around the sun.

Future of Capitalism

This rather lofty preamble is an excuse for some shaky predictions about the future of capitalism. One looks first at the simple trends:

---

*Reprinted from the *Harvard Business Review*, January-February 1959.

**Dr. Boulding was formerly Professor of Economics, University of Michigan; he is now (1968) Professor of Economics, University of Colorado and President of the American Economic Association.

if we go on as we have been going, where do we get to? In the West the answer is clear; we go toward the "affluent society," if we have not already arrived. Poverty ceases to be a serious problem, except in isolated pockets; therefore equality no longer becomes a matter of major social concern. Economically, the society is an uproarious success; the revolutionaries and the grumblers are reduced to an impotent fringe. The society, like a bicycle, is stable because it moves. Stabilizers that are, we hope, built in ensure reasonably full employment.

In the event of large shifts in the composition of the national product, such as might be brought about by disarmament or by a decline in investment, we hope that government can step in to expand public services or private consumption to take up the slack. We may need, as J. Kenneth Galbraith suggests, better (public) camp grounds rather than better (private) camping equipment, but this is a minor adjustment and could easily be made.[1] The sky is pretty clear, and the ocean apparently boundless.

Turning toward the poor but noncommunist countries, we see a cloudier sky. From Thomas Malthus to Gunnar Myrdal there are prophecies of gloom. Haunting memories of the Irish famine brood over the exploding populations of Ceylon and of Formosa. The Marxian demon walks again in Myrdal's vision of Immiserization—not now of the working class, but of the poor countries. The rich countries get richer, the poor countries stay where they are, or barely manage to keep abreast of their exploding populations, and the gap between rich and poor widens all the time.

If this dismal picture is true, and if communism can point to high rates of economic development from a low base in Russia and China, even at high human cost, it will not be surprising if the poor countries fall like ripe plums, one after the other, into the communist lap. One toys with the idea that perhaps there is some critical level of economic development—a level which may differ from culture to culture—above which capitalism is stable, below which it is not. If so, we are in for a rough time.

Threshold Systems

We must, however, look beyond the trends to the trends of the trends. Are there more fundamental forces or cumulations of things which make for change in the way things are going?

History records many reversals of trend. Indeed, it is often when

---

[1] *The Affluent Society* (Boston, Houghton Mifflin Company, 1958).

the trend seems strongest that it is reversed; the mighty chariot of empire halts and is shattered at the moment of its greatest speed and majesty. It is this apparent discontinuity of historical systems, more than anything else, which seems to separate them from the smooth predictabilities of astronomy. It can be argued, indeed, that obsession with the continuous systems of Newtonian science has been a serious handicap in the development of social theory, and it might have been better for social scientists if they had never learned the slippery niceties of differential calculus.

A system is no less a system, however, because it is capable of sudden reversals of trend. Indeed, systems of this kind are common even in the physical world. They might be described as "threshold systems," where something accumulates invisibly behind a dam or threshold until a critical point is reached, and the dam spills or breaks, or the threshold is breached. Thus:

- Strains accumulate in the earth's crust for years on end and nothing happens, until one day there is an earthquake.
- An old building slowly weakens with no outward sign of deterioration, until one day it collapses.
- A man takes insult and humiliation day after day and presents an unruffled front to the world until one day he explodes into rage or collapses into nervous breakdown.

The processes of history show enough of this type of threshold phenomenon to make it well worthwhile to look for threshold systems in society. Where, for instance, do we have cumulative pressures of some kind which are boxed in behind a defensive or suppressive apparatus so that they do not manifest themselves until the box breaks?

Inquiries of this kind are more important for our image of future society than we might suppose at first sight. A social system as it exists at a point in time is a box; it consists, among other things, of a variety of institutions which socialize individuals by suppressing their discontents, either by external threats of punishment or by internal changes in preferences. On the whole, it is easier to maintain a social system in the short run by suppressing discontents than by allowing them expression. The suppression of discontents, however, leads to a rise in pressure on the system which may eventually result in its sudden collapse or transformation.

Dynamics of Discontent

Turning now to the alternative social systems which today are apparently struggling for world mastery, what can we say about the "hidden dynamic" of each—about the unseen discontents and frustrations which boil up within the tight walls of social sanction or even of internalized values, and which may lead eventually to sudden transformations of the systems themselves? This is an area where we do not know very much (though much more could be known if we cared to work at it), but where we are justified in hazarding some guesses.

One difficulty is that we are not faced with pure or unchanging systems: both capitalism and communism change with the years, sometimes quite rapidly. Indeed, up to a point, the more they are able to change, the more likely they are to survive in the long run, for the more likely they are able to adjust to discontents as they accumulate, rather than to dam them up until the system breaks. It is useful, however, to look at a mixed social system as a mixture of pure components—even though a system is more like a compound than a simple mixture, owing to the fact that the presence of one component always modifies the other.

Market vs. Budget

Two pure systems by which an individual may be related to his society can be identified as *market-justified activity* and *budget-justified activity*. Capitalism is traditionally supposed to have more of the first, communism more of the second.

If the individual relates himself to his society in a way which produced suppressed discontents, then the social system is a threshold system in danger of eventual bursting. Bearing this vital rule in mind, let us look at the systems just mentioned:

> A pure market system is one in which the individual obtains his livelihood by selling his services or products on an open market to anyone who will buy them. If the market is to be competitive, there must, of course, be many buyers, at least potentially. The activity of the seller is justified because he can find someone who will enter into a commodity-exchange relationship with him.
>
> By contrast, the budget-justified activity takes place within the framework of a hierarchical organization; it is included in a plan, or budget, which guides and coordinates the activities of the whole organization. And the individual performing such an activity derives his income not from a person with whom he has an exchange relationship, but from some official who is following a previously agreed-on plan. In a pure budget system the whole economy is organized hierarchically like a single firm, and every activity is justified by its conformance to a previously formulated plan.

Neither capitalism nor communism—as we know them today—are pure systems. They are distinguished by the proportions of market-justified and budget-justified activity they contain, but in fact they are mixtures. Thus, modern capitalist societies contain also a great deal of budget-justified activity, while the communist societies permit an important margin of market-justified activity, particularly in foodstuffs and small services. It is probable, indeed, that a pure system of either kind would be unworkable.

To complicate the matter still further (there is something in the universe which does not like pretty dichotomies), there are in all societies *market-justified budgets and budget-justified markets*:

> A market-justified budget is that drawn up by a private firm or organization which derives its revenue primarily from the sale of the goods or services which it produces. The revenues are then distributed among the various departments according to an internal budget. This is to be distinguished from the power-justified budgets of governments and governmental organizations, where the origin of the revenue is not primarily the sale of services but the exercise of sovereign power, through either the collection of taxes or the creation of money.
>
> A budget-justified market arises when the revenues which originate in budgets are spent in markets. Designated people in the organizational structure spend these revenues, not specifically according to a previously determined plan, but in the purchase of goods or services from individuals who are not included in the plan as such. Thus, governmental organizations use the revenue that is provided by the budget to purchase labor, management, and goods of all kinds. The private corporation also budgets money to its various departments, which spend the money in market purchases.

Ropes vs. Fences

These distinctions may not seem at first sight to have much to do with the future of capitalism. Nevertheless, they are of vital importance in assessing the trends of the trends.

Capitalism, for all its inevitable use of budgets both in government and in business, is deeply committed to the institution of the market; it might almost be described as a market-justified system. If the institution of the market produces satisfactory results—that is, manageable discontents—capitalism has a good chance of surviving in one form or another because of the sheer human value of its most characteristic institution.

Communism, on the other hand, is a budget-justified system,

rejecting the market as a basic institution and seeking to organize all human activity, especially all economic activity, in the budget-justified activity of the one-firm state.

The dispute is essentially over whether the market or the budget should be the dominant institution which coordinates the activity of the individual in the great ongoing processes of society. The outcome of this struggle will depend in large measure on the relative strains, or suppressed discontents, which each method of coordination produces. Every method of coordination produces discontents, if only because all coordination involves limitations of some kind on the freedom of the individual.

The individual whose behavior is limited by the market is conscious of an *over-all* limitation, in that he has only a certain amount to spend, and thus there are things which he cannot afford. He is less conscious of any specific restriction on his freedom; although tied to the rope of his financial resources, he is not fenced in by specific prohibitions. By contrast, the budget-limited individual is much more conscious of *specific* limitations. The budget to which he must conform is a set of specific commands and prohibitions. In effect, he is fenced in rather than roped.

Because of these differences, the nature and direction of the aroused discontents are also different. Market limitations may produce one of two reactions:

(1) If the individual feels himself to be unduly restricted by his lack of income, he can set about increasing his income. This type of restriction I call *private discontent*. The individual goes to night school, moves West, changes his job, marries a rich wife, or embezzles money. In each case the discontent is directed against himself, rather than against the system, and the efforts of the individual are directed toward changing his own position within the system rather than toward changing the system as such.

(2) The other possible reaction to market limitation is *political discontent*, that is, discontent not so much with the position of the individual within the system, as with the system itself. This is reflected in pamphleteering, joining political parties or pressure groups, making and hearing speeches, campaigning, voting, manning the barricades, and so on. The individual attributes the restrictions on his freedom to an impersonal system rather than to his own defects, and his discontent accordingly takes on a political form.

The future of a market system depends very much on which of these two forms discontent takes. If it takes predominantly the personal form, the system is not only secure but will prosper, provided that the discontent expresses itself in productive and creative activity rather than in predatory or merely redistributive activity. If, however, the discontent takes predominantly a political form, the system itself is liable to rapid or even revolutionary change, the more so because energies which might have been spent in productive activity within the system are now spent in trying to destroy it.

In the United States, on the whole, discontent has taken the personal form. There has been some political activity and some system change, often of a useful nature, but the main expression of discontent has been in private activity for private betterment, and this has brought with it public riches.

In Russia and in China, on the other hand, the opportunities for private expression of discontent seemed to be so meager that much of the energy that in the United States has gone to improving the system went in those countries to overthrowing it. And, of course, the more energy is devoted to overthrowing a system, the more poorly the system works and the greater the apparent justification for an overthrow.

Finding Scapegoats

It does not necessarily follow from this, however, that the communist economies have no political future. Such an easy conclusion cannot be justified by the propositions just outlined.

I venture the hypothesis—which needs to be tested—that a budget-limited system produces more discontent than a market system, and that this discontent is more likely to be suppressed, but that it is more likely to be directed against subsystems within the larger system than against the budget system itself. The budget limitation is felt as something specific, imposed on the individual by a hierarchical superior. Budgets, therefore, have a high human cost in terms of frustration. All the discontent produced, however, is likely to be directed toward easily identifiable scapegoats *within* the hierarchical structure; it is discharged at a lower level than system criticism. For example:

The disgruntled workman blames the foreman, the straw boss, or the supervisor, whether in General Motors or in the Soviet Union. There is a certain feeling that the "old man" is just fine, and the system is dandy, but the so-and-so John Doe who sits in the lower echelon of authority is the one who really messes things up. If discontent becomes too great, there may be a subsystem revolution; Doe goes, but the "old man" stays on and the system remains.

The larger the system and the larger the organization, the more steps there are in the hierarchy and the harder it is for the "old man" to know what is going on down the line—and the more likely we are to find accumulating and undischarged discontents. The bigger the organization, also, the more demanding the top roles, and the more chance there is, on sheer principles of probability, that people will move into roles which are too big for them and in which they may make fatal mistakes.

Freedom vs. Justice

Up to this point I have not mentioned equality, the distribution of income, or surplus value. This may seem to some like discussing the future of Denmark without Hamlet. I would not, indeed, argue that these matters are irrelevant; I do, however, hold them to be secondary.

The concept of surplus value is an important one as it refers to a surplus of production from any sector of the economy over and above the consumption necessary to support the productive activity. (Ancient civilization rested in general on the ability of the coercive power to extract economic surplus from the agriculturist.) And the class of idle rich—whose contribution to the economy and even to the cultural life is tenuous indeed, while they consume resources for which better uses can be proposed—is a significant feature of many societies.

Nevertheless, the battle between capitalism and communism is seen less and less as the traditional battle of the poor against the rich. There is not much difference between the "bloated capitalist" of socialist imagination and the commissar luxuriating in his state-owned limousine and spending his week ends in an elegant *dacha* in the country.

The problem of inequality, and especially the problem of inequality of economic power, is simply not solved by communism. Indeed, the communist state represents a concentration of economic power far beyond the wildest dreams of a Rockefeller or a Carnegie. If General Motors were to expand to absorb the whole American economy, its president might then have as much economic power as that which lies in the hands of Khrushchev. As it is, even Tito wields as much economic power as the head of the largest American corporation, while Khrushchev and Mao wield very much more. There is not much economic difference between the poverty of the sharecropper under capitalism and the poverty of the forced laborer in the communist labor camps.

What I am suggesting is that the problem of economic justice and freedom is in no way solved by communism; neither is it solved by pure capitalism. This remains a problem to be solved in its own right, no matter what the form of the society. Some aspects of it may be solved more easily under communism, some under capitalism; but on the whole this is not the issue between the two forms of society, and there is nothing in either form of society which guarantees a satisfactory solution to these problems.

Striking a Balance

I am hospitable to the hypothesis that the market institution in some form is an almost indispensable adjunct of human freedom, partly because the market system, by its very nature, restricts personal choice less than the budget system does, and partly because I do not see how to organize a system with wide distribution of economic power except through market coordination. On the other hand, I also entertain, perhaps a little less cheerfully, the notion that there are many needs which the market cannot satisfy, and that, if some basic minimum standard of human life and decency is to be established in a society, extensive use must be made of coercive power and budget machinery.

The tension between the market and the budget as competing coordinators of activity is therefore mixed up in some degree with the tension between freedom and justice, either of which may have to be paid for by some sacrifice of the other. Those for whom justice in distribution is a major objective are frequently prepared to sacrifice a good deal of freedom in order to attain the desired distributional condition. But those who see in the desire for justice a compulsion which easily becomes both inordinate and destructive—as when, for example, children fight over and often destroy their shares in some treat—are more inclined to sacrifice an ideal justice in the interest of greater freedom, or even in the interest of mere order.

Just as the problem of justice versus freedom in society is not whether we should have one or the other, but how much of each is most desirable, so also the struggle of the market against the budget does not raise the question of which to have, but how much of each to have. We may see here perhaps a distant gleam of hope for an eventual reconciliation of capitalism and communism. The political discontents which arise out of the market experience develop mainly when the market is not functioning properly, especially in times of deflation and inflation. It is certainly not beyond our wit and knowledge in these days to eliminate the major sources of market breakdown, so that on this score we may hope to see a sharp reduction in the sources of market discontent.

The discontents which arise out of budgets and large-scale organizations are more intractable. Nevertheless, there is some hope that by becoming aware of the high human cost of organizational control we may be able to devise information and control systems even in large organizations which have as *one* of their conscious aims the reduction of personal frustration and tension among members of the organization. This may involve the development, within the framework of an organization, of limitations which take the form of general restraints, like a limitation of total expenditure, rather than of particular restraints, like conformity to a detailed, prearranged budget or plan.

Hope of Reconciliation

In one's more optimistic mood, therefore, it is possible to visualize a true dialectical synthesis of the market and the budget in which each will play its proper part in the coordination of human activity, and in which neither one will inherit the peculiar pathological features to which each institution is subject today. Such a synthesis may be a long way off, but belief in the possibility of its coming may draw both capitalist and communist societies toward it.

So far the capitalist societies seem to have been moving toward a synthesis much faster than the communist societies, which are more entangled in the strait jacket of an obsolete ideology. Capitalism does not hesitate to use budget coordination where this seems clearly desirable, nor does it hesitate to modify the market institution in the direction of greater stability. It can be argued rather cogently that the capitalist societies drew the right inferences from the Marxist criticism and learned the right lessons from Marx, whereas the communist societies learned mainly the wrong things from him!

Nevertheless, there are signs that communist societies can learn too, and that they can move toward greater freedom, more market institutions, looser planning, more individual property, and so on. (The recent news from China about the creation of great communes is a forcible reminder, however, that just the opposite can still happen.) Much depends on the external environment; the greater the external pressure on any society, the less likely it is to make desirable adaptations, and the more likely it is to devote its energies to self-justification. But if the capitalist world can treat the communist world with a firmness which is not devoid of sympathy and understanding, the sheer logic of social systems and human need should move it in the direction of greater freedom.

The more we can perceive communism as a disagreeable stage on the road to a truly free and workable society, the faster we are likely to move toward this great end.

Clashing Symbols

Now, however, we come to the social dynamics of the third order—the trends of the trends of the trends. Here we face peculiar difficulties in systems analysis, because at this level the important systems are symbolic in nature, and have to do with the vast imaginative furniture of the human mind:

- In the first-order system we simply project the trend, and suppose that what has been happening will continue.
- In the second-order system we look at the accumulating tensions and discontents of the society to see where system breaks or trend changes may occur.
- At the third level we must look to the symbolic *content* of these tensions, for it is this which determines the direction and even the magnitude of the tensions.

A man—or a society—may accumulate a good deal of vague dissatisfaction without much happening. Let somebody invent a symbol or an ideology around which the vague dissatisfaction can crystallize, however, and social movements are under way. Without the invention of the concept of parity, for instance, it is doubtful whether American agricultural discontent would have crystallized into the form it took, nor would it have been so politically powerful. Without the invention of the concept of surplus value, socialism would never have attained the direction and power which it has achieved.

One gets the feeling sometimes that the struggles of men and societies are echoed, or perhaps even parodied, by the struggle of symbols in some Platonic heaven, and that just as Homer saw the gods fighting above Troy, so above all ignorant armies on the darkling plain, bright shapes of symbols struggle for the possession of men's minds. The cross and the crescent, the flags and the books, the bears and lions and eagles, goddesses of liberty and justice and freedom, symbols of race, class, religion, and ideology, ideas like surplus value or the Hidden Hand—all these struggle in the cloudy content of the human imagination. They are the genes of social organization, intricately building the fabric of churches, nations, empires, parties, universities, and families.

One good symbol can beat a thousand battalions, and the strength of the strong is as wax in the imaginations of the imaginative. The Pharaohs and the Caesars are dust, but the Jews, who apparently had nothing but imagination, have outlasted them all.

Capitalism's Weakness

We know very little, however, about what gives power to a symbol. Synthetic symbols have never been very successful, and the great symbols have arisen not among those who consciously direct, or think that they direct, the larger destinies of men and nations, but among the poor and despised and ignorant. At this point, therefore, there is an enormous gap in our conscious knowledge of social systems which makes even middle-range prediction hazardous. Even now in some obscure Nazareth or Mecca there may be someone who will write the history of the next 1,000 years, but there is no way of telling who he is or where he might be.

One thing seems sure: the market is a symbol-poor system. This is perhaps because of its very rationality. Exchange is an activity which does not involve deep emotions; it is a simple, rather abstract activity of little symbolic value. The passing of the collection plate is not the high emotional point of a church service, nor is the paying of taxes the act which symbolizes the deepest and most dramatic element in the relation of an individual to his country, however necessary these activities may be.

Consequently, the market as an institution does not gather to itself strong symbols and powerful loyalties. No matter how successful the market is in extending freedom and in lessening frustration, still nobody loves it. Nobody even hates it very much or for very long. In the pantheon of symbols, therefore, the market does not have a god to represent its interests, and its position in the struggle of symbols is thereby weakened. The saint and the patriot, the prophet and the reformer, alike despise it—and tolerate it merely as a useful beast of burden.

By contrast, the budget acquires a vicarious charisma from the organization which it coordinates. Organizations are superhuman, if not divine. They represent a power beyond that of the individual; they become colossi which throw bridges across straits and rockets into space. They attach to themselves the great virtues of loyalty, devotion, and self-sacrifice. They are watered with the blood of martyrs and nourished with the flesh of heroes. Our attitude toward them is deeply ambivalent; they destroy us and elevate us at the same time.

There is little wonder that organizations like the church and the state are so deeply affected with symbolic value, some of which rubs off even on the corporation. It is little wonder that socialism has stirred the hearts of men as capitalism has not, and that it has filled the minds of men with its bright but deceitful dreams of the future.

Conclusion

Are we to conclude, then, that the future is with the most powerful symbol; that the market, because of its very rationality and common-senseness, is doomed to go down before the budget, which cloaks its chains in the borrowed garments of symbolic virtue? This would be premature. All that's symbol is not sense, and sense is not without defenses in the world of symbols. Nonsense, no matter how precious, no matter how well-entrenched behind powerful symbol and organization, has the ultimately fatal disadvantage of being nonsense. And when good sense is combined with a good symbol, the combination is powerful indeed.

I do not despair, then, of the market; it is not incapable of finding powerful symbols. However, I am not sure that its defenders have always been wise in their choice of symbols. There are those, for instance, who try to identify the market economy with the symbol of freedom. This rings hollow to those who feel the market mainly as a limitation (even though it may be a better limitation than the alternatives). It rings particularly hollow to the poor and hungry.

There are those also (often the same people) who try to link the market economy with symbols of nationalism, like the "American way of life." This unfortunately smacks overly much of imperialism and militarism; and if there is any place where the budget reigns supreme, it is in the Pentagon, which is by far the largest socialist enclave in the American economy.

Just as a wild suggestion thrown to the wind, might there not be more hope for the market as a symbol of peace? Free exchange is the type of noncoercive coordination where each party benefits. In the past, the trader and merchant have traditionally been men of peace; they have even been despised as such. The market is an important mechanism for resolution of conflicts through the opening up of a myriad of alternatives. Capitalism is an ideology of compromise and finagle, of accommodation and adjustment.

The budget, on the other hand, focuses and intensifies conflicts. It resolves them only by exercising coercive hierarchical force. Marxism and nationalism are both ideologies of conflict. The communist and the legionnaire have at least this in common: they believe in knocking the enemy down, not in buying him off.

Peace is an ambivalent symbol; we hate and love it at the same time. But ambivalence makes a symbol all the more powerful; we can neither escape it nor subdue it. In our day, because of the changed technology of war, the demand for peace becomes more and more urgent. The market institution (with the added support, perhaps, of some political analogues of the market) offers hope of co-ordination without coercion, of the values of differentiation without the violence of organizational conflict.

If this is the case, the market may have a bright future. A world weary of coercion, inflated ideologies, and useless and destructive conflicts may find in it a symbol of that peace which it needs so desperately, and which does not pass understanding.

Index